Banknotes and Banking
in the
Isle of Man 1788–1994

Banknotes and Banking in the Isle of Man 1788–1994

A GUIDE FOR HISTORIANS AND COLLECTORS

by Ernest Quarmby, MIScT.

SECOND EDITION

SPINK
London 1994

First Edition 1972
Second Edition 1994

ISBN 0 907605 51 6

Published by Spink & Son Limited, London SW1Y 6QS

© Ernest Quarmby 1994

COUNTY RESERVE

SUFFOLK COUNTY COUNCIL LIBRARIES & HERITAGE	
Library Services UK	14/05/97
HoB:Col	£19.95
769·5594	28 9

Typeset and printed Pardy & Son (Printers) Ltd., Ringwood, Hampshire

To Benny

For her encouragement and enthusiasm

Contents

Introduction to First Edition

Recent increasing interest in the field of banknote collecting and the lack of published information on Manx notes since Clay's work[1] over a century ago has led to research in this series for the purpose of making information available for the benefit of libraries, museums and collectors.

Records of many of the early banks of issue have long since disappeared, especially in cases where the bank concerned failed or was compelled to wind up its business. Two world wars this century with their attendant salvage drives have added to the loss of business documents being destroyed or disposed off. Added to this many records have been destroyed due to lack of storage space and these combined factors have not eased the task of research. Fortunately the Manx banks which had the right of note issue until recent years have preserved their records, especially in cases of bank amalgamations in which the note registers, etc. of antecedent banks have been preserved.

The object of this research is to provide detailed listings of notes issued in the Isle of Man including the various paper currencies used in the Internment Camps during the 1939–1945 War. It is realised that these were not official bank issues but they are included for the sake of completeness. Also included are a few Bills which have been found in collections. The well known card money has regretfully been omitted since it was felt this was a specialised study of its own.

Introduction

Introduction to Second Edition

Since publication of the first edition over twenty years ago much new information has been discovered, particularly details of numbers of notes outstanding and of extant notes, the latter being from a careful record of any Manx notes found in collections or passing through dealers and auctioneers. This information is of particular value since it will give a more accurate record of the rarity of notes which is of interest to the collector. A few new note issues have been discovered in archival collections and these are included. As mentioned, in the first edition the card money had been omitted, this is now included.

Catalogue Numbers

Also, since publication of the first edition, a number of new note varieties have been reported, especially proofs and printers' essays. To incorporate these into the existing numbering system required several suffix letters and would have made the system look untidy. Therefore, after much careful thought and discussion with dealers and collectors, it is proposed to have a completely new numbering system and in order to avoid confusion with the old system, card money has been allotted numbers 1–200, pre-Government and internment camp notes will be numbered 201–435 and Government notes 451–. A table showing the old and new numbers is given in Appendix IV.

Arrangement

Card money is arranged in alphabetical order of issuer and banks are arranged in chronological order of foundation, followed by an historical note regarding the bank. A description of the notes with details of each note issue is given with additional information where necessary. Separate issues are regarded as changes in design of note, change of colours or change of signatures. This arrangement has been modified in some instances to avoid repetition and to maintain continuity due to bank amalgamations. Although not in strict chronological order it is more convenient to list currency or issued notes first followed by artist's sketches, printer's proofs, etc. This method makes it easier to present descriptions of the latter by comparison with issued notes and to point out differences between them. In the case of Government notes this arrangement is reversed.

Illustrations

All main varieties of design are indicated by photographs where specimens have been available. In the case of card money this has not been possible due to the condition of specimens available so fewer pieces are illustrated. Notes from the Manx Museum Collection are published by kind permission of the Trustees of the Manx Museum and National Trust. Illustrations of negotiable bank notes are reproduced with kind permission of the issuing or retiring authority, ie. notes of Dumbell's Banking Company, Parr's Bank, London County Westminster & Parr's Bank and the Westminster Bank by permission of National Westminster Bank Limited. Manx Bank, Mercantile Bank of Lancashire, Lancashire & Yorkshire Bank, Martins Bank and Barclays Bank by permission of Barclays Bank Limited, and Lloyds Bank Limited, Isle of Man Bank Limited and the Isle of Man Government for permission for their respective note issues.

Unless otherwise stated all illustrations of card money are full size and those of bank notes are half-size.

Dimensions

The dimensions quoted are average values on several notes which may vary slightly due to small variations in the cutting at the final stages of note production. On earlier notes the dimensions are more variable since in some cases the notes were printed in several subjects per sheet which was then cut or torn by hand.

Colours and Printing Errors

Printing inks may vary in tint due to aging or effect of general handling where acids or grease may alter the colour slightly. Where possible the colours given are those of notes in extremely fine condition. Varieties of ink shades are not listed but attention is drawn to them where necessary. No errors have been recorded amongst the pre-Government notes but a few have occurred in the Government issues. They are mainly due to printing defects caused by pieces of paper falling on the sheet prior to printing. Misplaced serial numbers and miscut notes are also known. In 1980/81 a small number of one pound notes were discovered devoid of signature and a few twenty pound notes of the special Millenium issue are known with the overprint missing. All these varieties are rare due to the careful scrutiny of notes during manufacture.

Rarity

A guide to the rarity of Manx notes is included and based on the number of specimens seen and details in the note registers which indicate the number of notes still outstanding. This number does not necessarily mean that all the outstanding notes are in existence since it is known that many have been lost or destroyed. For example, during World War 2 many Manx notes sent from various banks in the UK were lodged at Liverpool ready for return to the Isle of Man and as consequence of war operations were lost in the blitz. No details of these lost notes will ever be known and this of course reduces the numbers of extant notes. With some of the modern Manx notes there are examples of less than 900 notes and in some cases the maximum number of specimens is less than 20. Numbers of notes seen or reliably reported since 1968 are indicated and although these figures do not intend to account for all extant notes they will present an accurate picture of the survival ratio and rarity.

With exception of the Government notes all Manx notes have a degree of rarity due to two main factors. Firstly, notes of failed banks were quickly disposed of by the holders in an effort to redeem them, or if this was not possible, the notes would simply be disposed of as useless pieces of paper. Secondly, in the case of banks that ceased note issue in 1961 a large percentage of their notes have now been paid in leaving only comparatively few still outstanding. This point may be further illustrated by quoting some actual figures.

The Isle of Man Bank having the greatest note circulation of £150,000 had only £10,222 in one pound and five pound notes still outstanding on 1 August 1993.[2] This figure is made up from 8,772 one pound and 295 five pound notes. For the Westminster Bank with a limit of £25,000, 2,018 pound notes remain and 176 for its antecedent banks. Martins Bank limited to £25,000 have 1,378 notes outstanding and 446 for its antecedent banks. The licence limit set for Barclays was £10,000, the lowest of the banks of issue, and only 583 notes remain outstanding. For Lloyds Bank, with a limit of £15,000, the number is 818. Since some notes have been lost or destroyed the above figures will be reduced.

Another determining factor in considering rarity occurs in notes of the nineteenth century. If a bank failed or was amalgamated there would be a number of unissued notes on hand which were preserved for some reason and eventually became available as curiosities. One instance of this occurred when the Dumbell's Banking Company ceased payments and a number of unissued notes were found at the bank, along with a supply of notes signed by the manager but requiring the accountant's signature before being ready for issue. Notes with the single signature or none are not as rare as those bearing the two signatures, since the latter notes were quickly disposed of by holders and eventually redeemed. Therefore issued notes have a greater rarity than unissued notes.

Degrees of Rarity

Under the Rarity heading in the text the degree of rarity is given according to the Table below which is based on the number of specimens located, coupled with data from the note registers. Also the number of specimens known plus those in archives, the latter term embraces museums and banks holding archival collections.

R8	Unique
R7	2–10 specimens
R6	11–20 specimens
R5	21–30 specimens

R4	31–50 specimens
R3	51–100 specimens
R2	101–250 specimens
R	251–500 specimens
S	501–1000 specimens
C	> 1000 specimens

Positional Code Letters (Plate Letters)

Previously termed Plate Letters the more correct name of Positional Code Letters is adopted to conform with standard practice. Many of the notes printed by Waterlow & Sons Limited incorporate minute letters in the design as a means of identifying impressions on the printing plates and an aid to monitoring wear or damage to that particular impression. This use of code letters was important evidence in the famous Portuguese Bank Note case in 1925.[3] From the examination of several hundred notes it has been possible to show that these letters were used in a certain sequence and combination with each other, and a detailed search on the notes indicates that these letters change at approximately every thousand notes printed. The location of the letters is given at the appropriate point in the listing.

Replacement Notes

The use of replacement notes by many note issuing authorities to replace damaged or defective notes from the printing processes is well known. Owing to the requirements of maintaining details of serial numbers in the note registers, identifiable replacement notes were never used by the commercial banks in the Isle of Man. However, a careful study of positional code letters has revealed a few notes bearing out of sequence letters and it would appear that some defective printings were discovered at the printers and the sheets of notes in question were replaced by some sheets from another print run all prior to the printing of serial numbers. These particular notes have not been listed as a separate variety. In recent years replacement notes have been used by the printers of the Isle of Man Government notes and details are given at the appropriate point.

Signatures

Until the 1950s many of the Manx notes were hand signed, a task of some proportion involving much time in handling. As new notes were required the manager and assistant manager or accountant appended their respective signatures in a special non-fading ink. After checking, details were entered in the note register to record the serial number, date and signatories of each note. When the notes were retired at a later date a date-stamp was applied against the entry in the note register and the note cancelled and stored until ready for destruction in the presence of officials of the bank of issue and Clerk of the Council.

Hand signing of individual notes decreased to some extent when the

Westminster Bank and Martins Bank had the necessary signatures reproduced in facsimile in 1929. Barclays' notes were hand signed until 1954 but Lloyds Bank continued hand signing until 1961. Due to the higher issue of notes the Isle of Man Bank had used facsimile signatures of the manager since about 1915, but still required the assistant manager's signature until 1961. The five pound notes were all hand signed from 1894 to 1961.

Note Licences

The actual note licence issued to each bank was a simple document signed by the Lieutenant-Governor in which the limit of the note issue was stated. Usually the period of the licence was for twelve months commencing on 1 November. The licence fee was twenty pounds until 1921 when the fee was increased to fifty pounds and in addition to this the sum of two pounds for each thousand pounds of the total amount of the licence. For example a bank with a licence limit of twenty-five thousand pounds paid a total fee of one hundred pounds per annum.

During the course of circulation some notes would become dirty or defaced. These would be gradually withdrawn and cancelled prior to destruction. New notes to replace withdrawn notes could not be put into circulation until a certificate was issued by the Clerk of the Council indicating the destruction of old notes in his presence. Usually the notes were destroyed in batches of five hundred or multiples thereof. A record was also made of the serial numbers of notes destroyed at a particular time.

Weekly returns were made showing the number of notes held in each branch of the bank, this total deducted from the number of uncancelled notes in the note register showed the actual number of notes in circulation.

Note Registers

These are books in which the bank of issue maintains a record of all its note issues. Details being dates appearing on the note, the signatories and dates of issue. The serial numbers appear in columns against which the date of retirement is later entered. After checking to see all withdrawn notes have been correctly marked off an additional entry may be made in a list of notes destroyed on a particular date with signatures of officials of the bank and Clerk of the Council who witness their destruction. The balance of the note account shows the number of notes on hand and in circulation. New notes could not be placed in circulation as replacements for withdrawn notes until the latter had been destroyed. Thus it is possible to follow the course of a note from issue to destruction.

The English based banks maintained their Note Registers during and since the period of withdrawal of their own notes and all registers back to 1882 have survived. In the case of the Isle of Man Bank the massive volume of notes being returned from an authorised circulation of £150,000 was so great that it was impossible to mark off withdrawn notes and only a total outstanding has been made in the annual returns. This has meant the loss of earlier registers prior to 1948 for one pound notes and therefore no details of dates on notes are known except for those specimens actually examined. Fortunately the corresponding five pound note register has survived and a full listing of dates gleaned from this.

Types of Notes

Essay. Initial drawing in pencil or watercolours prepared by the note printer and submitted for approval to the appropriate authority before work commences on the actual engravings. May also be prepared by invitation or speculation. These are unique items.

Die Proof. On acceptance of the Essay the dies are engraved usually by more than one engraver each of whom specialises in various aspects of work, ie. portraits, vignettes, ornamental work, lettering, etc. Pulls are produced at various stages to check on progress of the engraving. Die proofs are rarely available to collectors.

Printer's Proof. The combined work of each engraver is incorporated on a master die and proofs from this are submitted for approval. When these have been approved steel printing plates are then prepared with as many impressions of the master die as it is intended to print notes per sheet. These notes may also have the word CANCELLED as overprint, typescript, hand written or perforated. Proofs may be printed on paper different from currency notes, ie. without watermark or security thread and may also be printed on card.

Colour Trial. The Printer's Proof may be submitted in a variety of colours from which the final choice is taken. These Colour Trials are usually unique.

Promotional Note. As currency note but printed in different colours. These were prepared by the printers as examples of their work for promotional purposes and in this respect differ from colour trials which were part of an official commission. It is realised that the difference between the two classifications may be ill-defined but usually promotional notes would bear a printer's reference number quite separate from the serial number. Where absolutely known the term promotional note or colour trial is clearly shown in the text.

Specimen Note. Notes in their final form and colour as prepared for issue endorsed SPECIMEN and all zeros serial number. These notes may also be punch cancelled through the facsimile signature. The main purpose of Specimen Notes is for publicity purposes, consequently only a small number are prepared, usually one hundred sets. Another type of Specimen Note exists in which sets of notes endorsed SPECIMEN, are mounted and framed by the printers for display purposes. Occasionally specimen notes occur in which a regular serial number is used, ie. as found on currency notes. In the nineteenth century specimen notes consisted of uniface printings on large cards from the printing plate overprinted SPECIMEN, PROOF or CANCELLED.

Currency Note. The note in its final form as issued to the public.

Unissued Note. Note as prepared ready for circulation but lacking serial numbers or signatures. In the period of hand signing of notes a number would be signed by the manager and passed to the assistant manager or accountant for his signature. Examples exist in which only one signature was appended and for some reason or other were never countersigned.

CHAPTER 1

Manx Features on Notes

Many famous landmarks have featured on Manx notes since the first issue and to avoid repetition a short note about each is given.

Old Fort

Prior to 1818 a small fort stood on Pollock Rock on which part of the Victoria Pier in Douglas Harbour is now erected. George Waldron, an historian, relates that Queen Boadicea's brother, Caratack, concealed the Queen's nephew from the Romans who were in pursuit of him after having vanquished the Queen and slain her children.[4] Some authorities in the early nineteenth century regarded the structure as the most ancient in the British Isles, An old account of Douglas details "a most considerable fort, strongly built of hard stone, round in form, upon which are mounted tower and four pieces of ordnance. It is commanded by a constable and a lieutenant. The constable and two of the soldiers, which are there on continual pay, are bound to lie in this fort every night and keep watch and ward upon the rampart betwixt the fort and the town".[5]

Tower of Refuge

A few hundred yards to the north of the Victoria Pier lies the Conister or St. Mary's Rock which has caused the destruction of many vessels. On one occasion the R.M.S. "St. George" foundered on the rock and only after strenuous efforts of Sir William Hillary, founder of the Royal National Lifeboat Institution, were all the crew saved. A result of this incident was the idea of erecting a tower to serve as a warning to mariners and to provide temporary shelter in case of shipwreck. The architect was John Welch and the structure completed in 1832 at a cost of £254.12.0 (£254.60), of which Sir William paid £78.6.0 (£78.30).[6]

Douglas Harbour

Before 1872 steamers moored at the Old Red Pier if the tide was favourable but at low water the unfortunate passengers were transferred from the steamers to the shore by means of barges. By arrangement with the British Government in 1866 the Island was allowed, in consideration of an annual contribution to Imperial funds of £10,000, to apply surplus revenue for local purposes. A pier due of threepence per passenger was levied by the Manx authorities and paid by the shipping company. This revenue was allocated for harbour works and permitted considerable modification to be carried out. The Victoria Pier was opened for use in 1872 and has been subjected to many improvements since. Work on renewal of the Old Red Pier commenced in 1930 and on completion named the King Edward VIII Pier in May 1936. Another protective structure is the Battery Pier completed in 1879, and the whole harbour facility offers access at all times.

Laxey Wheel

Regarded as one of the marvels of the Island, the wheel was constructed by John Casement in 1854 for pumping water from the adjacent lead mines. During the latter part of the nineteenth century the Laxey Mines were very prosperous, with an output of more than two million pounds value between 1831 and 1884 when lead, copper, silver and zinc were produced in economic quantities. Some indication of the mine's prosperity is shown by the fact that its £80 shares were selling for £1,200 in 1854.

On 27 September 1854 the giant wheel was named the "Lady Isabella" by the chairman of the Great Laxey Mining Company, George William Dumbell, in honour of the wife of the Lieutenant-Governor, Sir Charles Hope. The wheel has a diameter of 72.5 feet and a breadth of 6 feet. In operation the pump was capable of withdrawing water at the rate of 250 gallons per minute from a depth of 1,800 feet, with a power rating of 200 horse power. The mines closed many years ago due to low economic output and the machinery left to decay. The wheel itself may have rusted away but for the efforts of E.C. Kneale, a Laxey joiner and builder, who completely renovated and repaired the wheel, thus preserving it for the benefit of the many tourists who visit Laxey each year.[7,8]

Castle Rushen

Early records indicate the existence of the fortress of Castle Rushen at Castletown since Norse times. Although Norse in origin many of its features are of the fourteenth century. Structural development of the Castle occurred during the reign of several rulers by additions or modifications to the original building and James, seventh Earl of Derby used it as a residence for several years. Its present function is for the courts and installation of new Governors.[9]

Peel Castle & St. Germain's Cathedral

This fortification, sited on St. Patrick's Isle at Peel, was the centre of early Manx religious and civil history and dates from the tenth or early eleventh century. After the garrison ceased in the eighteenth century the buildings fell into ruin. St. Germain's Cathedral is the smallest cathedral within the Anglican community and was erected ca. 1130. Since 1710 the nave has been roofless and by 1772 the chancel had completely gone to ruin. Plans are in hand for the cathedral to be restored. A unique feature was the crypt-prison in existence as late as 1780. A flight of stone steps in the south wall of the chancel afforded access to the prison, described as a bitterly cold, dark, comfortless place in which were confined heretics, drunkards, adulterers, brawlers and "prophaners" of the Sabbath.[10, 11]

Albert Tower

The Albert Tower was erected by the inhabitants of Ramsey to commemorate the unexpected visit of Prince Albert on 20 September 1847. On that occasion the royal yacht anchored in Ramsey Bay when returning from a royal visit to Scotland. The Prince landed on the south shore and asked the first person he met, the local barber, if he would escort him to the summit of Frissel Hill. As the Prince stood enjoying the view news of his arrival reached the Governor then resident at Castletown. The Governor ordered his carriage and quickly travelled to Ramsey some 26 miles distance. Unfortunately he arrived too late and barely caught a glimpse of the royal ship disappearing below the horizon.

The Tower, constructed of granite, is 45 feet high and 16 feet square with access to the roof by a staircase inside the building. Above the door a suitable inscription records the event.[12]

Tynwald

The Isle of Man is famous for its own government which differs in many respects from that of the English parliament particularly in its Norse origin. The name "Tynwald" is derived from the Scandinavian "Thing" (= an assembly) and "vollr" (= a field). It is composed of the Governor with Upper and Lower Chambers, and is also applied to the outdoor ceremony held each year on 5 July on Tynwald Hill at St. John's.[13]

Tynwald Hill consists of a four tiered conical mound traditionally composed of earth from each of the seventeen parishes. The diameters are 256, 163, 102 and 60 feet, stepped at 3 feet intervals. At the actual ceremony the top tier is occupied by the Lieutenant Governor, the Lord Bishop of Sodor and Man who is the sole remaining baron of the Isle of Man, the Deemsters, and two members nominated by the Lieutenant Governor and elected by the Keys. The Legislative Council, or Upper Chamber, headed by their Speaker occupy the third tier and the Keys, or 24 members elected by the six Sheadings and four principal towns occupy the second tier with the clergy and Captains of the parishes who were formerly militia company commanders, on the lowest tier.

Tynwald Court assembles each year on the 5 July when the Lieutenant Governor, the clergy, Captains of the parishes, the coroners and representatives of the town assemble in St. John's Church for a short service followed by a ceremonial procession to Tynwald Hill to take up their positions. After the opening preliminaries the Lieutenant Governor calls on the First Deemster to read all Acts of Tynwald passed by the Legislature since the last ceremony. Owing to the length of each Act only the titles are read together with their dates of Royal assent. Usually the Laws are read in Manx and English.

After the conclusion of the ceremony on Tynwald Hill the officials return in procession to the Chapel where the Lieutenant Governor, Legislative Council and the Keys hold Tynwald Court and transact any further business.[14]

Triune and Motto

A feature of Manx notes is the Triune and motto which has appeared on all notes since their inception. The Triune or Triskellis was adopted as the official crest of the Island in the fourteenth century. Many of the Norse kings used the Viking ship as their emblem and it was towards the end of the Scandinavian period that the Triune came into use. The Triune has been used since ancient times and is known on Greek pottery of the sixth century BC. From Greece the design went to Sicily and then to Scandinavia. Alexander III of Scotland was also familiar with device and adopted it for use in the Isle of Man.[15]

The three legs were modified by addition of spurs and armour and assumed the familiar form of modern times. Later the Latin motto QUOCUNQUE JECERIS STABIT (= Whatever way you throw me I shall stand) was added and first used on Manx coinage in 1668. The heraldic description of the Manx Arms is Gules, three legs, armed, conjoined in fesse at the upper parts of the thigh, flexed in triangle, garnished and spurred or.

Manx Exchange Rates

Prior to 1840 there was a separate rate of exchange for Manx currency against British currency when there were fourteen Manx pence to the English shilling, a state of affairs which created much confusion. Outside of towns Manx money rates were used but within towns English money rates were in use. To overcome this Tynwald passed an Act in May 1840 to make the two currencies on a par. The apparent loss of two pence per shilling caused dissatisfaction among the Manx which led to riots in Douglas with destruction of property. Eventually law enforcement quelled the unrest and the Act of Tynwald came into effect on 21 September 1840.

CHAPTER 2

Card Money

Regretfully these had to be omitted from the first edition due mainly to lack of suitable specimens, many of those which have survived are in poor condition. Details of issuers of card money are not easy to find so this section will not be as comprehensive as desired. Very few specimens of card money have been located in private collections so the majority will only be found in the Manx Museum and in some instances the only information has been recorded by Clay.[16] No detail of rarity has been given for each card since apart from the Bowstead issues the rarity R7 may be assigned to all other cards, and R3 to the Bowstead shilling and half-crown cards, and R4 for the five shillings.

The use of card money as a substitute for small coinage in Canada and Russia is well known. The Isle of Man had an extensive range of cards in the early nineteenth century brought about by a chronic shortage of small change on the Island. Only pence and halfpence were issued during the reign of George III (1760–1820) and these were insufficient to meet the needs of the population. In an attempt to overcome this situation a number of Manx business houses issued their own currency in the form of pieces of card in denominations from threepence to seven shillings. Train attributed introduction of card money to the repeal of the 1737 Act in 1814 but many pieces antedate this, therefore Train's observations are incorrect since the earliest card known was issued by Edward Gawne in October 1805.

As with many other tokens fraudulent issues appeared and some cards were circulated by issuers who had not the slightest intention of redeeming them or even attached difficult conditions to their exchange for coin or notes, ie. acceptance of at least one pounds worth at a time. Difficulties of circulation were also experienced with some cards issued in the north of the Island not being accepted in the south and vice-versa.

A contemporary motto was "Every man his own banker" and many of the cards had little or no financial backing. Counterfeiting was so bad that even genuine cards were sometimes not immediately accepted by the issuers. For several years the Manx coped with this inconvenient medium of exchange and the situation was exacerbated by the indurability of the actual cards rapidly becoming affected by handling so that they became almost illegible and of course made detection of counterfeits a difficult task. One well documented story relates how a member of the Bar collected over £300 in fines and received this in card money instead of coins and notes. All this had to be checked and counted before departure on a long ride home where, on arrival and being exhausted, he threw the bundle into a cupboard until the following morning. On checking the contents they had stuck into a large mass due to the action of lather from the horse. An estimate of the number of these cards was in the order of 2,700. No further comments were recorded!

Many of the issuers were bankers of prominence such as George Quayle, Edward Gawne and George Copeland. Being men of integrity the public accepted their cards without hesitation. Other issuers were not so honest and one such issuer on being asked to redeem his cards replied that he had not put them into circulation with the intention of paying out on them again.

The cards were not of a very complex design and this eased the task of counterfeiting. Usually of varied colours, ie. blue, brown, green, pink, yellow with black print, and some examples are known with different colours on obverse and reverse which were printed separately and stuck together to yield the final product. Details of date, serial number and signature were appended by hand. A multitude of shapes were used, round, oval, octagonal, oblong. Very few specimens have survived in good condition and most extant cards may be described as fair to fine in condition and sometimes almost illegible. No documentary evidence survives in the form of ledgers or similar records to indicate numbers issued or outstanding as is the case with bank notes. A further point regarding card money is that occasionally an example is found which has been cut in two and stitched. Apparently the card would be bisected to yield two cards of half value and then sewn together on redemption. This has been observed on a five shilling card.

In August 1815 several prominent residents called a meeting to petition the Legislature with a view to restraining circulation of card money, both genuine and counterfeit. A resolution was passed to the effect that only cards issued by George Quayle, banker of Castletown, would be accepted in payment unless other issuers appointed resident agents in Douglas and to maintain regular daily hours of business. This petition was presented in October 1815 and favourable acceptance announced the following month. A special Tynwald Court held on 1 December 1815 considered measures to be adopted which eventually led to the Bankers' Notes Act, 1817 under which no notes or cards below one pound could be issued and those in circulation had to be redeemed by 1 October 1817 after which date they were invalid. This Act laid the foundations to the Manx banking system under which note licences were required prior to issue of bank notes.

For convenience, issuers of card money are arranged in alphabetical order along with some contemporary newspaper announcements giving extra details of interest.

BANKS, James – Douglas

1 No further information known relating to issuer or denominations used. Banks died in 1826. The following appeared in the local paper in June 1809.[17]

CARD MONEY
James Banks begs leave to inform the Public, that his Card Notes are cashed, as usual, at his Office, in Douglas.

An unfair attempt to injure him by executing *a Run*, which must necessarily be productive of temporary Inconvenience, even to the *Most Solvent* issuer of Notes, seems altogether (upon the best Information he can procure) to have originated in a *Monopolizing* Principle, highly discreditable in any but particularly so, when done with a view to depress one *Name* thereby for the purpose of personal convenience, by the issue of *another* upon whom the public certainly have no *better* security.

J.B. begs to observe, that his Relatives in this country are numerous and respectable: that they have come forward, and are ever ready to support his credit, when necessary, against any illiberal attacks from whatever quarter they may arise, as he has been sufficiently shown in the present Instance, by the Quality of his notes that he has been duly discharged since Saturday last. And he pledges himself still to preserve that Faith with the Public, which however unkindly or interestedly *defamed*, he is happy to say he has never yet been *broken*.

BEATSON, John – Douglas

John Beatson was in the printing business as early as 1812 and in the following year George Copeland became his partner. Their work was of a high quality but the partnership was short-lived due to the death of Beatson on 4 July 1814, aged 44. Born in 1770 he married Isabella Brew on 22 December 1807. Beatson was a wine merchant and agent for Atlas Fire Insurance, whose tokens featured Atlas in the design. In association with Copeland they issued bank notes for one guinea. Copeland called in and redeemed all Beatson's cards in September 1814.

CARD ISSUES

Beatson's cards are known to have circulated as early as April 1811 when a statement was published regarding refusal to pay cards.[18]

> Some evil disposed Person having been the means of circulating a report, stating that I had refused payment of my *Card Notes* – I hereby offer a reward of *Five Guineas* to anyone who will give such information as may lead to Discovery of the Slanderer; and a further reward of *Five Guineas* to any Person who can prove that payment of them has been refused in any one instance, either by myself or those officiating for me, or that it has at any time been necessary to make a second Application.
>
> J. Beatson

2   One Shilling
Obv: PAYABLE TO THE BEARER ON DEMAND AT J. BEATSONS' WINE AND LIQUOR VAULTS/DOUGLAS (Date). *Rev:* Probably displays triune. *Format:* Circular, 50mm. dia. black print on white. *Date:* 1 January 1813.

3   One Shilling
Similar to (2) above but octagonal, 50mm. dia. dated 1 January 1815.

4   Two Shillings & Sixpence
Obv: 2/6/ISLE OF MAN centre top in two lines. NO. (serial number) to left, ENTD.
(date) to right. Below TWO SHILLINGS AND SIXPENCE/PAYABLE TO THE
BEARER ON DEMAND/AT JOHN BEATSON'S/WINE AND LIQUOR STORES
/2/6 BRITISH. DOUGLAS in five lines. *Obv:* Figure of Atlas on the Globe.
PAYABLE IN GOLD OR BANK NOTES./THE CHANGE TO BE PAID IN BY
THE BEARER./ATLAS FIRE OFFICE in three lines. *Format:* Oblong, 64 x 38mm.,
black print on yellow. *Date:* July 1814.

5   Two Shillings & Sixpence
Similar to (4) above but black print on blue.

6   Five Shillings
Obv: ISLE OF MAN top centre, ENTD. (serial number) 181 (date) below. FIVE
SHILLINGS/PAYABLE TO THE BEARER ON DEMAND/AT JNO. BEAT-
SON'S/WINE AND LIQUOR STORES,DOUGLAS. in four lines. 5/- at lower left.
(signature) at lower right. *Rev:* Figure of Atlas on the Globe. PAYABLE IN
BANK NOTES OR BILLS IN/LONDON./THE CHANGE TO BE PAID IN/BY
THE BEARER/FIRE-----OFFICE. in five lines. *Format:* Oblong, black print on
pink. *Date:* July 1812.

7   Five Shillings
As (6) above but oblong octagonal, black print on yellow, dates unknown.

8   Five Shillings
As (7) above but oblong octagonal, black print on pink, dated 4 July 1815.

9   Five Shillings
?Similar to (6) above, but oval, black print on pink. dated 1815.

BELL, J. – Douglas

10   Threepence
Obv: DOUGLAS NO: (serial number) ENTERED (date). PAYABLE TO THE
BEARER ON DEMAND/THREEPENCE/BRITISH/AT THE OFFICES OF (in
three lines, centre) J. BELL and THREEPENCE below. *Rev:* no details known.
Format: circular, no other details. *Date:* 7 May 1816.

BOWSTEAD, John – Kirk Andrews (Kirk Andreas)

Bowstead's cards are the type most frequently found in comparison with cards of
other issuers. At least 48 sets have been recorded for this issuer, along with
several single specimens of the two lower values. The five shillings is the scarcest
piece.

11 John Bowstead. One shilling card dated 1 February 1814, signed by John Bowstead. [*H. F. Guard*]

11 One Shilling
Obv: BRAWSE KIRK ANDREWS ISLE OF MAN at top. NO (serial number) ENTD. (date) below. ONE SHILLING in centre; PAYABLE TO THE BEARER ON DEMAND, below, 1s in circular panel, BRITISH above. In lower right corner, year, with signature of J. Bowstead at lower left. *Rev:* Triune within garter and motto. *Format:* Oblong, 57 x 40mm., black print on buff or yellow. *Dates:* 1 February 1814, 1 February 1815, 1 September 1815, 10 January 1816, 12 January 1816, 1 February 1816.

12 Two Shillings & Sixpence
Obv: Similar to one shilling cards but TWO SHILLINGS & SIXPENCE in centre. 2/6 in oval, BRITISH above in lower left corner. Signature of J. Bowstead at lower right, 181 (date) below. *Rev:* Triune within garter and motto. *Format:* Oblong, 65 x 47mm., black print on yellow or buff. *Dates:* 21 February 1815, 1 September 1815, 1 January 1816, 13 January 1816, 14 February 1816, 20 February 1816.

12 John Bowstead. Two shillings & sixpence card dated 20 February 1816, signed by John Bowstead. [*H. F. Guard*]

13　John Bowstead. Five shillings card dated 1 February 1816, signed by J. Bowstead. [*H. F. Guard*]

13　Five Shillings

Obv: ENTD. (date) with figure 5 in circle dividing date. Serial number above. PAYABLE TO THE BEARER ON DEMAND/FIVE SHILLINGS BRITISH in two lines, centre; BRAWSE KIRK ANDREWS/ISLE OF MAN in two lines, below with signature of J. Bowstead. All within oval frame. *Rev:* Triune within garter and motto. *Format:* Oval, 62 x 49mm., black print on yellow or buff. *Dates:* 1 January 1816, 20 January 1816, 1 February 1816.

BREW, Thomas – Lezayre

14　Two Shillings & Sixpence

Obv: ISLE OF MAN top centre; NO: (serial number) 2/6 ENTD. (date) below. PAYABLE TO THE BEARER ON DEMAND/TWO SHILLINGS AND SIXPENCE BRITISH/AT THE MANUFACTORY in three lines. LEZAYRE below with signature of T. Brew. *Rev:* PAYABLE IN GOLD OR BANK NOTES/THE CHANGE TO BE PAID IN BY BEARER in two lines. *Format:* Oblong, black print on white, dated 1810.

Thomas Brew died in 1833.

CALEY, John & GAWNE, Patrick & Daniel – Jurby

Issued cards for half-crown and five shillings. No other details known. John Caley died in 1831.

CALLISTER, Edward – Ballashamroch

Obv: No details known. *Rev:* Sailing ship in full sail, fish below. *Format:* Black print on green reverse, no other details known.

19   Two Shillings & Sixpence
Obv: ISLE OF MAN top centre; NO. (serial number) 2/6 ENTD. (signature of James Dugdale) below. I PROMISE TO PAY THE BEARER ON DEMAND/TWO SHILLINGS AND SIXPENCE/BRITISH in three lines. Signature of Edward Callister below. BALLASHAMROCH and date in lower left corner. *Rev:* PAYABLE IN GOLD OR BANK NOTES above sailing ship and harbour. THE CHANGE TO BE PAID IN BY THE BEARER. *Format:* Black print on white. No other details known.

CASTLETOWN NEW CARD BANKING COMPANY – Castletown

A proposal to establish this business was announced in 1808 when the following notices appeared in the local press.[19]

Castletown New Card Banking Company
Whereas great Inconveniences have arisen to the Public, from the several Card Makers residing in various parts of this Island, not having regular Hours appointed for Business, and frequently absenting themselves, and, when from Home, leaving no ostensible Person to answer the Demands upon them; the aforesaid Company, in order to obviate the above Inconveniences, are about to establish a Card Bank, upon a most liberal and permanent footing. Constant attendance from eight in the morning until nine at night.

It will not be necessary to observe to a discerning Public, the various Advantages accruing from this Establishment, as more than ordinary attention is paid to the Security of the Parties concerned.

More Banks !!!
Douglas, 3 Aug. 1808
A Card Company Bank
Some Gentlemen of Fortune, and well known Responsibility, intend opening a Bank, in Douglas, solely for the accommodation of the Inhabitants and strangers in the Isle of Man; each card will be of the value of Ten Shillings, which will be made payable in every Part of the Island (without any delay or any excuses whatever), and at their Banking House in London. The Cards are now preparing in England; the Engraving part will be executed by a well known Italian artist; and the finishing of them will be unique in its kind, asking most brilliant and magnificent Quadrille or Whist Counters; a set of them being framed, will form a elegant assortment of miniatures, which will always of themselves bear an intrinsic value, superior to their nominal.

The Banking House will be from 10 o'clock in the morning till 5 in the afternoon, Winter and Summer. Two Dozen Clerks from one of the first Banking Houses in the English Metropolis are expected to arrive by the next Packet, to superintend the Company's Concerns. It will be conducted on such a grand and liberal scale, that the Public will receive great advantages, while the Proprietors merely content themselves with its Praises.

N.B. A Paper Mill has been contracted with, who are to furnish to the Company, and to them exclusively, a peculiar firm wrought Papier Maché, as materials for these Notes, therefore all fine Linen Rags will be handsomely paid for, being brought to the Cat & Fiddle near the Marine Hotel

Every Man his own Banker, & success to Banking[20]

The Card Company Bank

The Proprietors of the above Bank, beg leave to acquaint the Public (the Clerks being arrived, together with an experienced Cashier and an experienced Teller) that, having purchased that large, commodious, and beautiful mansion, next the Marine Hotel, they intend opening the Bank and commencing business on Monday next, Money advanced and Bills discounted, at Six per cent Interest, upon good Security, to any amount not exceeding One Hundred Thousand Pounds. – at the Solicitation of their House in London, the Bank of England, with an enlarged Liberality, have issued to them to the amount of Twenty Thousand Guineas in Gold, and an adequate Quantity of Silver, part of which is arrived and deposited at their Bank, the Remainder is expected by the Duke of Athol, from Liverpool soon. Two stout and able-bodied Men are wanted, to act as Porters, and to assist in keeping off the Crowd, so that Gentlemen in coming to the Bank may have free Ingress and Egress, good security will be required with them, as a handsome Salary will be allowed, and their chief employment will be to carry the Cash to customers.

Wanted to purchase SIX Large Iron Chests, with good locks, for which a liberal price will be paid.

These are the only details known about this bank. No examples of their card money have been recorded.

CHRISTIAN, William – Douglas

Christian was in business as a brewer but little else is known about him.

21 One Shilling

Obv: DOUGLAS top centre; printed date, 1812, under. NO. (serial number) ENTD. (date) below. PAYABLE/TO THE BEARER ON DEMAND/AT THE BREWERY OFFICE in three lines. Signature of William Christian across bottom. ONE SHILLING BRITISH in lower frame. All within circular frame. *Rev:* No details. *Format:* Octagonal, black print on white, dated 1812, and also 1814 over 1812.

21 William Christian. One shilling card dated 1814, signed by William Christian. Example of card bisected to yield portions circulating at sixpence each and rejoined later. [*H. F. Guard*]

22 Sixpence
Obv: No details. *Rev:* No details. *Format:* Black print on white, dated September 18—.

CHRISTIAN, William – Ballahow, Kirk Onchan

No further details known.

CHRISTIAN, William – Kirk Andreas

No further details known

COPELAND, George – Douglas

Business partner of John Beatson, further details under that name. Cards were printed by Silvester, 27 Strand, London. All cards were called in for redemption on 18 November 1815.

25 One Shilling
Obv: Circle divided into three. ONE/BRITISH above, signature of G. Copeland centre, SHILLING and Triune below. All within ornamental frame. *Rev:* Triune, motto round, laurel leaves to left and right. DOUGLAS ISLE.OF.MAN above. JANUARY.THE.FIRST.1814 below. All within ornamental frame. *Rev:* Circle

25 George Copeland. One shilling card dated 1 January 1815, signed by George Copeland. [*H. F. Guard*]

divided into three. *Format:* Octagonal, 50 x 50mm., black print on white. *Dates:* 1 January 1814, 1 January 1815.

26 Two Shillings and Sixpence
Obv: DOUGLAS ISLE OF MAN across top, date below to right. NO (serial number), ENTD. (date), below; TWO SHILLINGS AND SIXPENCE ON DEMAND in centre. 2/6 BRITISH, lower left; G. COPELAND 7 CO. lower right. *Rev:* Horse's head within circle. G.C.& Co. in oval below. *Format:* Oblong, black print on pink. *Date:* 1 January 1815.

CORKHILL, William – Kirk Maughold

27 Two Shillings and Sixpence
Known to have been issued but no further details.

28 Five Shillings
Known to have been issued but no further details.

CORLETT, Thomas – Douglas

No information on issuer.

29 Sixpence
Obv: SIXPENCE STERLING/6D/(illegible name). *Rev:* PAYABLE IN GOLD OR NOTES/TO LESSEN THE INCONVENIENCE ARISING FROM/THE SCARCITY OF COPPER CURRENCY/TO BE PAID IN BY THE BEARER. in four lines. *Format:* Octagonal, black print on white.

30 One Shilling

The only evidence of this denomination being issued is the following from the local press.[21] The request for redemption may account for no specimens having survived.

A Forgery having been committed upon the Shilling Notes of Thos. Corlett, the Public are hereby desired to take no more of them, but to send on what they have for immediate payment.

COSNAHAN, James – Lark Hill, near Douglas

An announcement in the local press refers to redemption of cards by his widow in March 1813.

31 Three Shillings

Obv: ISLE OF MAN/NO. (serial number) 3/- ENTD. (date)/PAYABLE TO THE BEARER ON DEMAND/THREE SHILLINGS BRITISH/AT JAMES COSNAHAN'S/LARK HILL, NEAR DOUGLAS in six lines. Signature below. *Rev:* Ship within circle. PAYABLE IN GOLD OR BANK NOTES/THE CHANGE TO BE PAID IN BY THE BEARER in two lines. *Format:* Oblong octagonal, black print on pink.

Following discovery of alteration of three shilling cards to circulate as seven shillings the following notice appeared.[22]

Having accidentally heard there has been an attempt made by some fraudulent Person or Persons to *alter* my Three Shilling Notes, which are in circulation for *Seven* shilling; I take the earliest Opportunity of cautioning the Public against taking any of my Notes which may appear to exceed the sum of *Three Shillings* British, having never issued any above that amount.
Lark Hill, July 9, 1806

COWLE, Charles – Ballaghawe, Kirk Andreas

Known to have issued cards, no further details.

COWLE, Thomas & GAWNE, Thomas – Ramsey

32 Five Shillings

Obv: RAMSEY above centre, NO. (serial number) to left, 5/- centre, (date) to right. ON DEMAND PAY THE BEARER/FIVE SHILLINGS BRITISH ACCEPTED in two lines, centre. THOMAS COWLE AND THOS. GAWNE below right. *Rev:* TO PREVENT IMITATION BY BAD SILVER above. PAYABLE IN GOLD OR BANK NOTES/THE CHANGE TO BE PAID IN BY THE BEARER in two lines, centre. G.C.& Co. lower right. *Format:* Oval, black print on pink obverse, blue reverse. *Date:* 10 April 1806.

COWLEY, Daniel – Curraugh Beg, Bride

33   Sixpence
Obv: CURRAUGH BEG, BRIDE top centre, I PROMISE TO PAY THE BEARER/
ON DEMAND SIXPENCE BRITISH in two lines. (date) below. DANIEL COW-
LEY lower right. *Rev:* blank. *Format:* Oblong, black print on white. *Date:* 26 April
1817.

CRAINE (or CRANE) – Douglas

No details regarding issuer or his cards.

DAVIES, T. & Co – Douglas

Davies was in business as a merchant in Douglas and acquired the Phoenix Press
from Mills.

35   Two Shillings & Sixpence
Obv: DOUGLAS (date)/TWO SHILLINGS AND SIXPENCE/PAY TO THE
BEARER ON DEMAND/AT THE OFFICE OF T. DAVIES & CO. in four lines.
Rev: uncertain. *Format:* Oblong, black print on yellow. *Date:* 3 May 1815.

DINWOODY, William – Castletown

No issued cards have been located and possibly they were prepared but never
issued. The printing plates are now in the Manx Museum.

36   William Dinwoody. Unissued one shilling card money. The printing plates for this card
now repose in the Manx Museum. [*H. F. Guard*]

36 One Shilling
Obv: CASTLETOWN in upper border. ISLE OF MAN in lower border.NO. (serial number)ENTD. (date) ON DEMAND I PROMISE/TO PAY THE BEARER in four lines; signature space below. ONE SHILLING BRITISH curved inside border. *Rev:* PAYABLE/AT THE OFFICE OF/WILLM. DINWOODY/CASTLETOWN. *Format:* Circular, 52mm. dia. black on white obverse, orange on white reverse.

37 One Shilling
As (36) but printed on uncut rectangle, 102 x 63mm. black print on both sides.

DUNLOP, Anthony – Balnahow

Obv: No details. *Rev:* PAYABLE IN BANK NOTES/OR BILLS ON LONDON/ DUNLOP BALNAHOW in three lines. *Format:* Oval, black on blue.

FORBES, Edward – Douglas

Forbes was in business with Wulff as his partner as the Isle of Man Bank (1827). Details will be found under that bank later.

39 Five Shillings
Obv: ISLE OF MAN/NO. (serial number) BRITISH ENTD. (date)/5/FIVE SHIL-LINGS/PAYABLE TO THE BEARER ON DEMAND/AT THE OFFICE OF EDWD, FORBES/(signature)/DOUGLAS (date). *Rev:* PAYABLE IN GOLD OR BANK NOTES. *Format:* Oval 65 x 50mm., black on pink obverse, black on blue reverse. *Date:* 1812.

FORBES, Edward & Son – Douglas

40 Two Shillings & Sixpence
Obv: ISLE OF MAN/NO. (serial number) ENTD. (date)/TWO SHILLINGS & SIXPENCE/PAYABLE TO THE BEARER ON DEMAND/AT THE OFFICE OF EDWD. FORBES & SON/DOUGLAS/BRITISH 18 (date). *Rev:* unknown. *Format:* Oval, 60 x 45mm., black print on white.

41 Two Shillings & Sixpence
As (40) but impression of obverse design on uncut card. Printing plate in the Manx Museum.
   The following notice regarding forgeries of this card appeared in the local press.[23]

   Whereas, a Forgery has lately been discovered on the HALF-CROWN NOTES or tickets of Edw. Forbes of Douglas. It is hereby requested that the Holders of any of the Half-Crown Notes or Tickets of Edw. Forbes or Edw. Forbes & Son, may send them in immediately for Payment.

And as it is possible that many Individuals are now in possession of some of the Forged Half-Crown Notes or Tickets, and have taken the same on the Credit of Edw. Forbes, it is their Determination and wish to prevent such Individuals from sustaining any loss.

They do hereby give Notice
That all persons of good character, who can prove satisfactorily that they have taken such forged notes in Payments shall receive the amount and same from the Date thereof; but that after the said five Days have expired no Forged Notes will be paid on any Account.

42   Five Shillings
Obv: ISLE OF MAN/5/FIVE SHILLINGS/PAYABLE TO THE BEARER ON DEMAND/AT THE OFFICE OF EDWD.FORBES SON/(signature)/DOUGLAS 1812. in seven lines. *Rev:* Plain. *Format:* Oval, 66 x 50mm. black print on pink obverse, blue reverse. *Date:* 1812.

43   Ten Shillings
Obv: ISLE OF MAN/NO. (serial number) ENTD. (date) /10/BRITISH/TEN SHIL-LINGS/PAYABLE TO THE BEARER ON DEMAND/AT THE OFFICE OF EDWD.FORBES/DOUGLAS 1815. *Rev:* no details. *Format:* Circular, 55mm. dia., colour unknown.
Impression taken from printing plate in the Manx Museum.

44   Ten Shillings
As (43) but uniface print on 120 x 70mm. card. Black on white. Reads 'Print from plate 23 May 1915' on reverse.

FORBES, Richard

45   Five Shillings
Only detail known is that this has black print on yellow, oval, dated 4 July 1813.

GAWNE, Edward – Mount Gawne

Gawne was a prominent banker and further details are given under the entry for his bank.

46   Two Shillings & Sixpence
Obv: MOUNT GAWNE/ENTD.(serial number) 2/6 (date)/I PROMISE TO PAY THE BEARER/TWO SHILLINGS AND SIXPENCE/BRITISH ON DEMAND/ EDWD.GAWNE. in six lines. *Rev:* PAYABLE/IN GOLD OR/BANK NOTES/THE CHANGE TO BE PAID IN BY/THE BEARER E.G. in five lines. *Format:* Oblong, black print on yellow obverse, black on pale blue reverse. *Date:* 2 October 1805.

47   Five Shillings
Obv: MOUNT GAWNE/NO. (serial number)/ENTD. (date)/I PROMISE TO PAY THE BEARER/FIVE SHILLINGS BRITISH/ON DEMAND/EDWD. GAWNE in

six lines. *Rev:* PAYABLE/IN GOLD OR/BANK NOTES/THE CHANGE TO BE PAID IN BY/THE BEARER E.G. in five lines. *Format:* Oval, black print on pink obverse and reverse. *Dates:* 5 December 1805, 8 December 1806.

Detection of forgeries of the five shilling card necessitated the following notice in the local press.[24]

> Whereas I have lately discovered a Forgery of my 5s Cards, the Public are cautioned to examine the Signature, and requested to send in such cards as were actually signed by me, for immediate payment.
> Edw. Gawne
> Mount Gawne, 10 September 1806

GAWNE, Edward & Thomas – Mount Gawne

Listed in Clay as issuers of half-crown and five shilling cards, but probably only signatories to cards issued by Edward Gawne.

GAWNE, Thomas & COWLE, Thomas – Ramsey

48   Five Shillings
Obv: RAMSEY/NO. (serial number) 5/- (date)/ON DEMAND PAY THE BEARER/ FIVE SHILLINGS BRITISH ACCEPTED/ (signature) Thomas Cowle/Thomas Gawne in six lines. *Rev:* TO PREVENT IMPOSITION BY BAD SILVER/PAY-ABLE IN GOLD OR BANK NOTES/THE CHANGE TO BE PAID IN BY THE BEARER/G.C.& Co. in four lines. *Format:* Oval, black print on pink obverse, black on blue reverse. *Date:* 10 April 1806.

GAWNE & MOORE – Peel?

No further details known.

GIBBONS & MADDRELL – Douglas

No further details known.

GRAYSON & McBRIDE – Douglas

No further details known.

G. & M.

Probably one of the three previous issuers. No details of denominations, dates, shape or colour. Design depicts Crest of Lion's head with G&M in oval. Illustrated in Clay.[25]

JOUGHIN, William – Kirk Andreas

Notice in the press referring to redemption of his cards.[26] Shortly afterwards Joughin gave notice that he would attend to exchange his cards.[27] Later a Coroner's Sale of his property was held to meet his debts.[28]

54   Two Shillings & Sixpence
No further details known.

55   Five Shillings
No further details known.

KAIGHAM, John – ??

No further details known.

KANAN (or KANEEN), Daniel – Kirk Andreas

No further details known.

KELLY, William – Union Mills

Proprietor of the combined corn and woollen mills. Kelly appointed Francis Goodair of Duke Street as his cashing agent in September 1814.

57   Two Shillings & Sixpence
Obv: ISLE OF MAN at top, date at upper right. Flail and fleece in centre. NO. (serial number) 2/6 ENTD. (initials)/I PROMISE TO PAY THE BEARER ON DEMAND/TWO SHILLINGS AND SIXPENCE/BRITISH Wm. Kelly (signature) in four lines. *Rev:* PAYABLE IN GOLD OR BANK NOTES (view of mills)/THE CHANGE TO BE PAID IN BY THE BEARER. *Format:* Octagonal oblong, black on pink obverse, black on buff reverse. *Date:* 1815.

58   Five Shillings
Obv: ISLE OF MAN in curved line at top. NO. (serial number) 5 ENTD. (initials). Flail and Fleece. I PROMISE TO PAY THE BEARER/ON DEMAND FIVE SHILLINGS/BRITISH Wm. Kelly (signature)/UNION MILLS (date). *Rev:* PAYABLE IN GOLD OR BANK NOTES/(view of mills)/THE CHANGE TO BE PAID IN BY THE BEARER. *Format:* Oval, 70 x 55mm. black on pink. *Dates:* 4 September 1811. 29 August 1816.

KENNISH, Peter – Kirk Maughold

59 One Shilling
Obv: KIRK MAUGHOLD ISLE OF MAN/NO. (serial number) ENTD./ ONE
SHILLING/PAYABLE TO THE BEARER ON DEMAND/BRITISH 1s below at
lower left. Peter Kennish (signature) (date) below, at lower right. *Rev:* probably
plain. *Format:* Oblong, 62 x 45mm. black on white. *Date:* 1816.

60 Two Shillings & Sixpence.
No further details known.

61 Five Shillings
Oval, black print on white. Dated 4 October 1806.

KETLER, A. & GUDGE, James & Co. – Ramsey

62 Two Shillings & Sixpence
Obv: RAMSEY/NO. (serial number) 2/6 (serial number) 1806/ON DEMAND PAY
THE BEARER/TWO SHILLINGS & SIXPENCE BRITISH/ACCEPTED. Jas.
Gudge (signature). A. KETLER. *Rev:* TO PREVENT IMPOSITION BY BAD
SILVER/PAYABLE IN GOLD OR BANK NOTES/THE CHANGE TO BE PAID
IN BY THE BEARER/G.K. & CO. *Format:* Oblong, black on pink obverse, black
on blue reverse. *Date:* 1806.

63 Five Shillings
Obv: RAMSEY (in curved line)/NO. 5 1806/ON DEMAND PAY THE BEARER/
FIVE SHILLINGS BRITISH/ACCEPTED. (signature) in five lines. *Rev:* PAY-
ABLE/IN GOLD OR/BANK NOTES THE/CHANGE TO BE/PAID IN BY/THE
BEARER/G.K.& Co. in seven lines. *Format:* oval, 60·x 45mm., black on white
obverse, black on blue reverse. Reverse printed at ninety degrees to obverse.

KEWLEY, Thomas – The Nab, Marown

No further details known. Noted for refusing to accept his own cards.

KILLEY, Philip – Douglas

65 Two Shillings & Sixpence
No further details known.

66 Five Shillings
Obv: I PROMISE TO PAY THE BEARER AT MY/OFFICE, CATTLE MARKET
ST., ------/FIVE SHILLINGS IN CASH/ 5/- PHILIP KILLEY. *Rev:* No details.

KILLEY, William – Kirk Michael

67 One Shilling
Obv: KIRK MICHAEL ISLE OF MAN in curved line/BRITISH/NO. (serial number) 1 ENTD. [two lines illegible]/ONE SHILLING Wm. Killey (signature). *Rev:* PAYABLE IN GOLD OR BILLS ON LONDON. mainly illegible]. *Format:* Circular, 45mm. dia. black on white. *Date:* ?.

68 Five Shillings
Obv: KIRK MICHAEL ISLE OF MAN in curved line/NO. (serial number) 5 ENTD (date)/I PROMISE TO PAY THE/BEARER ON DEMAND/FIVE SHILLINGS. Wm. Killey (signature). *Rev:* no details. *Format:* Oval, black on blue. *Date:* ?

KISSACK, William – Ramsey

69 One Shilling
Announcement in local press regarding forgeries of this denomination.[29]

70 Five Shillings
Obv: ISLE OF MAN in curved line/NO. (serial number) ENTD. J. Kissack (signature)/PAYABLE TO THE BEARER ON DEMAND/FIVE SHILLINGS BRITISH/AT WILLIAM KISSACK'S OFFICE IN RAMSEY/ 5 Wm. Kissack (signature)/4 October 1806 (date). *Rev:* PAYABLE IN/GOLD, BANK NOTES/OR PAYABLE UPON DEMAND./THE CHANGE TO BE PAID/IN BY THE BEARER. *Format:* Oval, 57 x 40mm., black on white. *Date:* 4 October 1806.

71 Five Shillings
Details similar to (70) but of slightly larger format. Oval, 60 x 43mm., black on orange.
    The five shilling cards were also forged and the following notice appeared in the press.[30]

FORGERY
Whereas it has been discovered that the Five Shilling Notes or Cards of Mr. William Kissack have been forged, and that several such Forgeries are now in Circulation.

Notice is hereby given
That any persons giving Information to the said William Kissack against the Forger, or the Issuer of such forged Notes or Cards, so as they may be prosecuted to conviction, shall receive Five Pounds Reward.
    And the holders of such forged Notes or Cards, or of the real Notes or Cards, of Wm. Kissack are hereby requested to take Notice, that the Same will be taken up or cashed by the said William Kissack, at Ramsey. Mr. Robert Cannell of Douglas, Mr. William Kelly of Castletown, and Mr. Hugh Clucas, High Bailiff of Peeltown.

LACE, Daniel – Jurby

No further details known.

LLEWELLYN, John – Castletown

Llewellyn was a lawyer and High Bailiff of Peel.

73 Five Shillings
Obv: CASTLETOWN ISLE OF MAN/NO. (serial number) 5 (date)1813/ON DE-
MAND I PROMISE TO PAY THE/ BEARER/FIVE SHILLINGS/BRITISH/JOHN
LLEWELLYN. in seven lines. *Rev:* plain. *Format:* Oval, black on pink obverse,
black on green reverse. *Date:* 1813.

74 Five Shillings
Variety as (73) but legends on reverse. SUCCESS TO THE LAW, EVERY MAN
HIS OWN BANKER. have been used.
   In 1808 Llewellyn gave notice of intention of issuing cards when the following
notice appeared in the press.

> Mr. Llewellyn begs leave to inform the Public, that in the present
> dearth of *good* Silver Coin, he proposes and intends issuing small
> Bank Notes, similar in some respects to the Notes at present in
> circulation in this Island, but differing from them all in one very
> material respect. In order to ensure credit to his Notes and *Safety to
> the Public*, he has lodged upon Record in the Rolls Office undeniable
> Security for Payment of the Notes which he intends to issue, to the full
> amount and extent thereof.
> Castletown, 7 July 1808[31]

McWHANNELL, Llewellyn – Ramsey

Was also the owner of the Ramsey & Isle of Man Bank. Further details of
McWhannell will be found under bank notes.

75 One Shilling
Obv: RAMSEY/ISLE OF MAN/NO. (serial number) ENTD. (signature)/ONE
SHILLING BRITISH/PAYABLE TO THE BEARER ON/DEMAND in six lines.
Rev: No details. *Format:* Octagonal.

76 Two Shillings & Sixpence
Obv: Apparently design is similar to John Bowstead's card (12). *Format:* Oblong.

77 Five Shillings
Obv: ISLE OF MAN (in curved line at top)/NO. (serial number) 5 ENTD. (signature)/ON DEMAND I WILL PAY THE BEARER/FIVE SHILLINGS BRI-TISH/IN CASH OR BANK NOTES/RAMSEY 1815 in six lines. *Rev:* no details. *Obv:* Oval, colour not known. *Date:* 1815.

MOORE, Charles – Ballcamaish, Kirk Andreas

Apart from a press notice to redeem his cards no further details are known.

MOORE, Edward & Co. – Douglas

No further details known.

MOORE, Edward & James – Douglas

79 One Shilling
Obv: (illegible)/DOUGLAS/(date)/ONE SHILLING BRITISH/PAYABLE TO THE/BEARER ON DEMAND/IN BANK NOTES OR BILLS ON LONDON/JAS. MOORE/AT THE MANUFACTORY. in nine lines. *Rev:* Triune and garter within motto. *Format:* Oval, black on lake red obverse, black on light green reverse. *Date:* 7 January 1815.

80 Two Shillings & Sixpence
Obv: NO. (serial number) ENTD. (signature) Moore/TWO SHILLINGS & SIX-PENCE/ PAYABLE TO THE BEARER ON DEMAND/AT....OFFICE IN DOUG-LAS/James Moore (signature)/1814 in six lines. *Date:* 1814.

81 Two Shillings & Sixpence
Obv: LINEN MANUFACTORY/NO. (serial Number) DOUGLAS/TWO SHIL-LINGS & SIXPENCE/PAYABLE TO THE BEARER ON DEMAND/AT THE OFFICE OF/JAS. MOORE/BRITISH/ 2/6 /ENTD. (signature). *Rev:* Triune and motto within garter. *Format:* Oblong, 65 x 50mm., black on white.
   A copper printing plate for the reverse is now in the Manx Museum. The back bears the inscription 'T. Large, Junr. Little New Street'. This may have been the engraver.

82 Five Shillings
Cards of this denomination were subjected to forgery and the following appeared in the local press.[32]

New Forgery on the Small Notes

Twenty Guineas Reward

Whereas a Forgery has lately been discovered on the Five Shilling Notes, or Tickets issued by Messrs. Edw. & Jas. Moore of Douglas in the year 1804, (for Convenience of their general Linen Manufactory through the Island) at which Time small Change, or any other Substitute could not be obtained. They hereby offer a Reward of Twenty Guineas to any person or persons who will communicate to them such Information as may lead to a conviction of the Offender or Offenders, with an assurance of their Names being kept secret.

The following is a Description of the Forged Notes, so as to distinguish them from the Real or good Notes.

They appear to be principally executed with a pen and if there is Merit in Villainy, such they do possess – from Falsity imitating Truth, and bearing a Strong Resemblance in Parts. In the words *Payable to the Bearer on Demand* the Forgeries which have appeared are all cracked purposely through that Part, as if by Accident – the Signature of *'Edw. Moore'* is much worse written, and begun further from the small circle of '5s British' than in the real. The Pink colour, or Red, on the Back of the Notes, is much Paler, and the circle on the Back, which should contain around it 24 points, as in the Copper Plate, is irregular in the Forgeries – containing in some 25, 26, 27 and in others 28 Points. Several of the Numbers are such as Edw. & Jas. Moore have never issued.

Strong Suspicions are entertained, in a certain ingenious Quarter, where there is a good Penman, and, with attention to the foregoing remarks, it is fully expected that the villain or villains will be discovered, as it is probable that many Individuals are now in possession of some of the Five Shilling forged notes, and have taken them as real, on the stability and credit of Edw. & Jas. Moore, it is their determination and wish to prevent such Individuals from sustaining any loss. They do, therefore, hereby request that all their Notes or Tickets, of Five Shillings each, may be sent in for immediate Payment, within Seven Days of this Date; and all Persons of good character, who can prove satisfactorily that they have really taken such forged Notes in Payment, shall receive the amount of them in Gold, Silver, or Bank Notes, on Demand, but after the said Seven Days Notice, no forged Notes will be paid by them on any account. – and for the further accommodation of those who may live distant from Douglas, attendance (for the payment of the aforesaid Notes) will be given, on Wednesday next the 22nd Inst. at Downes's Inn, Castletown; on the next day, Thursday the 23rd. at Long's, Peel, and the following day, Friday the 24th. at Smiths', Ramsey; from One O'clock till Four.

Their Notes of Two Shillings & Sixpence each are entitled to the usual confidence of the public; no attempts of Forgery having appeared against them.

MOORE, James – Douglas

83   One Shilling
Only information known is that the card is circular, black print on lake-red and dated 7 January 1815.

84   Two Shillings & Sixpence
Known to be oblong format, black print on pink. Dated 7 January (year?).

MOORE, John -"The Hills", Peel

85   Two Shillings & Sixpence
Obv: PEELTOWN ISLE OF MAN/NO. (serial number) ENTD. (date)/I PROMISE TO PAY/THE BEARER ON DEMAND/TWO SHILLINGS & SIXPENCE BRITISH/ 2/6 John Moore (signature). *Rev:* JOHN MOORE/PEEL TOWN round the legend PAYABLE IN GOLD. *Format:* Oblong 65 x 45mm black on white obverse, black on blue reverse. *Date:* unknown.

86   Five Shillings
Obv: PEELTOWN ISLE OF MAN/NO. (serial number) ENTD. (date)/I PROMISE TO PAY/THE BEARER ON DEMAND/TWO SHILLINGS & SIXPENCE BRITISH/ 5/- John Moore (signature). *Rev:* JOHN MOORE OF PEELTOWN round. *Format:* Octagonal, 65 x 45mm., black on buff or pink obverse, black on green or blue reverse. *Date:* 1808
   A press report in 1812, details conviction of a forger of Moore's cards by 100 lashes, £50 fine and six months in gaol.

MOORE, Peter – Douglas

Peter Moore's business premises were situated in Junction Street, Douglas.

88   Peter Moore. Half-crown dated 5 July 1811, signed by Peter Moore. [*H. F. Guard*]

88　Two Shillings & Sixpence
Obv: ISLE OF MAN/NO. (serial number) ENTD. N. Moore (signature)/TWO
SHILLINGS & SIXPENCE/PAYABLE TO THE BEARER ON DEMAND/AT
THE OFFICE OF PETER MOORE, JUNR./DOUGLAS in six lines. BRITISH, 2/6
below at lower left. (date)18 at lower right with Peter Moore (signature) below.
All within oblong frame with incurved corners. *Rev:* plain. *Format:* Oblong, black
print on pink. *Dates:* 27 January 1809, 5 July 1811, 5 July 1815.

89　Five Shillings
The only reference to this denomination is a press report about forgeries.[33]

FORGERY
Whereas, a Forgery has been lately discovered on the Five Shilling
Notes of Peter Moore of Douglas, it is hereby requested that the
Holders of any of his Five Shilling Notes may send them in immediately for payment and as it is possible that many Individuals are now in
possession of some of the forged Five Shilling Notes, and have taken
the same on the Credit of Peter Moore, it is his determination and
wish to prevent such Individuals from sustaining any loss.

MOORE, William & COWLEY, John – ?

90　Two Shillings & Sixpence
Oval format, black on pink. Only detail known.

MORRISON, William – Kirk German

No details known.

OATES, William – Douglas

92　Two Shillings & Sixpence
Obv: DOUGLAS.ISLE OF MAN/NO. (serial number) ENTD. (date)/I PROMISE
TO PAY/THE BEARER ON DEMAND/TWO SHILLINGS & SIXPENCE BRI-
TISH. in five lines. 2/6 at lower left, Wm. Oates (signed) at lower right. *Rev:*
WILLIAM OATES DOUGLAS ISLE OF MAN in frame. PAYABLE IN/GOLD OR
BANK NOTES/THE CHANGE TO BE PAID/IN BY THE BEARER. in four lines,
below. *Format:* Oblong, 60 x 45mm., black on white obverse, black on yellow
reverse.

93　Two Shillings & Sixpence
As (92) but oval format (may have originally been oblong cut to shape).
61 x 45mm., black on pink obverse, black on blue reverse.

94   Five Shillings
Obv: DOUGLAS.ISLE OF MAN/NO. (serial number) ENTD (date)/I PROMISE
TO PAY/THE BEARER ON DEMAND/FIVE SHILLINGS BRITISH. in five lines.
5/- at lower left, Wm. Oates (signed) at lower right. *Rev:* WILLIAM OATES,
DOUGLAS./ISLE OF MAN in frame./PAYABLE IN/GOLD OR BANK NOTES/
THE CHANGE TO BE PAID/TO THE BEARER. *Format:* Oval, 60 x 45mm., black
on pink obverse, black on blue reverse.

95   Five Shillings
Variety as (94) but reverse reads PAYABLE IN BANK NOTES OR BILLS/THE
CHANGE TO BE PAID IN BY THE BEARER. *Date:* 1 February 1806.

QUAYLE, George & Co. – Castletown

Further details of this business are given under the entry for bank notes.

96   One Shilling
No further details known.

97   Two Shillings & Sixpence
Obv: ISLE OF MAN BANK/NO. (serial number) FOR THE CONVENIENCE OF
PUBLIC round 2/6. (date) ENTD. Thomas Caveen ? (signed)/PAYABLE TO THE
BEARER ON DEMAND/TWO SHILLINGS & SIXPENCE/ (signature)/TO THE
CASHIER. *Rev:* no details. *Format:* Oblong, black on white.

98   Two Shillings & Sixpence
Obv: ISLE OF MANN BANK/NO. (serial number). FOR THE CONVENIENCE
OF THE PUBLIC round 2/6 (date)/ENTERED 1811/ON DEMAND PAY THE
BEARER/TWO SHILLINGS AND SIXPENCE BRITISH/GEO. QUAYLE & CO./
TO THE CASHIER. *Rev:* PAYABLE/IN BANK OF ENGLAND NOTES.... [re-
mainder illegible]. *Format:* Oblong, black on pink obverse, black on blue reverse.
Date: 3 August 1811.

99   Five Shillings
Obv: ISLE OF MAN BANK/FOR THE CONVENIENCE OF THE PUBLIC round
5/- /ON DEMAND PAY THE BEARER/FIVE SHILLINGS BRITISH/GEO.
QUAYLE & CO./ (date). *Rev:* no details. *Format:* Oval, black on pink. *Date:* 13
January 1811.

**QUAYLE, John, TAUBMAN, John & MOORE, Norris – Ballaugh & Castle-
town**

100   One Shilling

101   Three Shillings & Sixpence

102 Seven Shillings
Apart from a brief reference in Clay no other details are known of the above three denominations.

QUIGGIN, Philip & John – Kirk Michael

103 Two Shillings & Sixpence
No further details known.

104 Five Shillings
No further details known.

QUILLIAM, John – Maughold

105 Sixpence
No further details known.

106 One Shilling
No further details known.

RAY, James – Kirk Michael

107 Two Shillings & Sixpence
No further details known.

108 Five Shillings
No further details known.

RAY, William

109 Two Shillings & Sixpence
Only detail known is that this card is black on blue oblong.

110 Five Shillings
Obv: KIRK [illegible]/ 5 /I PROMISE TO PAY/THE BEARER ON DEMAND/ FIVE SHILLINGS BRITISH/W. Ray (signed) in six lines. *Rev:* unknown. *Format:* Oval, black on blue.

RONEY, John – Port Erin

111 (Denomination unknown)
Obv: no details. *Rev:* PAYABLE AT THE OFFICE OF JOHN RONEY, PORT IRON (sic). *Format:* Oblong, black on green reverse.

SAYLE, William – Lezayre

112   Sixpence
Oblong, black on white obverse, dated 22 June 1816. Only details known.

113   One Shilling
Oblong. No other detail known.

SPITTAL, Andrew & Co. – Douglas

No further details known.

TAUBMAN & STEPHEN – Ballaugh

No further details known.

TEARE, John – Ballawhaine, Kirk Andreas

No further details known.

TEARE, John – Ballaugh

117   Ten Shillings
Obv: ISLE OF MAN in curved line at top/NO. (serial number)ENTD.(signature)/
PAYABLE TO THE BEARER/ON DEMAND/TEN SHILLINGS BRITISH/AT
JOHN TEARE'S/IN BALLAUGH (curved) 10 (date) (signature). *Rev:* PAYABLE
IN GOLD/OR BANK NOTES/THE CHANGE TO BE/PAID IN BY THE/
BEARER. *Format:* Octagon, 77 x 52mm. Brown on white obverse and reverse.
    A notice regarding encashment of the cards appeared in the press in 1817.[34]

VONDY, Thomas – Jurby

118   Two Shillings & Sixpence
No further details known.

VONDY, Thomas – Lezayre

No further details known.

W(........) – Douglas

119   Threepence
Circular card, black on white, dated May 1816. No other details.

CHAPTER 3

Foundations of Manx Banking

Isle of Man Bank (Taubman & Kennedy) – Manx Fencibles – George Quayle
& Company – Bridson & Harrison – Moore's Bank – Mount Gawne Bank –
Spittall's Bank – Ramsey & Isle of Man Bank – Douglas Bank Company –
Beatson, Copeland & Company.

ISLE OF MAN BANK (Taubman & Kennedy)

Towards the end of the eighteenth century the idea of founding a Manx bank was
formulated by two men, Taubman and Kennedy, who formed a partnership to
establish a bank in Castletown under the title of Isle of Man Bank. The bank does
not appear to have commenced business and the only evidence now remaining is a
single known specimen of an unissued five pound note dated 1 January 1788. A
second specimen formerly reposed in Castle Rushen but was stolen ca. 1974 and
not recovered.

201   Isle of Man Bank (Taubman & Kennedy). Unissued five pounds note dated 1 January
1788. This is the earliest Manx note known. [*H. F. Guard*]

31

Note Issues

201   Five Pounds

Issued: ? *Obverse:* Circular panel displaying Triune, motto round, FIVE POUNDS to left; ISLE OF MAN BANK to right with printed date 1st. JANUARY 1788 below. I PROMISE TO PAY (blank for name)/OR BEARER ON DEMAND FIVE POUNDS STERLING/AT THE COMPANY'S OFFICE HERE in three lines, centre. FOR TAUBMAN & KENNEDY below with space for signature(s). At left-hand side an oval panel enclosing T&K. BUTTERWORTH, SCRIP, below; all within scroll work. NO. (serial number) centre left, ENT. (name) at lower left. KIRKWOOD, SCULP, below. *Reverse:* plain. *Printer:* Butterworth. *Colour:* Grey-black print on white paper. *Watermark:* ISLE OF MAN BANK/T&K in two lines. *Dimensions:* 215 x 124mm. *Rarity:* R7 (1 known).

ROYAL MANX FENCIBLES

In the first edition it was not possible to present much detail of a particular note which was then assigned the tentative title of "Castle Rushen Guinea Note". Since then some letters have been located in the Manx Museum which throw more light on this note. Study of the correspondence now indicates the note was issued by the Royal Manx Fencibles.

Fencible Corps were used in Great Britain to occupy barracks vacated by regular soldiers when serving abroad, being disbanded when the regulars returned and so lacked continuity but did receive pay and allowances accorded to the regular army. All were volunteers. The Isle of Man raised four corps of fencibles from 1779 to 1811. The second corps, titled "Royal Manx Fencibles" was raised by the Duke of Atholl in February 1793. Two of the officers were Lieutenant Mark Quayle and Captain John Taubman who were later partners in the Isle of Man Bank founded by George Quayle.[35] The Paymaster was Mark H. Quayle appointed on 24 April 1796. Only one issued note has been traced, dated 20 December 1798, and signed by Mark H. Quayle as Paymaster.

202   One Guinea

Issued: 1795?. *Obverse:* Vignette of Castle Rushen, ISLE OF MAN above, ONE GUINEA in gothic script below. CASTLE RUSHEN divided by vignette. NO. (serial number) left; (date) 179– right. ON DEMAND I PROMISE TO PAY THE BEARER/ONE POUND ONE SHILLING BRITISH VALUE RECEIVED. in two lines. ENTD. (signature) lower left with space for principal signature lower right. Vertical ornamental scrollwork at left with Triune and motto within laurel branches, crowned. *Reverse:* plain. *Printer:* unknown. *Colour:* Black print on thick white paper. *Watermark:* horizontal lines. *Dimensions:* 234 x 123mm. *Rarity:* R7 (2 known + 4 in archives)

203   One Guinea

As (202) but printed on thin white watermarked paper. *Rarity:* R7 (3 known + 2 in archives)

202 Royal Manx Fencibles. Unissued one guinea note. [*H. F. Guard*]

204 One Guinea
As (202) but printed on thick white unwatermarked paper. *Rarity:* R7 (1 known +
1 in archives)

205 One Guinea
As (203) but printed on thin white unwatermarked paper. *Rarity:* R7 (3 known + 3
in archives)

ISLE OF MAN BANKING COMPANY (George Quayle & Co.)

The formation of this bank was due to the efforts of John Taubman and George
Quayle[36]. George, born in 1751, was the eldest son of John Quayle, Clerk of the
Rolls and the Duke of Atholl's seneschal in the Island. He was well known as a
captain in the first regiment of the Royal Manx Fencibles, which had been raised
in 1779, and was later responsible for the formation of a corps of yeomanry, later
disbanded after the Peace of Amiens in March 1802. John Taubman, son of John
Taubman and Dorothy Christian, also had military connections, holding the rank
of major and acting as commandant of the South Manx Volunteers.
　　It was whilst in London that George Quayle met John Taubman and discussed
an outline plan for the establishment of Quayle's bank. An agreement was drawn
up and signed by the two partners on 25 March 1802 but a few weeks later two
other partners, James Kelly and Mark Hyldesley Quayle, were admitted. Very
little is known about Kelly, who later left the partnership. Mark H. Quayle was a
younger brother of George. Born in 1770 he succeeded his father as Clerk of the
Rolls in 1797 and died seven years later, aged 34. Mark's son, of the same name,

was one of the influential figures in the founding of the Isle of Man Banking Company in 1865, which is dealt with in a later chapter. The original agreement required some modification and was signed on 25 April 1802. Some of the terms of the partnership are of interest. The title of the bank was adopted as the Isle of Man Banking Company with George Quayle as manager, with the responsibility of signing all banknotes and bills. Under the terms of the deed the partners were to enter into the business of banking for a term of fourteen years with the head office at Castletown and sub-offices elsewhere in the Island. Each partner was required to advance the sum of five hundred guineas by 1 June 1802 in order to give a capital of £2,100. A limit to the note issue was imposed, fixed at £4,200 in denominations of one guinea and five guineas. Any excess of the note issue was only allowed at the manager's discretion, but not to exceed the value of Bank of England or Royal Bank of Scotland notes on deposit.

It was decided that no profits or interest were to be taken on the first annual account, but instead these were to be added to the original capital. This was to be continued until the capital amounted to £2,500, the partners to be allowed interest at 4% per annum. Provision was made in case any of the partners died during the partnership, where the partner's share of capital and effects were to pass to the surviving partners.[37]

Business commenced in May 1802 at Bridge House, Castletown, the residence of George Quayle, and continued until the death of Mark H. Quayle (Snr.) in 1804. In the following year, on 11 September, James Kelly was paid out of the partnership and on the same day the bank's liability to the Mark H. Quayle estate was discharged. This now left the two original partners who continued the business until 29 May 1807, when George Quayle wrote to the depositors indicating that the partnership with John Taubman was to be terminated and, if desired, the depositors were invited to continue their business with Quayle on the same terms as previously. Quayle continued the business alone until 7 September 1810, when a new partnership was formed with Edward Cotteen and Patrick Townshend Lightfoot. This new partnership continued for a few years until some differences of opinion on business policy arose. On 16 December 1816 a notice appeared in the Manx press that the partnership was dissolved by mutual consent in relation to Cotteen, but indicated that Quayle and Lightfoot would continue together with effect from 1 January 1817. But the bank had now entered a phase of difficulties and rumours had already circulated in the Island leading to several prominent residents of Castletown, Peel, Douglas and Ramsey showing their support by accepting Quayle's notes.

Further difficulties occurred and on 18 April 1817 the business was assigned to a group of trustees who received from Quayle and Lightfoot a sale in trust of all their property. Within six months George Quayle had sold sufficient of his property to discharge his mortgage and all depositors then informed to submit for payment any negotiable bills, notes and cards by 30 August, after which the amounts were made up and a dividend paid in full.

The principal reason for failure of Quayle's bank was due to advances exceeding deposits coupled with over-issue of its own notes. Examination of the balance sheet for 31 December 1816 shows advances of £19,167 and deposits of only £15,501, clearly not a healthy state for a bank to be in.[38] In the early nineteenth century it was not unusual for advances to be made without security, since in a small community such as the Island a man's social status was held in esteem and for a man in this position to be asked for security for an advance was unthinkable. In view of the state of the bank's affairs some credit is due to George Quayle for his efforts in preserving the name of his bank and his ability to ensure no hardship on the holders of his cards and notes.

Note Issues

206 One Pound
Issued: unknown. *Obverse:* Vignette of Castle Rushen within garter bearing bank's title ISLE OF MAN BANK. £1 and (date) 18—— upper right. NO. (serial number) to left and right of vignette. ONE POUND in gothic script below. ON DEMAND WE PROMISE TO PAY THE BEARER/ONE POUND BRITISH AT THE COMPANY'S/OFFICE IN BANK OF ENGLAND NOTES OR BILLS ON LONDON in three lines. Gothic ONE at lower left. ENTD. (signature) below. Space for signature(s) at lower right. Triune and motto on circular plaque within laurel branches, crowned, at left. *Reverse:* plain. *Printer:* Blake, Change Alley, London. *Colour:* Black print on white paper. *Watermark:* Decorated border, ISLE OF MAN BANK in centre. *Dimensions:* 226 x 131mm. *Rarity:* R7 (1 known).

207 One Guinea
Issued: May 1802. *Obverse:* Vignette of Castle Rushen, ISLE OF MAN BANK above, CASTLETOWN to left; (date) 18—— to right. NO. (serial number) on either side of vignette. ONE GUINEA below. ON DEMAND I PROMISE TO PAY THE BEARER/ONE POUND ONE SHILLING BRITISH AT THE COMPANY'S OFFICE/IN BANK OF ENGLAND NOTES OR BILLS ON LONDON in three

207 Isle of Man Banking Company (George Quayle). One guinea note dated 6 November 1809, signed by George Quayle and Thos. Caveen. [*Manx Museum*]

lines, in centre. ENTD. (signature) lower left, principal signature at lower right. Ornamental scrollwork at left-hand side with Triune and motto on plaque within laurel branches, crowned, to right. *Reverse:* plain. *Printer:* Blake, Change Alley, London. *Colour:* Black print on white paper. *Watermark:* Decorated border, ISLE OF MAN BANK, centre. *Dimensions:* 226 x 131mm. *Rarity:* R7 (1 known). The only known specimen bears the signatures of George Quayle and Thos. Caveen.

208   Five Guineas
Reference has been made to notes of this denomination being issued, but no specimen has been located and no further details are known.[39]

209   Ten Pounds
Issued: unknown. *Obverse:* Vignette of Castle Rushen ISLE OF MAN BANK below, NO. (serial number) to left and right. WE PROMISE TO PAY THE BEARER/ON DEMAND TEN POUNDS BRITISH AT THE/COMPANY'S OFFICE, IN BANK OF ENGLAND NOTES OR BILLS ON LONDON in three lines. TEN POUNDS at lower left. Space for signature(s) at lower right. ISLE OF MAN BANK in vertical panel at left, Triune and motto on plaque within laurel branches, crowned, to right. *Reverse:* plain. *Printer:* Silvester, 27 Strand, London. *Colour:* Black print on white paper. ISLE OF MAN BANK within decorative frame. *Dimensions:* 238 x 125mm. *Rarity:* R7. No issued notes have been examined and it is probable they were prepared but not issued due to the bank ceasing business.

209   Isle of Man Banking Company (George Quayle). Unissued ten pounds note. [*H. F. Guard*]

210   Bridson & Harrison. Unissued one guinea note. [*Manx Museum*]

BRIDSON & HARRISON

Little is known of this bank whose partners were Thomas Harrison, senior, Paul Bridson and Thomas Harrison, junior. Their office was in Douglas and were only in business for a short time.

Note Issues

210   One Guinea
Issued: unknown. *Obverse:* Vignette of sailing ship and an oval panel bearing the letters HBH in script separating the denomination ONE GUINEA. NO. (serial number) at upper left of vignette; ISLEMAN at upper right. ON DEMAND I PROMISE TO PAY THE BEARER/ONE POUND ONE SHILLING STERLING VALUE RECEIVED/AT THE OFFICE OF MESSRS. BRIDSON & HARRISON DOUGLAS/FOR THOS. HARRISON, SENR. PAUL BRIDSON & THOS. HARRISON JUNR. in four lines. ENTD. (signature) at lower left. Space for principal signature at lower right. At far left is the Triune and motto with a floral decoration above and below. *Reverse:* plain. *Printer:* unknown. *Colour:* Black print on white paper. *Watermark:* none. *Dimensions:* 232 x 100mm. *Rarity:* R7 (1 known, in archives).

EDWARD & JAMES MOORE

Edward and James Moore were well known in the Island as linen manufacturers, using their card money as small change due to a lack of sufficient coinage. With the exception of a few brief references in Clay very little information has been found regarding this bank, which was in business in Douglas as early as 1804 when a notice was published in the Manx press explaining that their card money would be paid in British money and not Manx money.[40] The partnership was dissolved by mutual consent on 1 July 1814 but continued as two separate firms. Edward Moore then entered into partnership with Benjamin Starey and continued the banking business for a while. No terminal date of the bank is known.

Note Issues

211   One Guinea
This denomination was issued prior to 1814 but due to lack of specimens no further details are known.

212   Five Pound Bill
Bills for five pounds were also issued payable to bearer or Benjamin Starey, who later formed a partnership with Edward Moore.[41]

Obverse: Vignette of Pier Head, Douglas. with ships, ISLE OF MANN in centre with crown above, Triune below. NO. (serial number) at upper left, (date) 18——— at upper right. FIVE POUNDS centre, ——— ONE DAYS AFTER SIGHT I PROMISE TO/PAY ——————————————OR THE BEARER FIVE POUNDS/BRITISH AT MR. BENJAMIN STAREY'S POULTRY,/LONDON. VALUE RECEIVED in three lines. FOR EDWARD & JAMES MOORE. (signature) at lower right, ENTD. (signature) at lower left. EDWARD & JAMES MOORE vertical, left. *Reverse:* plain. *Printer:* unknown. *Colour:* Black print on white paper. *Watermark:* unknown. *Dimensions:* 209 x 136mm. *Rarity:* R7 (1 known, in archives).

MOUNT GAWNE BANK

This bank was founded by Edward Gawne a brewer and land-owner in business at Mount Gawne near Port St. Mary. On 1 November 1817 a note licence was granted to Gawne to issue up to £5,000 in one pound and one guinea notes. This limit was later increased to £10,000 on renewal of his licence in 1821 and maintained in 1826, 1829, 1835 and 1836.[42] Edward Gawne had his card money circulating as early as 1806 but it was not until November 1817 that he commenced his note issue. The bank ceased on the death of Gawne on 4 October 1837.

Note Issues

Under the note licence granted on 1 November 1817 Gawne was permitted to issue one pound and one guinea notes. Specimens of the latter have not been located and it is possible they were never issued. Two designs of pound notes are known.

213 Mount Gawne Bank. One pound note dated 7 September 1817, signed by Edward Gawne and Edw. G. Smith. [*H. F. Guard*]

Numbering of the first issue commenced at 1, dated 7 November 1817, to a total of at least 6600 and followed by notes dated 6 August 1818 when the notes recommenced at number 1 to at least 2200. Notes dated 7 September 1818 continued with this numbering system. No issued notes after these dates have been examined, therefore further details of the numbering system are not available.

213   Issue 1 (1817–18..) One Pound
Issued: 7 November 1817. *Obverse:* Vignette of main bank premises, MOUNT GAWNE above, ISLE OF MANN below; all dividing title MOUNT GAWNE and BANK. Date at upper right. ONE POUND below vignette NO. (serial number) to left and right. ON DEMAND I PROMISE TO PAY THE BEARER ONE POUND/ BRITISH, AT MY OFFICE VALUE RECEIVED. Principal signature below, right. ENTD. (signature) left. Vertical panel at left-hand side worded EDWARD GAWNE and printer's imprint. *Reverse:* plain. *Printer:* I. Rowe, Change Alley, London. *Colour:* Black print on white paper. *Watermark:* None. *Dimensions:* 190 x 103mm. *Rarity:* R6 (11 known + 5 in archives).

214   Issue 2 One Pound (18..-1837)
Issued: Not known. *Obverse:* Vignette of bank premises, ISLE OF MAN above, MOUNT GAWNE BANK below. NO. (serial number) either side of vignette. ON DEMAND I PROMISE TO PAY/THE BEARER ONE POUND BRITISH AT/MY OFFICE. VALUE RECEIVED. in three lines. 18(date) and principal signature at lower right, ENTD. (signature) at lower left. ONE POUND in vertical panel at left-hand side. EDWARD GAWNE in vertical panel at right-hand side. *Reverse:*

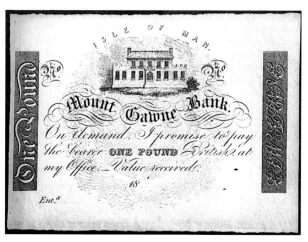

214   Mount Gawne Bank. Unissued one pound note. [*Manx Museum*]

Triune and motto within cable border, all within scrollwork. *Printer:* E. Smith. *Colour:* Black and blue print on white paper. *Watermark:* Letters E G M G in the four corners, (= Edward Gawne Mount Gawne) and two vertical oblong panels. *Dimensions:* 157 x 115mm. *Rarity:* R7 (1 known, in archives)

JOHN SPITTALL & COMPANY

This business is known to have been in existence as early as 1809 under the partnership of Andrew and John Spittall. Application for a note licence in October 1817 and October 1818 permitted the issue of one pound and one guinea notes, but no specimens have been located. No application for renewal of the licence was made in 1819 and it is presumed the bank closed in that year.

RAMSEY & ISLE OF MAN BANK

There is uncertainty when Llewellyn McWhannell commenced his banking business in Ramsey but he was active in 1810 as evidenced by one of his card currency notes for half-crown dated 26 January 1810.[43] In November 1817 a licence was issued for 1,400 one pound notes of the first issue which circulated for five years. At a Council Meeting held at Castletown on 29 November 1822 McWhannell applied for licence to issue £4,000 but was informed that the wording on his existing notes was not in accordance with Section 6 of the 1817 Act in which he omitted to state his notes could be exchanged for Bills on London. McWhannell was then directed to alter his notes at the earliest opportunity or risk imposition of a fine. It was at this meeting that Council members made comparisons with a contemporary Holmes' note (230) and it can be assumed that McWhannell took them at their word and had not only the promissory legend altered to the same as the Holmes' note but somehow his note design came to have a strong resemblance. Notes of the second design (218) appeared to have been issued early in 1823 soon after the Council meeting.

McWhannell's note licence was reduced again in November 1823 to £3,000. No figures are known for 1824 and 1825 but in November 1826 the limit was £5,000. Shortly afterwards, early in 1827, his business closed causing distress to account holders and later, in December, a notice was published requesting holders of McWhannell's notes to send them to the Rolls Office for payment.

Note Issues

217   Issue 1 (1817–1823) One Pound
Issued: November 1817. *Obverse:* Vignette of unidentified building dividing RAMSEY BANK, ISLE OF MANN above. ONE POUND below, NO. (serial number) to left and right. I PROMISE TO PAY THE BEARER ON DEMAND/ ONE POUND BRITISH FOR VALUE RECEIVED/THIS————————DAY OF— ———————————————— (signature) in three lines. ENTD. (signature) to left. Vertical panel at left displaying sailing ship with agricultural implements above and below. *Reverse:* plain. *Printer:* unknown. *Colour:* Black print on white paper. *Watermark:* none. *Dimensions:* 219 x 137mm *Rarity:* R7 (1 known, in archives)

217   Ramsey & Isle of Man Bank. Unissued one pound note. [*Manx Museum*]

218 Ramsey & Isle of Man Bank. Unissued one pound note. Although first examination indicates this to be an issued note, the details are in error and is a spurious item.

218 Issue 2 (1823–1827) One Pound

Issued: c.January 1823. *Obverse:* Vignette of Ramsey Bay and harbour with sailing ships. RAMSEY & ISLE OF MAN BANK above, I PROMISE TO PAY THE BEARER/ON DEMAND ONE POUND BRITISH IN/BANK NOTES OR BILLS ON LONDON. RAMSEY (date) 18——————— in four lines. ENTD. (signature) to left NO (serial number) to right with space for principal signature below. ONE POUND in panel above lower border. Vertically, at left LMcW monogram flanked by ornamental design. All enclosed in engine-worked frame. *Reverse:* Three engine-worked panels, centre panel superimposed on other two. ONE in centre. *Printer:* unknown. *Colour:* Black print on white paper, reverse same. *Watermark:* none. *Dimensions:* 152 x 128mm . *Rarity:* R5. (10 known + 26 in archives).

Notes of this issue were printed in eight subjects per sheet then cut into singles. In about 1950 a number of uncut sheets were discovered in Douglas serving as lining paper on shelves. No issued notes have been recorded with the exception of one note bearing the fictitious date 27 October 1810 and supposed to be signed by Llewellyn McWhannell. This is a spurious item.

218A   One Pound

An unissued note as (218) but printed on paper bearing the watermark KILLOWS 1825. No other details known. Rarity: R7 (3 known).

DOUGLAS BANK COMPANY

Also known as Littler, Dove & Company the bank commenced business on 29 November 1811 initially at Fort Street, Douglas until premises were ready in Duke Street, which was their only office. The partners were William Scarlett

Littler, the Reverend Robert Littler and James Dove. An advertisement in the contemporary Manx press gave details of the bank's function and readiness to meet payments on their tokens, this was to reassure the public who had been subjected to rumours of false plans and intentions regarding the company. Tokens below the sum of twenty pounds tendered for redemption were exchanged for one pound notes, above this amount bills of exchange upon Spooner, Attwoods & Company of London were issued. Until the bank's own notes were prepared and ready for issue, notes and card currency of other banks were used.[44]

Shortly after the company was founded some differences of business policy arose between the partners which led to Robert Littler's plans to leave the Island, but before he could depart James Dove sued for £1,000 resulting in Littler's arrest and detention. Chancery Court proceedings on behalf of Littler against Dove commenced on 3 January 1812 when the arrest was waived and the banking business ceased to operate after only a few weeks existence.[45]

Note Issues

219   One Pound (1811–1812)
Issued: December 1811. *Obverse:* DOUGLAS, ISLE OF MAN across top, NO. (serial number) below. I PROMISE TO PAY THE BEARER ON DEMAND/THE SUM OF ONE POUND BRITISH AT/MESSRS. SPOONER, ATTWOODS & CO. BANKERS LONDON/ENTERED THE —————————DAY OF ————— —————18(date)/FOR THE DOUGLAS BANK COMPY. in five lines. ONE at lower left, signature at lower right. Vignette in panel at left displays a female figure representing Hope supporting a shield bearing the Triune and motto with sailing ships in the background and monogram LD&Co above. NO. (serial number) below. *Reverse:* plain. *Printer:* R & E Williamson, 8 Brook Street, West Square, London. *Colour:* Black print on white paper. *Watermark:* none. *Dimensions:* 197 x 107mm. *Rarity:* R7 (4 known + 1 in archives).

219   Douglas Bank Company. Unissued one pound note. [*H. F. Guard*]

220   Douglas Bank Company. Unissued five pounds note. [*H. F. Guard*]

220   Five Pounds (1811–1812)
Design exactly as for the one pound note (219) except that promissory legend reads I PROMISE TO PAY THE BEARER ON DEMAND HERE/THE SUM OF FIVE POUNDS BRITISH BY BILLS PAYABLE/AT MESSRS. SPOONER, ATTWOODS & CO. BANKERS LONDON. *Rarity:* R7 (2 known).

221   Ten Pounds (1811–1812)
Details as for five pounds (220) note except promissory legend reads I PROMISE TO PAY THE BEARER ON DEMAND HERE/THE SUM OF TEN POUNDS BRITISH BY BILLS PAYABLE/AT MESSRS. SPOONER, ATTWOODS & CO. BANKERS LONDON/. *Rarity:* R7 (1 known) The only extant note bears the false date 25 May 1840.

221   Douglas Bank Company. Unissued ten pounds note. This note bears the false date 25 May 1840. [*H. F. Guard*]

BEATSON, COPELAND & COMPANY

The banking partnership of John Beatson and George Copeland commenced about 1811, when they issued their penny and halfpenny tokens, followed by card money for one shilling, half-crown and five shillings. The partners maintained a wine shop in Douglas, which also served as their banking premises, and acted as agents for the Atlas Fire Insurance Company whose emblem appeared on the tokens.[46]

Another facet of their business partnership was a successful printing works responsible for printing and publishing many famous Manx books.[47] Little information about the actual banking business can be traced and after the death of John Beatson on 4 July 1814 some attempt may have been made by George Copeland to continue the business alone, since a one guinea note is known of the same design as the initial issue, but with Copeland's name only. A point of interest about the bank's clerk, John Stuart Dalton, is that he later became a librarian at the Liverpool Public Library and Museum, in William Brown Street, until his death in August 1868.

Note Issues

222   One Guinea (1813–1814)

Issued: September 1813. *Obverse:* Vignette displays the Old Fort, Douglas. DOUGLAS ISLE OF MANN above, denomination £1.1 at upper right, printed date SEPT. 14th 1813, below. NO. (serial number) either side of vignette. WE PROMISE TO PAY/THE BEARER ON DEMAND/ONE POUND, ONE SHILLING,/ BRITISH, AT THE COMPANY'S OFFICE IN BANK/NOTES OR BILLS ON LONDON VALUE RECD/FOR BEATSON, COPELAND & CO in six lines. ENTD (signature) to left, space for principal signatures to lower right. The bank's title in

222   Beatson, Copeland & Company. One guinea note dated 14 September 1813, signed by John Beatson, George Copeland and J. S. Dalton. [*H. F. Guard*]

223 Beatson, Copeland & Company. Unissued one guinea note bearing name of George Copeland only. [*Charles Clay*]

224 Beatson, Copeland & Company. Unissued ten pounds Bill. [*Manx Museum*]

ornate style within a vertical panel with Triune and motto appears to the left. *Reverse:* plain. *Printer:* Silvester, 27 Strand, London. *Colour:* Black print on white paper. *Watermark:* none. *Dimensions:* 144 x 117mm. *Rarity:* R7 (3 known + 3 in archives). Notes usually bear signatures of John Beatson & George Copeland and also J.S. Dalton (Clerk).

223 One Guinea
A note of the similar design as (222) but bearing name of George Copeland only, unissued. *Dimensions:* 165 x 133mm. *Rarity:* R7 (1 known)

224 Ten Pounds Bill
Obverse: Vignette of the Old Fort, Douglas. DOUGLAS ISLE OF MANN above, NO. (serial number) at upper left and right. £10.0.0 at upper right. TO MESSRS. JONES, LLOYD, & COMPNY. BANKERS, LONDON/AT ——————————— — DAYS SIGHT PAY TO OUR ORDER/TEN POUNDS STERLING FOR VALUE RECEIVED,/AND PLACE IT TO ACCOUNT OF THE MACCLESFIELD BANK,/ FOR BEATSON, COPELAND, & COMPY. in five lines. TEN POUNDS to left, ENTD. (signature) below. Space for principal signatures at lower right. At extreme left a vertical panel with the bank's title in ornate script and Triune and motto within laurel branches to right. *Reverse:* plain. *Printer:* Silvester, 27 Strand, London. *Colour:* Black print on white paper. *Watermark:* Pattern. *Dimensions:* 197 x 120mm. *Rarity:* R7 (2 known + 1 in archives).

CHAPTER 4

Tynwald Act, 1817

Douglas & Isle of Man Bank (Holmes') – Wulff & Forbes – Isle of Man Joint Stock Bank – Isle of Man & Liverpool Joint Stock Banking Company – Isle of Mann Commercial Banking Company – Bank of Mona

THE ACT OF 1817

Public feeling about the number of card notes in circulation led to a meeting of prominent residents in August 1815 to consider a course of action to restrain the increasing quantities of cards, both genuine and counterfeit, in circulation. A resolution was passed that only cards issued by George Quayle's Bank would be accepted in payment, unless the issuers of other cards appointed resident agents in Douglas, keeping regular daily business hours. The bank notes presented in payment also had to be approved by the person tendering the card notes. A small committee was set up to investigate any complaints against issuers of card notes not complying with the conditions.[48] A few days later a meeting was held at Castletown under the chairmanship of Robert Kelly, the High Bailiff. The results of this meeting were similar to that held in Douglas.[49]

These two meetings resulted in positive steps for suppressing the numbers of card notes in circulation. A petition was presented to the Manx Legislature in October 1815 requesting regulations in relation to card notes. Favourable acceptance of the petition by the Lieutenant-Governor was announced in November and a special Tynwald Court held on 1 December 1815 considered measures to be adopted.[50]

A direct result of these meetings was the Bankers' Notes Act, 1817, reproduced in full in Appendix I. Under this Act all card and other notes under twenty shillings were abolished under a penalty of fifty pounds. Notes below twenty shillings in circulation were to be paid in by 1 October 1817 after which they were invalid. Further regulations required all issuers of notes to apply for a licence to issue bank notes of one pound or above for which a fee of twenty pounds per annum was paid. Licences were renewed each year and if necessary the limit of note issue was adjusted. An important feature of the Act was that all notes issued were covered by securities in the form of real or personal estate, so in the event of a bank failing the holders of the notes would be paid.

DOUGLAS & ISLE OF MAN BANK (Holmes')

Originally founded in 1815 under the partnership of Henry Holmes and his three sons, Henry, John and James, the business continued until the father retired from the bank in 1819 leaving the concern entirely in the hands of his three sons. As with some previous Manx banks the business of banking was a subsidiary portion of a general trading business and Holmes' bank was no exception. The Holmes' were fish-curers established at Derbyhaven with interests in the running of passenger and cargo vessels, iron, salt, coal, wines, spirits, groceries, etc. and owned extensive property in the Island and England. Diverse interests such as these naturally incurred speculation, not always successful, and later resulted in the bank's downfall.

In 1826 the father died leaving legacies totalling £20,000 to be paid from his estate, of which only £8,000 was paid by 1853 when the bank closed, still owing £12,000. The business was now completely in the hands of the three sons and without their father's guidance. From this point the banking was carried out entirely to the sons' satisfaction, but possessed a deal of confidence of the people in the Island and in Liverpool. The 1840s witnessed the railway mania and money was advanced by Holmes' on railway scrip in 1845 continuing through 1846 and 1847. Financial losses were incurred, but the partners maintained these were the fault of brokers mishandling their business by bad investments.

Henry Holmes died in 1848 leaving his property to his brothers, James and John, the latter dying a short time later, leaving the youngest brother as survivor. James was now the sole owner and manager, but blindness and advanced years did not make his banking business easy to conduct. He finally died, age 75, on 7 November 1853, when the amount of money on deposit was £206,000 with £20,000 of notes in circulation, indicating the licence limit of £12,000 had been greatly exceeded. This led to stricter control by regular inspection and auditing of banking accounts. Other liabilities were discovered and the total amounted to £300,000.

Immediately the note licences were granted in 1817, Holmes' secured a limit of £12,000 the highest for the Manx banks that year. This was increased to £21,000 in 1821 but reduced in 1826 to £20,000. Another reduction to £15,000 occurred from 1829 to 1836, when the limit was further reduced to £10,000 remaining at this figure until 1842, when it was increased to £12,000 and maintained at this figure until closure except for the years 1845 and 1846 when the limit was raised to £25,000.[51]

Numbering of the notes did not appear to follow a particularly tidy pattern. Initially notes appeared to have been numbered in blocks of 10,000 with a prefix letter being advanced alphabetically. After letter W was reached in 1839 a new sequence was introduced, omitting the prefix letter and numbering from 1 to a total in excess of 10,000. In 1847 the numbers commenced at 1 again and may have continued in this way until the bank closed in 1853. These figures indicate a total note issue of ca. 300,000 notes in 38 years and are relatively the most common note of this period.

Many Holmes' notes were discovered in the strong room of George Quayle's bank at Castletown about 1940, when a search was made in the various rooms which had not been entered for almost a century. A vivid description of this search has been recorded elsewhere.[52]

225   Douglas & Isle of Man Bank (Holmes). Unissued one pound note of first issue. [*H. F. Guard*]

Note Issues

Only two designs of one pound notes were issued.

225 Issue 1 (1815–1824). Notes signed by James Holmes and John Holmes.
Issued: 1 June 1815. *Obverse:* Vignette of harbour scene and sailing ships. ISLE OF MAN above, NO. (serial number to left and right. WE PROMISE TO PAY/ THE BEARER ON DEMAND ONE POUND/BRITISH IN BANK NOTES OR BILLS ON/LONDON/DOUGLAS (date) 1815/FOR HENRY HOLMES JUN. JN. HOLMES/& JAS. HOLMES. in seven lines. ENTD. (signature) at lower left, ONE POUND below. Principal signatures at lower right. To the left HY HOLMES & SONS in vertical panel. *Reverse:* Triune and motto, HENRY, JOHN AND JAMES HOLMES. DOUGLAS ISLE OF MAN round. *Printer:* unknown. *Colour:* Black and pink print on white paper, black print on reverse. *Watermark:* none. *Dimensions:* 154 x 125mm. *Rarity:* R7 (1 known + 1 in archives). The latter is an issued note, numbered A433, dated 1 June 1815.

226 Essay Note – I (1815)
Design as for (225) above, but obverse displays the Liver Bird in a dark brown tint which appears in black on the reverse. Above this on the reverse Henry Holmes wrote the following instructions to the printer 'N.B. Legs of Man in the centre and the Manks motto and then Holmes's Payable at Douglas, Isle of Man. and flourishes round which it would be impossible to imitate.' Around the Liver Bird Holmes wrote 'Holmes Payable at Douglas, Isle of Man'. *Rarity:* R8 (1 known, unique)

227 Essay Note – II (1815)
Similar note to (226) but the Liver Bird now appears in red print on the reverse only. Round this Holmes had written 'Holmes's Payable at Douglas, Isle of Man'. *Rarity:* R8 (1 known, unique).

228 Essay Note – III (1815)
Similar to previous essay (227) but reverse has penned inscription modified to HOLMES'S [PAYABLE? illegible] DOUGLAS, ISLMAN (sic) round Liver Bird with pen flourish at right. *Rarity:* R8 (1 known, in archives, unique).

230 Issue 2 (1824–182.). Notes signed by John Holmes, James Holmes & Thomas Tattersall.
Between 1822 and 1825 a new design was introduced, the exact date of which has not been determined but the imprint Perkins & Heath was the printers' title between July 1822 and May 1829. The earliest known date of the second design is 2 May 1825, which suggests this design appeared during the period 1822–1825. It will be noticed that notes of the second design omit the father's name due to his retirement from the bank in 1819.

Issued: 1824?. *Obverse:* Vignette of Douglas Bay and Harbour DOUGLAS & ISLE OF MAN BANK above. WE PROMISE TO PAY THE BEARER/ON DEMAND ONE POUND BRITISH IN/BANK NOTES OR BILLS ON LONDON. in three

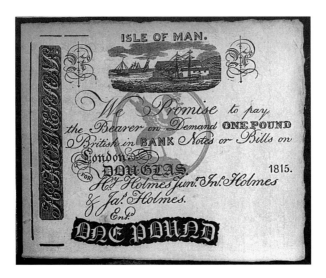

226   Douglas & Isle of Man Bank (Holmes). Unaccepted essay for proposed one pound note issue. [*H. F. Guard*]

227   Douglas & Isle of Man Bank (Holmes). Unaccepted essay for one pound note issue. [*H. F. Guard*]

lines. ENTD. (signature) DOUGLAS (date) NO. (serial number) in one line below promissory legend. FOR HY. HOLMES JUNR, JN. HOLMES & JAS. HOLMES. in one line. Principal signature at lower right. ONE POUND at lower left. At left is an ornamental panel with monogram in centre, with NO. (serial number) below. *Reverse:* Triune and motto, centre. HENRY, JOHN & JAMES HOLMES.DOUG-LAS.ISLE OF MAN round. Decorative panels in each corner. *Printer:* Perkins & Heath, London. *Colour:* Black print on white paper, reverse same. *Watermark:* none. *Dimensions:* 145 x 110mm. *Rarity:* R7 (1 known + 1 in archives). *Dates:* 2 May 1825, 3 May 1825.

231   Issue 3 (182.-1845). Notes signed by John Holmes & James Holmes.
Specification as for (230). *Rarity:* S (132 known + 41 in archives). *Dates:* see below.

[1595]	14 May 1838
[W 250]	14 January 1839
[11605]	2 January 1840
[2287–10057]	January 1841
[1686–8647]	2 January 1843
[9275–16956]	1 January 1844

Majority of notes of this issue are in well circulated condition and it has not been possible to determine finer points of dates and serial numbers with some of the specimens available. Details of known serial numbers are shown above with the lowest and highest numbers for each date. It will be seen that in some cases only one specimen for a particular date has been recorded.

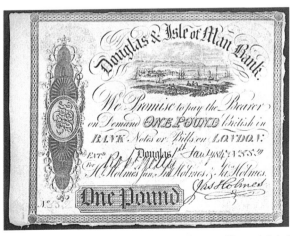

232   Douglas & Isle of Man Bank (Holmes). One pound note of Issue 4 dated 1 January 1847 signed by James Holmes and Robert Kelly. [*H. F. Guard*]

232   Issue 4 (1846–1853). Notes signed by James Holmes & Robert Kelly.
Notes as issued note (231). *Rarity:* R6 (7 known + 4 in archives). *Dates:* see below.

[23259–23444]	1 January 1846
[70–557]	1 January 1847
[5511]	1 May 1847

Although the terminal year for this issue is given as 1853 no notes have been recorded after the single known note dated 1 May 1847. As mentioned earlier James Holmes' blindness did not make the task of running a business easy and it is possible that notes dated after 1847 do not exist. Notes of this issue are more likely to turn up in quite good condition.

ISLE OF MAN BANK (Wulff & Forbes)

The second bank bearing this title was established at Douglas in 1826 under the partnership of John Wulff and Edward Forbes, the latter being the father of Professor Edward Forbes, FRS the eminent naturalist. For the first seven years the bank appears to have functioned normally but from 1833 became indebted to their London agents, Williams, Deacon & Company who, during the course of the next three years, were obliged to send many letters expressing dissatisfaction at the bank's business, especially in connection with the overdraft at the London agent due to the discounting of bills drawn on Wulff & Forbes.

No improvements in the financial position of Wulff & Forbes occurred, who were unable to offer securities required by Williams, Deacon. Early in 1836 Wulff & Forbes requested time to pay and declared their intention of converting the bank into a joint stock company. Two prospectuses were published on 3 and 19 May 1836 and Williams, Deacon viewed these favourably by allowing Wulff & Forbes time to liquidate their liabilities which now totalled £35,000.[53]

Note Issues

233   One Pound (1826–1836). Notes signed by J. Wulff, E. Forbes & T.L. Caley.
Issued: ?1826. *Obverse:* ISLE OF MAN BANK across top, Triune and motto in upper left corner with oval panel enclosing initials JW & EF. WE PROMISE TO PAY THE BEARER ON/DEMAND ONE POUND BRITISH IN BANK/NOTES OR BILLS ON LONDON AT OUR OFFICE IN DOUGLAS in three lines, centre. (date) in panel to left NO. (serial number) to right and repeated below date. FOR JOHN WULFF & EDWARD FORBES at lower right with space for principal signatures, usually the two partners. ONE POUND to left of signatures. The clerk's signature appears in the ENTD. space vertically at left. *Reverse:* Vignette of Neptune seated, with decorative devices in four corners. *Printer:* Perkins &

233   Isle of Man Bank (Wulff & Forbes). One pound note dated 22 June 1829, signed by John Wulff, Edward Forbes and T. L. Caley.

Bacon, London. *Colour:* Black print on white paper, reverse same. *Watermark:* none. *Dimensions:* 160 x 95mm. *Rarity:* R6 (2 known + 13 in archives).
   Numbering of the notes commenced at A 1–1000, B 1–1000, ... to S 676 being the highest serial number recorded. Notes prefixed F to S were all dated 22 June 1829 and notes prior to this are believed to be dated 1826 though this has to be confirmed should a specimen be located. The total issued was ca. 17,000. It is uncertain if all prefix letters A-S were used.

ISLE OF MAN JOINT STOCK BANKING COMPANY

The business of Wulff & Forbes was converted into a joint stock bank and opened for business on 12 July 1836 at Douglas, with a capital of £47,500 composed of 2,500 shares at £4 each and 7,500 shares at £5 each. A further 2,500 shares were allotted to Wulff & Forbes without payment. John Wulff was one of the five directors holding this position until his death about 1840 or 1841. Edward Forbes continued in the capacity of manager with the authority to sign bank notes, bills, etc. Williams, Deacon acted as the London agents.
   Within six months the bank was in financial difficulties due to an increasing overdraft with Williams, Deacon, who informed the Joint Stock Bank that unless business was conducted more favourably the account would be closed. Clearly a similar state of affairs to that which had existed when dealing with Wulff & Forbes before becoming a joint stock company. Correspondence in 1837 reveals a little of the bank's financial position, with overdrafts of £14,000 (March), £16,800 (June) and £15,000 (August). During the next two years the financial position appears to have been the same and on 26 December 1839 Williams, Deacon, who had shown much patience, indicated their intention of closing the Joint Stock Bank, but expressed a reluctance due to the standing of many of its shareholders. An attempt was made by the Joint Stock Bank to reduce this overdraft but before long this was increased.

The gradual deterioration of the Joint Stock Bank eventually resulted in the bank's closure on 14 August 1843 under the direction of the Court of Chancery, due to defalcation by the manager by means of circulating false bills. At this time the bank's liabilities were £14,000 on notes, £6,000 unpaid drafts and £45,000 deposits. There were also £62,000 advances and £15,000 in securities lodged against the note issue. The largest debt to Williams, Deacon & Company amounted to between £70,000 and £80,000.

Note Issues

Only notes of one pound were issued. Numbering of notes was continued from the Wulff & Forbes system commencing at S 1 with an extra hand-written number added to indicate a running total, ie. S201/17,201. On reaching Z 1000, the prefix letter returned to A 1 but the running total was omitted.[54] Wulff & Forbes notes were allowed to remain in circulation for the benefit of the new bank until the Directors produced the necessary security for issue of their own notes.[55]

234   Issue 1 (1836–1838). Notes signed by Edward Forbes (Manager), T.L. Caley (Cashier) and J. Macquillin (Accountant).
Issued: 1836. *Obverse:* Vignette displays two female figures supporting a shield bearing the Triune with motto below. The figure to the left holds a cornucopia and that at the right a pair of scales. ISLE OF MAN JOINT STOCK BANK in upper frame, DOUGLAS in lower frame. ONE with NO. (serial number) below, at either side of vignette, DOUGLAS to left and (date)18—— to right. ISLE OF MAN BANKING COMPANY/PROMISE TO PAY THE BEARER ON/DEMAND, ONE POUND BRITISH/IN CASH OR BILL ON LONDON AT THEIR OFFICE HERE.

234   Isle of Man Joint Stock Bank. One pound note dated 1 January 1838 signed by Edward Forbes, T. L. Carey and J. Macquillin. [*H. F. Guard*]

in four lines. BY ORDER OF THE DIRECTORS to lower right with spaces for signatures of Manager and Cashier below. ONE at lower left, ENTD. (signature) ACCOUNTANT below. All enclosed in frame. *Reverse:* Vignette of Tower of Refuge, ISLE OF MAN JOINT STOCK BANK round. All within ornamental border. *Printer:* W.H. Lizars, Edinburgh. *Colour:* Black print on white paper, reverse same. *Watermark:* none. *Dimensions:* 140 x 122mm. *Date:* 1 January 1838. *Rarity:* R7 (1 known).

235   Issue 2 (1838–1841)
Notes as (234) but signature of John C. Charles replaces that of T.L. Caley. *Date:* 1 May 1838. *Rarity:* R7 (1 known, in archives).

236   Issue 3 (1841–1843). Notes signed by R.W. Fletcher (Manager), T.L. Caley (Cashier) and J. Macquillin (Accountant).
Notes as (234). *Date:* 4 January 1843. *Rarity:* R7 (1 known, in archives).

237   Printer's Proof
Design as issued note (234) but omits ONE, NO. DOUGLAS and 18—— in areas adjacent to vignette. Printer's imprint appears on the reverse only. *Rarity:* R8 (1 known, in archives).

237   Isle of Man Joint Stock Bank. Printer's proof of one pound note. [*Royal Bank of Scotland*]

ISLE OF MAN & LIVERPOOL JOINT STOCK BANKING COMPANY

This bank was established in 1836 with its head office at Douglas and a subsidiary office at Liverpool. The note licence permitted a limit of £10,000 in one pound notes.[56] The bank only remained in business for about two years when it was wound up due to insufficient capital for business to continue in both Liverpool and Douglas. Many of the Manx shareholders were successful in the formation of the Isle of Mann Commercial Banking Company and the manager, William Dickie, later acted as manager for the Commercial Bank.

Note Issues

238 One Pound (1836–1838). Notes signed by William Dickie (Manager) and J. MacLeod (Clerk).
Issued: 21 July 1836. *Obverse:* Vignette of Douglas Harbour, ISLE OF MAN & LIVERPOOL JOINT STOCK BANKING COMPANY above, DOUGLAS to left (date)18——— to right. I PROMISE TO PAY THE BEARER ONE POUND/ BRITISH, ON DEMAND IN BANK NOTES OR BILL ON/LONDON, AT THE COMPANY'S OFFICE IN DOUGLAS centre. (serial number) below to left and right. FOR THE DIRECTORS AND COMPANY (signature) MANAGER below. Arms of the Bank consisting of two shields displaying the Triune and Liver Bird with motto UNION IS STRENGTH below, appear at the left with ONE in panel below. In lower left corner ENTD. (signature) for Clerk. *Reverse:* Triune and motto in circular panel with bank's title round. ONE to left, POUND to right. Upper vignette of two cherubs and lower vignette displays two female figures.

238 Isle of Man & Liverpool Joint Stock Bank. One pound note dated 21 July 1838, signed by Willim Dickie and J. Macleod. [*H. F. Guard*]

Printer: Perkins, Bacon & Petch, London. *Colour:* Black print on white paper, reverse same. Note has three deckle edges, one plain. *Watermark:* none. *Dimensions:* 185 x 108mm. *Rarity:* R6 (2 known + 9 in archives)

239   As (238) but paper bears watermark of bank's title and horizontal bars. Unissued. *Rarity:* R7 (1 known).

240   As (239) but all four edges of note are clean cut. Unissued. *Rarity:* R7 (3 known + 2 in archives)

ISLE OF MANN COMMERCIAL BANKING COMPANY

On cessation of business of the Isle of Man & Liverpool Joint Stock Banking Company in 1838 several of the Manx shareholders established another joint stock bank under the title of Isle of Mann Commercial Banking Company.

Under the deed of co-partnership[57] all the bank's business was strictly confined to that of banking with severe penalties for any member transgressing this. The management consisted of seven members forming a board of directors with trustees appointed to hold the bank's property. The capital of £60,000 was composed of 6,000 shares of £10 each with a limit of four hundred shares to any shareholder.[58] 3,000 shares were subscribed on foundation and business commenced on 29 March 1838 in Douglas. The bank restricted its business to the Island and made no plans to establish branches other than in the Isle of Man.

One of the requirements of the board of directors was that four members should be resident in the Island, these were William Duff, William Kelly, Gavin Torrance and Francis Hall Richmond. Two other directors were resident in Scotland. The seventh member of the board was the bank's manager, William Dickie, formerly with the Isle of Man & Liverpool Joint Stock Banking Company.

The note licence in 1842 permitted £13,500 to be issued in one pound notes, and in 1845 the limit was increased to £24,000.[59] Issue of five pound notes commenced about January 1847 but the licence limit was reduced to £19,850.

Owing to the financial stress of 1848 the bank's directors were obliged to suspend payment resulting in the winding up of the company. In 1849 a branch of the City of Glasgow Bank was established in its place with the new title of Bank of Mona. A committee of shareholders was appointed to wind up the affairs of the Commercial Bank and on 3 December 1858, Robert Dun, Chairman of the Committee appointed to wind up the bank, advised shareholders that the City of Glasgow Bank had paid £884.14.6 (£884.72) for the Bank's remaining assets and were then in a position to declare a final dividend and wind up the affairs. The dividend was four shillings (20p) per share divided among 4395 shares.[60]

Note Issues

241   One Pound Issue 1 (1838–184.). Notes signed by William Dickie (Manager) and Henry Johnson (Accountant).
Issued: 1838. *Obverse:* Vignette of Douglas Harbour with sailing ships and early steam vessels. ISLE OF MANN COMMERCIAL BANKING COMPANY above,

£1 in upper left and right corners. NO. (serial number) either side of vignette, DOUGLAS at left (date) 18—— to right. I PROMISE TO PAY THE BEARER ON/ DEMAND ONE POUND BRITISH./IN BANK NOTES, OR BILL ON LONDON/ AT THE COMPANY'S OFFICE HERE in four lines. FOR THE DIRECTORS AND COMPANY below, with (signature) MANAGER at lower right. Lower left is ENTD. (signature). Other vignettes appear at lower left and right displaying allegorical figures representing Trade and Commerce. All within frame. *Reverse:* Central vignette of Peel Castle with Triune below, surrounded by ornate border embracing two cherubs. All within ornamental frame. *Printer:* W.H. Lizars, Edinburgh. *Colour:* Black print on white paper, reverse same. *Watermark:* none. *Dimensions:* 154 x 122mm. *Date:* 15 November 1844. *Serial numbers:* [17498–20480]. *Rarity:* R7 (2 known, in archives).

242   One   Pound   Issue   2   (184.-1848).   Notes   signed   by   William   Dickie (Manager) and John S. Jackson (Accountant).
As (241). *Date:* 1 May 1848. *Serial numbers:* [A2257–A6572]. *Rarity:* R7 (2 known + 1 in archives).

243   One   Pound   Issue   3   (1848–1849).   Notes   signed   by   John   S. Jackson (Manager) and J.J. Karran (Accountant).
As (241). *Date:* 1 May 1848. *Serial numbers:* [A 9247–A 14877]. *Rarity:* R7 (2 known + 1 in archives).

243   Isle of Mann Commercial Banking Company. One pound note dated 1 May 1848, signed by John S. Jackson and J. J. Karran. [*H. F. Guard*]

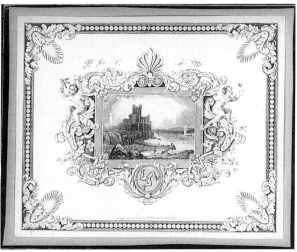

244/245   Isle of Mann Commercial Banking Company. Printer's proofs for obverse and reverse of one pound notes. [*Royal Bank of Scotland*]

244   Printer's Proof – Obverse

As issued note (241). Prepared by Lizars. *Rarity:* R7 (2 known + 1 in archives).

245   Printer's Proof – Reverse

As issued note (241). *Rarity:* R7 (1 known, in archives).

246   Five Pounds (1847–1849)
No details of signatories are known since the only three extant specimens have the lower part of the note cut off this being the portion with the signatures therefore all three possible signature combinations may have been used. Known specimens bear the printed date 5 December 1846 but were not put into circulation until the following year.

Issued: 1847. *Obverse:* Vignette of Neptune and figures with a view of Douglas Bay and the Tower of Refuge in the background. ISLE OF MANN COMMERCIAL BANKING COMPANY below. DOUGLAS to left and printed date 5 DEC. 1846 to right, with two sets of serial numbers on either side of vignette. I PROMISE TO PAY THE BEARER ON/DEMAND FIVE POUNDS BRITISH/IN BANK NOTES OR BILL ON LONDON/AT THE COMPANY'S OFFICE HERE in four lines. FOR THE DIRECTORS/AND/COMPANY in three lines below, centre. (signature) MANAGER lower right. Other vignettes of female figures are located to the left and right centres. FIVE at lower left. *Reverse:* Vignette of harbour scene with two lions and the Union Flag and the White Ensign. The whole surmounted by the Triune and motto supported by female figures. 5 either side of central vignette. All within ornamental surround. *Printer:* W.H. Lizars, Edinburgh. *Colour:* Black print on white paper, reverse same. *Watermark:* none. *Dimensions:* 208 x 128mm. *Rarity:* R7 (1 known + 2 in archives).
　　Known specimens are cancelled by removal of lower portion of note containing signatures. The notes bear two printed numbers, that in black is the serial number which commenced at 001 and the second number in red indicates the total issue of this denomination in pounds, ie note number 001 had the red number 24505, 002

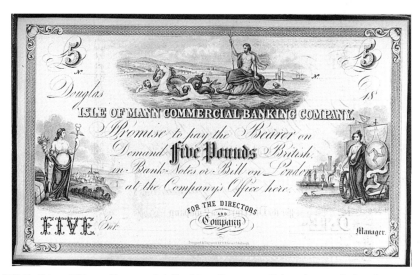

247/248   Isle of Mann Commercial Banking Company. Printer's proofs for obverse and reverse of five pound notes. [*Royal Bank of Scotland*]

248

had the number 24510, 003/24515 etc., so the bank accountant could quickly determine the sum issued by deducting 24500 from the red number. This method of numbering may have been introduced by J.J. Karran when he served as accountant, since a similar system was employed on the one pound notes of the Bank of Mona when Karran served in a similar capacity. Demand for five pound notes must have been quite small during the period of issue from early 1847 to about November 1849 when the bank ceased.

247   Printer's Proof – Obverse
As issued note (246). *Rarity:* R8 (1 known, in archives).

248   Printer's Proof – Reverse
As issued note (246). *Rarity:* R8 (1 known, in archives).

249   Artist's Sketch of Reverse (1846)
Original artist's design in pencil and watercolour. As reverse of issued note (246) but figure 5's of denomination omitted. *Printer:* W.H. Lizars, Edinburgh. *Rarity:* R8 (1 known).[61]

BANK OF MONA

On the termination of the Isle of Mann Commercial Banking Company in 1849 the City of Glasgow Bank established a branch under the name of Bank of Mona. This was the first occasion that a large modern bank commenced operating in the Island and although the parent bank was not a good example of a banking house, the Bank of Mona showed considerable energy and stability and many of its methods were adopted by later insular banks.

With branches at Castletown, Ramsey and Peel the bank was quite successful and figures for 1855 indicate a licence limit of £42,343 and £26,940 of notes in circulation. On 9 November 1857 the Western Bank of Scotland suspended payment giving rise to financial panic, especially in Edinburgh and Glasgow where the crisis was intense. This led to the City of Glasgow Bank suspending payment on 10 November and in turn the Bank of Mona ceased payments for a short time. After reopening of the parent bank on 14 December 1857 the Bank of Mona was able to resume business.

Up to 1869 custody of Chancery Court Funds was held by the Clerk of the Rolls but in that year it was decided to lodge these with the Bank of Mona and relieve the Clerk of liability, thus the bank became bankers to the Manx Government, a position held until the closure in 1878.

A sensational incident occurred in 1878 when Andrew William Gray, employed as chief cashier, attempted to rob the Douglas branch of £8,873 in gold with the aid of two accomplices on Easter Day, 21 April. In his defence at the subsequent trial Gray claimed to have been attacked and robbed of the keys to the bank. But the truth behind the incident lay in revelations of Gray's financial position. He had a salary of £100 per annum and embarked on business ventures, such as a livery stable, wine shop and intended acquiring a pub, also maintaining a trap and servant, much to the concern of the bank's manager, John K. Greig, who had issued an ultimatum to Gray requesting him to abandon his business interests or resign from the bank. Gray chose the latter course and his letter of resignation was received by the bank on the day preceding the robbery. Doomed to failure from the start the robbery was a futile affair, since Gray could not hope to leave the Island with the gold.

The trial commenced on 23 May 1878 and after a six day hearing a verdict of guilty was returned on the charge of robbery, but insufficient evidence resulted in the discharge of his two accomplices, Nix and Roberts. Apart from the robbery other charges were offered including defalcation of about £3,000 and a further trial was held on 9 July when Gray received a sentence of ten years penal servitude.[62][63]

On 2 October 1878 the City of Glasgow Bank failed due to a charge of theft and fraud against the directors, manager and secretary. The failure of the parent bank had no injurious effect to the Bank of Mona and all depositors were quickly paid in full.[64][65] After closure of the Bank of Mona all Manx banking was carried out by Dumbell's Banking Company and the Isle of Man Banking Company, followed in 1882 by the Manx Bank.

Note Issues – One Pound.

250   Issue 1 (1850–1857). Notes signed by John S. Jackson (Manager) and J.J. Karran (Accountant).
Issued: 1850. *Obverse:* Vignette of Queen Victoria, garter motto round; Lion and Tower of Refuge at left; Unicorn and St. Germain's Cathedral right. NO. (serial number) printed at upper left and right with another hand-written number above. BRANCH OF THE CITY OF GLASGOW BANK in small serif letters divided by

vignette. DOUGLAS left; (date) 18——— right. THE BANK OF MONA below
vignette. INCORPORATED BY ACT OF TYNWALD below. I PROMISE TO PAY
THE BEARER ON DEMAND/ONE POUND/IN BANK NOTES OR BY BILL ON
LONDON/AT THE COMPANY'S OFFICE HERE in four lines, centre. Vignettes
of allegorical females holding shields, left displaying Arms of City of Glasgow,
right, the Triune with mottoes below. FOR THE DIRECTORS AND COMPANY
OF THE BANK OF MONA below promissory legend. Two plaques showing Arms
of City of Glasgow and Triune with mottos, below, centre. (signature) ACCOUNT-
ANT at lower left, (signature) MANAGER at lower right. All enclosed within
ornamental border. Printer's imprint below border. *Reverse:* Vignette of Castle
Rushen and sailing ships. Panels of Triune within garter left; Arms of City of
Glasgow with garter and motto right. ONE POUND above, BANK OF MONA
below. BRANCH OF THE CITY OF GLASGOW BANK in small print within
lower border. Printer's imprint below. *Printer:* W.H. Lizars, Edinburgh. *Colour:*
Black print on white paper, black reverse. *Watermark:* ?Bank's title. *Dimensions:*
156 x 116mm. *Rarity:* R7 (Half notes only – 6 known, in archives). *Dates:* (incomplete data).

           51,001–57,000   8 November 1856.

**251   Issue 2 (1857–1859). Notes signed by John S. Jackson (Manager) and
J.J. Karran (Accountant).**
Issued: 1857. As (250) but the overprint BRANCH OF THE CITY OF GLASGOW
BANK now appears in large sans-serif letters. *Rarity:* (R5 (Half notes only – 1
known + 13 in archives) also 1 complete note, in archives.

           57,001–60,000   22 August 1857
           60,001–64,000   20 April 1858
           64,001–67,000   1 October 1858
           67,001–69,000   9 August 1859
           69,001–   22 November 1859

251   Bank of Mona. One pound note dated 1 October 1858, signed by John S. Jackson and J.
J. Karran. Overprint 'Branch of the ...' in large sans-serif letters. [*Manx Museum*]

252 Issue 3 (1860–1865). Notes signed by John S. Jackson (Manager) and J.J. Karran (Accountant).

Issued: 1860. As (250) but overprint BRANCH OF THE CITY OF GLASGOW BANK now appears in small serif letters. *Printer:* Gilmour & Dean, Glasgow. *Rarity:* R7 (Half notes only – 2 known, in archives) also 1 complete note, in archives.

252 Bank of Mona. Obverse and reverse of one pound note signed by John S. Jackson and J. J. Karran. Overprint 'Branch of the ...' in small serif letters. [*Manx Museum*]

253   Bank of Mona. Obverse and reverse of one pound note dated 11 October 1872, signed by John K. Greig and Alexander Irvin. [*H. F. Guard*]

253   Issue 4 (1865–1873). Notes signed by John K. Greig (Manager) and Alexander Irvin (Accountant).
Issued: 1865. Similar to (252) but denomination ONE appears in oval panels at upper left and right. Serial number appears either side of Bank's title. BRANCH OF THE CITY OF GLASGOW BANK now appears in the upper border. Promissory legend modified by addition of IN TERMS OF ACT OF TYNWALD./140 VICT. 1851 as extra two lines. *Rarity:* R7 (1 known). dated 11 October 1872.

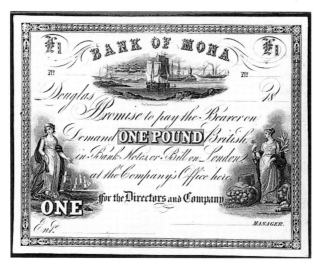

255   Bank of Mona. Unaccepted printer's proof for one pound note (1850). [*Royal Bank of Scotland*]

254   Issue 5 (1873–1878). Notes signed by John K. Greig (Manager) and John G. Greig (Accountant).
Issued: 1873. As (253). *Rarity:* R7 (1 known). dated 10 September 1874.

255   Printer's Proof of Obverse (1850)
Design similar to Isle of Mann Commercial Bank one pound (241) but with BANK OF MONA as bank's title. *Printer:* W.H. Lizars, Edinburgh. *Dimensions:* 161 x 126mm. *Rarity:* R7 (1 known, in archives). No issued notes of this design have been recorded, suggesting this may exist as proof only.

256   Artist's Sketch for obverse design (1850)
Original artist's design in pencil and watercolour of obverse. Basic design similar to issued note (250) but the Queen's head is uncrowned and threequarters view to left. CONSTITUTED BY ROYAL CHARTER below vignette, BY ORDER OF THE DIRECTORS OF THE CITY OF GLASGOW BANK below promissory legend. *Rarity:* R8 (1 known).[66]

257   Printer's Proof of Obverse (1850)
Design as issued note (250). CONSTITUTED BY ACT OF TYNWALD below vignette, FOR THE DIRECTORS AND COMPANY OF THE BANK OF MONA below promissory legend. *Printer:* W.H. Lizars, Edinburgh. *Rarity:* R7 (1 known).

258   Printer's Proof of Reverse (1850)
Design as issued note (250), but the overprint BRANCH OF THE CITY OF GLASGOW BANK is omitted. *Printer:* W.H. Lizars, Edinburgh. *Rarity:* R7 (1 known).

259   Printer's Proof of Obverse (1850)
Design as issued note (250) but reference to Act of Tynwald below vignette omitted. *Printer:* W.H. Lizars, Edinburgh. *Rarity:* R7 (1 known).

260   Printer's Proof of Reverse (1850)
As (258). Reverse of obverse proof (259). *Printer:* W.H. Lizars, Edinburgh. *Rarity:* R7 (1 known) (should be paired with (259)).

Note Issues – Five Pounds

261   Issue 1 (1867–1873). Notes signed by J.K. Greig (Manager) and Alexander Irvin (Accountant).
Issued: 1867. *Obverse:* Vignette of conjoined plaques bearing Triune and Arms of the City of Glasgow with corresponding mottos. DOUGLAS to left. (date) 18——— to right. NO. (serial number) to left and right. THE BANK OF MONA/ (INCORPORATED BY ACT OF TYNWALD) in two lines below vignette. PROMISE TO PAY THE BEARER ON DEMAND/FIVE POUNDS/IN TERMS OF THE ACT OF TYNWALD,/AT THE COMPANY'S OFFICE HERE. in four lines. FOR THE DIRECTORS AND COMPANY OF THE BANK OF MONA BELOW, with (signature) Acct. lower left and (signature) MANAGER lower right. All enclosed in ornamental frame. BRANCH OF THE CITY OF GLASGOW BANK in upper border, INCORPORATED BY ACT OF PARLIAMENT in lower border. *Reverse:* blank. *Printer:* Gilmour & Dean, Glasgow. *Colour:* Black and blue print on white paper. *Watermark:* no details. *Dimensions:* 206 x 128mm. *Rarity:* R7 (none known).

262   Issue 2 (1873–1878). Notes signed by J.K. Greig (Manager) and J.G. Greig (Accountant).
As (261). *Rarity:* R7 (none known).

263   Printer's Proof of Obverse (1867)
As issued note (261). *Rarity:* R7 (1 known, in archives).

CHAPTER 5

The Companies Act, 1865

ISLE OF MAN BANK LIMITED

Under its original name, the Isle of Man Banking Company Limited commenced business at Douglas on 1 November 1865, with the later addition of branches at Castletown, Ramsey, Peel, Port St. Mary, Port Erin, Laxey and four offices in Douglas.

Prior to its foundation banking in the Island was conducted by the Douglas & Isle of Man Bank (Dumbell, Son & Howard) and the Bank of Mona. Discussion for a joint stock bank had been taking place for some time, prompted by the financial stress in 1857 when Dumbell, Son & Howard were closed for a few weeks. This caused deep concern among local businessmen with the result that a prospectus for a bank of limited liability was published in the Island's newspapers in March 1858.[67] Many names appeared as subscribers to this proposal, prominent of which were Henry Bloom Noble and Samuel Harris, but initially no definite results ensued. The passing of the Companies Act, 1862 by the British Government effected a revival in the formation of the new bank. William Callister, former Holmes' Bank representative in Ramsey, and Mark Hyldesley Quayle, whose father was a partner in George Quayle's Bank in 1802, succeeded in asking the Governor, H.B. Loch, to give notice to Tynwald in 1864 for the introduction into the Legislature of a Bill "to provide for incorporation, regulation and winding-up of trading companies with limited liability."

There were further delays until 27 January 1865 when a meeting was held by five influential men. These were William Callister, Mark Hyldesley Quayle, William Fine Moore, Henry Bloom Noble and Samuel Harris. At this meeting a resolution was passed "That it is desirable forthwith to establish an Insular Bank with limited liability, and that such Bank be called The Isle of Man Banking Company Limited." A debate in the House of Keys a few weeks later met with strong opposition, but the promoters were not easily discouraged and indicated that the new bank might be registered in Liverpool under the English Act. But earlier opposition changed and this move was unnecessary, with the result that the Bill was passed on Tynwald Day 1865.[68]

During the period preceding the passing of the Act, a prospectus was formed with an agreed authorised capital of £150,000 in £10 shares, of which the promoters subscribed 3000, and 9000 offered for subscription by the public, the remaining 3000 being reserved for further issue. The application list closed on 19 August 1865 and one month later 9000 shares were allocated to 227 applicants, the original shareholders. The bank was the first Manx company registered under the 1865 Act and was allotted certificate number 1.[69]

The former accountant of the Bank of Mona, John James Karran, was elected as the first manager, holding this position until 1894 with a further fifteen years as director. Archibald Clarke, also a former Bank of Mona official, was appointed cashier. The one pound notes commenced issue in November 1865 when over five thousand went into circulation within a few weeks. One of the requirements of a note issue was the deposition of securities with the Manx government to cover the notes. At this time the bank was experiencing difficulty in obtaining bonds on land for this security, fortunately William Callister had in his private possession several mortgages on Manx properties which he passed to the government as securities for the notes. The later purchase by the bank for £8,000 Consols enabled these to be substituted for Callister's bonds which were then returned to him.[70]

The head office opened in Douglas on 1 November 1865 in Athol Street in premises close to the position of the head office today. Other branches were opened before the end of the year at Castletown and Ramsey followed by Peel on 8 February 1866, Port St. Mary in 1874, Port Erin in 1894 and Laxey in 1895. Further branches were established in Douglas, Onchan and Kirk Michael during the present century.

On the opening of the Regent Street branch in Douglas in 1900 one of the clerks was John Curphey, the former accountant of Dumbell's Bank. When the run on the banks incurred by the collapse of Dumbell's was at its peak, many depositors withdrew their money from other banks, including the head office of the Isle of Man Banking Company, and deposited it in the Regent Street branch. Curphey must have been quite popular with many depositors at Dumbell's and people thought their money would be safer in his hands and gave the term "Johnny Curphey's Bank" to the Regent Street branch.[71]

Records indicate deposits of £3,000 were made at the bank on the first day of business and by 7 November 1865 they reached £13,000. The bank's first General Meeting on 5 February 1866 showed deposits of £58,854 had been made up to 31 December previously, with a profit of £20 in this short time. In 1879 the 3000 shares held in reserve were offered at four pounds each and were readily taken up. Between 1880 and 1900 many changes occurred in the Island. Agriculture remained stable but fishing and mining declined. To compensate for this the Island became popular as a holiday resort. New facilities were made for accommodation in the form of hotels and boarding houses. The harbour was improved to meet the increase in steamship traffic and internal communications improved by the construction of railways.

Rivalry between the banks did not affect the business of the Isle of Man Banking Company which showed increasing deposits each year. The collapse of Dumbell's had its effect, but the bank emerged with greater prestige than before. Commencement of the war in 1914 terminated the Manx holiday season at the beginning of August and the problems associated with wartime conditions were successfully faced by the bank.

In 1925 the bank celebrated its sixtieth anniversary and in that year the bank's title was modified to its present form. A history of the bank by Pilcher G. Ralfe covering the first sixty years was published in that year to mark the Diamond Jubilee.[72]

Deposits and assets increased throughout the next forty years when the bank celebrated its centenary in 1965. The only other large event in the bank's history was the affiliation with the National Provincial Bank in 1961. When the initial announcement was made to the shareholders there was considerable surprise since it was felt that there would be loss of control by the shareholders, who, being Manx, were extremely proud of their bank. After much controversy control of the bank passed to the National Provincial. Since 1969 the bank has been part of the National Westminster Group but the Isle of Man Bank retains its name and autonomy.[73]

Another important event occurred in 1961 when note licences of all commercial banks operating in the Island were revoked in preparation for the Isle of Man Government note issue. The Isle of Man Bank was appointed to manage the note issue and now control all aspects of issue of new notes, withdrawal and eventual destruction.

Note Issues

Three basic designs of one pound notes were issued since 1865 and two designs of five pound notes since 1894 presenting a wide variety of prefixes, dates and signatures. Two hand-written signatures appear on the one pound notes until c1914 and thereafter the manager's signature is in facsimile. All issues of the five pound note bore two hand-written signatures.

One Pound Notes

264   Issue 1 (1865–1894). Notes signed by J.J. Karran (Manager) and Archibald Clarke (Cashier).

Issued: November 1865. *Obverse:* Vignette depicts view of Douglas Harbour from a print showing the arrival of Governor Piggott in 1862. £1 in upper left and right corners. THE ISLE OF MAN BANKING COMPANY/LIMITED in two lines below vignette. NO. (serial number) to left and right. PROMISE TO PAY THE BEARER/ON DEMAND ONE POUND AT THE OFFICE HERE/IN TERMS OF ACT OF TYNWALD. in three lines. DOUGLAS (printed date) below. ENTD. (signature) lower left, (signature) MANAGER lower right. ONE in large letters in centre of note. *Reverse:* Triune within circle, motto round, all within ornamental frame. THE ISLE OF MAN BANKING COMPANY above, LIMITED below. All within border with vertical blue lines to fill design. *Printer:* W.& A.K. Johnston Limited, Edinburgh. *Colour:* Black and brown print on white paper, blue reverse. *Watermark:* ISLE OF MAN BANKING COMPANY LIMITED. *Dimensions:* 168 x 120mm. *Rarity:* R7 (none known). *Serial numbers:* 00001–90000. *Dates:* various.

265   Artist's Sketch of Obverse (1865)
Artist's sketch in pencil and watercolour prepared by W.H. Lizars. Differs in some respects to the issued note (264). Vignette had to be modified by exclusion of a sailing vessel, NO. (serial number) either side of vignette placed below bank's

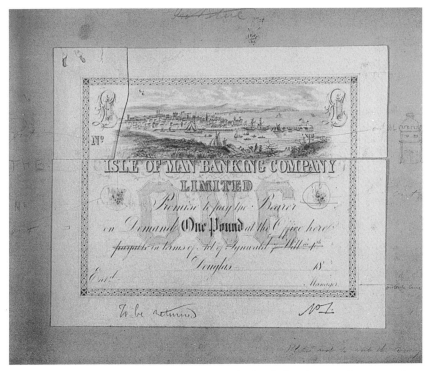

265 Isle of Man Banking Co. Ltd. Artist's pencil sketch for obverse of one pound note (1865). Showing detail of alterations required for the bank. [*Royal Bank of Scotland*]

title. Omission of floral decorations either side of promissory legend, final line of which read PAYABLE IN TERMS OF ACT OF TYNWALD WILLM. 4TH. Words PAYABLE and WILLM. 4TH later deleted. *Rarity:* R8 (1 known, in archives).

266 Printer's Proof of Obverse (1865)
As issued note (264) but printed in black only, portions printed in brown omitted, ie. figure 1 in denominations at upper left and right corners, and ONE in centre. *Rarity:* R7 (2 known, in archives).

267 Printer's Proof of Obverse (1865)
Final proof of issued note (264) printed in full colours. *Rarity:* R7 (1 known, in archives).

268 Printer's Specimen (1894)
Specimen of issued note (264) numbered 90000, dated 1 March 1894. Probably prepared as a printer's reference. *Rarity:* R7 (1 known, in archives).

266 Isle of Man Banking Co. Ltd. Printer's proof for obverse of one pound note omitting brown print. [*Royal Bank of Scotland*]

268 Isle of Man Banking Co. Ltd. Printer's specimen of one pound note dated 1 March 1894. [*Royal Bank of Scotland*]

269 Isle of Man Banking Co. Ltd. Obverse and reverse of one pound noted dated 1 May 1895, signed by Alexander Hill and Thomas Cubbon. [*H. F. Guard*]

269   Issue 2 (1894–1897). Notes signed by Alexander Hill (Manager) and T. Cubbon (Secretary).
Specification as (264) but title of counter-signatory now reads SECRETARY to indicate appointment of Thomas Cubbon to this position in 1894. *Rarity:* R7 (1 known).

                90001–111000   1 May 1895

270 Printer's Specimen (1895)
Printer's reference specimen, as (269), number 111000, dated 1 May 1895. *Rarity:* R7 (1 known, in archives).

271 Issue 3 (1897–1899). Notes signed Alexander Hill (Manager) and T. Cubbon (Secretary).
Specification as (269). The obverse printing plate has either been replaced or heavily retouched. Detail in the sky and sea areas in the vignette shows considerable strengthening. See (272) below. *Serial numbers:* 111001–126000. *Rarity:* R7 (none known).

272 Printer's Specimens (1897–1899)
Printer's reference specimens, basic design as (269) but stronger vignette as in (271) above. SPECIMEN overprint vertically at left and right. These specimens are the only evidence of serial numbers and dates in the absence of surviving issued notes. *Rarity:* R7 (3 known, in archives).

116000	2 June 1897
121000	2 May 1898
126000	22 February 1899

272 Isle of Man Banking Co. Ltd. Obverse and reverse (see following page) of printer's specimen one pound noted dated 2 June 1897. [*Royal Bank of Scotland*]

272 (reverse)

**273   Issue 4 (1899–1915). Notes signed by Alexander Hill (Manager) and
T. Cubbon (Secretary).**
Specification as (271) but reverse design now omits the vertical blue lines and
frame. *Serial numbers:* A.0001–O.10000. *Rarity:* R7 (4 known). Other dates to those
shown below exist.

A	0001– 5000	1 November 1899
A	5001–10000	1 January 1900
M	0001–10000	1 August 1914
N	0001–10000	1 September 1914
O	0001–10000	5 October 1914

274   Printer's Proof (1899)
Printer's proof of note with modified reverse design in which the vertical blue
stripes have now been removed. As (273) but no serial numbers, pencilled date 1st.
Novr. 1899. *Rarity:* R7 (1 known).

275   Printer's Specimens (1899–1900)
Printer's reference specimens. As (273) numbered A 5000, dated 1 November 1899
and A 10000, dated 1 January 1900. SPECIMEN overprint vertically at left and
right. *Rarity:* R7 (2 known, in archives).

**276   Issue 5 (1915–1926). Notes signed by T. Cubbon (Manager) and John R.
Quayle (Assistant Manager).**
Specification as (273) but title of counter-signatory now reads ASST. MANAGER.
Full details of serial numbers and dates are incomplete. 10,000 notes printed per

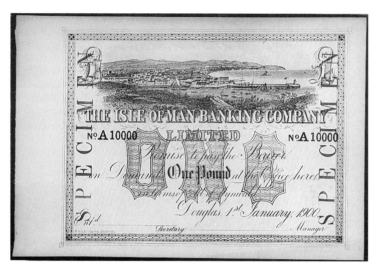

275 Isle of Man Banking Co. Ltd. Printer's specimen of one pound note dated 1 January 1900. [*Royal Bank of Scotland*]

276 Isle of Man Banking Co. Ltd. One pound note dated 1 March 1926, signed by Thomas Cubbon and John R. Quayle. This was the terminal date for this design.

date, except for terminal date. *Serial numbers:* P 0001–Z 10000, A/1 0001–O/1 5000.
Rarity: R4 (27 known + 4 in archives).

P 0001–10000	9 June 1915
Q 0001–10000	8 January 1916
R 0001–10000	3 May 1916
S 0001–10000	
T 0001–10000	
U 0001–10000	2 July 1918
V 0001–10000	6 March 1919
W 0001–10000	
X 0001–10000	18 February 1920
Y 0001–10000	12 November 1920
Z 0001–10000	10 May 1921
A/1 0001–10000	
B/1 0001–10000	
C/1 0001–10000	3 August 1922
D/1 0001–10000	30 September 1922
E/1 0001–10000	1 March 1923
F/1 0001–10000	21 June 1923
G/1 0001–10000	
H/1 0001–10000	2 April 1924
I/1 0001–10000	serial not used?
J/1 0001–10000	
K/1 0001–10000	
L/1 0001–10000	5 February 1925
M/1 0001–10000	7 May 1925
N/1 0001–10000	29 October 1925
O/1 0001– 5000	1 March 1926

By 1925 one pound notes had retained the same basic design for sixty years and as the bank was approaching its Diamond Jubilee it was felt that a change in design and format would be desirable. Also there was a change in the bank's title from Banking Company to Bank. It could be that the printers, Johnstons, were approached a year previously since a printer's proof dated 9 July 1924 exists (278). Notes commenced issue in mid-1926 and continued until replaced by the final design in 1934. One pound notes of the 1926–1934 period presented several signature varieties of counter-signatories after John R. Quayle was appointed manager. Owing to the high rarity of notes of this design information regarding prefixes and dates is very incomplete. Notes bearing prefixes J/2 and L/2 were signed in allocated blocks of serial numbers by different signatories on behalf of the Assistant Manager. In the absence of the Note Registers no other information is known but other prefixes may have existed allocated in a similar way.

277   Issue 6 (1926–1930). Notes signed by T. Cubbon (Manager) and John R. Quayle (Assistant Manager).
Issued: 1926. *Obverse:* Vignette of Douglas Harbour similar to (264) but shows low tide and fewer vessels. ISLE OF MAN BANK LIMITED below. 1 in ornamental design at upper left and right. INCORPORATED IN THE ISLE OF MAN 1865 AS/

277 Isle of Man Bank Ltd. One pound note dated 1 May 1926, signed by Thomas Cubbon and John R. Quayle. This was the first note issued of the new design. [*H. F. Guard*]

THE ISLE OF MAN BANKING COMPANY LIMITED/UNDER AN ACT OF TYNWALD, small print in three lines below bank's title. NO. (serial number) to left and right. PROMISE TO PAY THE BEARER/ON DEMAND ONE POUND AT THE OFFICE HERE/IN TERMS OF ACT OF TYNWALD/DOUGLAS (printed date), in four lines. ONE appears at centre within geometric design. (signature) ASST. MANAGER lower left (facsimile signature) MANAGER lower right. Lower corners display the old and new Arms of the Lords of Man. Printer's imprint below lower margin. *Reverse:* Triune and motto centre. ISLE OF MAN BANK LIMITED curved above, ONE POUND straight line below. All enclosed within geometric design. *Printer:* W. & A.K. Johnston Ltd., Edinburgh. *Colour:* Black and pink print on white paper, green and olive-green reverse. *Watermark:* ISLE OF MAN BANK LIMITED. *Dimensions:* 158 x 90mm. *Rarity:* R6 (12 known + 1 in archives).

O/1 5001–10000	1 May 1926
P/1 0001–10000	1 May 1926
Q/1 0001–10000	1 May 1926
R/1 0001–10000	1 December 1926
S/1 0001–10000	28 January 1927
T/1 0001–10000	7 June 1927
U/1 0001–10000	26 September 1927
V/1 0001–10000	15 February 1928
W/1 0001–10000	1 August 1928
X/1 0001–10000	19 November 1928
Y/1 0001–10000	31 January 1929
Z/1 0001–10000	
A/2 0001–10000	
B/2 0001–10000	
C/2 0001–10000	12 August 1930

278   Printer's Proof (1924)
Specification as issued note (277) but bears printed date 9 July 1924. No serial
number or signatures, cancelled by four punch holes. *Rarity:* R7 (1 known, in
archives).

279   Printer's Proof (1924)
Specification as (278) but devoid of serial numbers, date and signatures. *Rarity:* R7
(1 known, in archives).

**280   Issue 7 (1931–1932). Notes signed by John R. Quayle (Manager) and
W.K. Corlett (Assistant Manager).**
Specification as issued note (277). *Serial numbers:* (E/2 is the lowest known prefix
for this issue). *Rarity:* R7 (8 known + 1 in archives)

E/2	1 May 1931
F/2	1 December 1931
G/2	1 February 1932
H/2	29 March 1932
I/2	serial not used?

**281   Issue 8 (1932–1933). Notes signed by John R. Quayle (Manager) and
C.M. Watterson (p. Assistant Manager).**
Specification as (277). *Rarity:* R7 (3 known + 1 in archives).

J/2	1 October 1932
K/2	9 January 1933
L/2	4 September 1933

Blocks of serial numbers were allocated for different counter-signatories.

**282   Issue 9 (1932). Notes signed by John R. Quayle (Manager) and
W.W. Fargher (p. Assistant Manager).**
Specification as (277). *Rarity:* R7 (2 known).

J/2	1 October 1932

**283   Issue 10 (1933). Notes signed by John R. Quayle (Manager) and
J.W. Hampton (p. Assistant Manager).**
Specification as (277). *Rarity:* R7 (3 known).

L/2	4 September 1933

For nearly seventy years the note printing contract was held by Johnstons but in
1934 this was transferred to Waterlow's who produced the final one pound note
design. This final design yielded a number of signature combinations until 1961
when the note issue ceased.

280   Isle of Man Bank Ltd. One pound note dated 29 March 1932, signed by John R. Quayle and W. K. Corlett. [*H. F. Guard*]

281   Isle of Man Bank Ltd. One pound note dated 1 October 1932, signed by John R. Quayle and C. M. Watterson. [*H. F. Guard*]

283   Isle of Man Bank Ltd. One pound note dated 4 September 1933, signed by John R. Quayle and J. W. Hampton. [*H. F. Guard*]

Positional Code Letters on one pound notes

These will be located on the obverse of the one pound notes at junction of interlacing of lower frame and design surrounding lower left hand emblem, on the reverse they are located in the margin at junction of lower frame and design in lower left corner.

1934–1951

Notes printed in four subjects per sheet with the following layout:-

A/C	C/A
+	
B/D	D/B

ie for A/C A = obverse impression, C = reverse impression, From examination of any note for its positional code letter it is possible to determine which part of the printing plate was used for a particular note. Each quarter was used to print ca, 5,000 notes therefore 20,000 notes would be printed at each run thus yielding 20,000 notes bearing the same date and two prefix letters to the serial number. The table below indicates which impression would be used for a particular prefix. A few exceptions to this rule have been found and presumably these are from sheets left over from a previous run or possibly replacement notes.

Table 1

A/C	B/D	C/A	D/B
N/2	N/2	O/2	O/2
P/2	P/2	Q/2	Q/2
R/2	R/2	S/2	S/2
T/2	T/2	U/2	U/2
V/2	V/2	W/2	W/2
X/2	X/2	Y/2	Y/2
Z/2	Z/2	A/3	A/3
B/3	B/3	C/3	C/3
D/3	D/3	E/3	E/3
F/3	F/3	G/3	G/3
H/3	H/3		
J/3	J/3	K/3	K/3
L/3	L/3	M/3	M/3
N/3	N/3	O/3	O/3
	P/3	Q/3	
Q/3			R/3
S/3	S/3	T/3	T/3
U/3	U/3	V/3	V/3

1952–1961

By 1951 the printing plate, having produced 330,000 notes, required replacement and a new one was prepared using the next four positional code letter combinations. The layout being:-

E/G	G/E
+	
F/H	H/F

Table 2

E/G	F/H	G/E	H/F
W/3	W/3	X/3	X/3
Y/3	Y/3	Z/3	Z/3
A/4	A/4	B/4	B/4
C/4	C/4	D/4	D/4
E/4	E/4	F/4	F/4
G/4	G/4	H/4	H/4
I/4	I/4	J/4	J/4
K/4	K/4	L/4	L/4
M/4	M/4	N/4	N/4
O/4	O/4	P/4	P/4

This plate produced 200,000 notes. The gap in Table 1 for I/3 with positional code letters C/A and D/B suggests this prefix may have been used in printing 20,000 notes dated 30 August 1941 with H/3 and I/3 prefixes. It is possible that Waterlows may have delivered 10,000 notes with the I/3 prefix but these were not accepted by the Isle of Man Bank and therefore the next prefix, J/3, was used. No documentary evidence has been found to support this theory but it seems strange that this gap exists. The prefix I/4 was used at a later date but no evidence exists to indicate if the prefixes I, I/1 and I/2 were ever used.

284 Issue 11 (1934–1937). Notes signed in facsimile by John R. Quayle (Manager) and J.N. Ronan (Assistant Manager).
Issued: 1934. *Obverse:* Vignette of Douglas Harbour and Bay, 1 in the upper corners. ISLE OF MAN BANK LIMITED below. INCORPORATED IN THE ISLE OF MAN 1865 AS THE ISLE OF MAN BANKING COMPANY LIMITED/ UNDER ACT OF TYNWALD in two lines below bank's title. (serial number) to left and right. ONE POUND centre, PROMISE TO PAY/THE BEARER/ON DEMAND in three lines left, AT THE OFFICE HERE/IN TERMS OF/ACT OF TYNWALD in three lines right. DOUGLAS (date) below. (signature) ASST. MANAGER lower left (facsimile signature) MANAGER lower right. Lower corners display the old and new Arms of the Lords of Man. Printer's imprint in lower margin. *Reverse:* Triune and motto round, between geometric patterns. ISLE OF MAN BANK LIMITED above, ONE POUND below. Figure 1 in panel either side. All enclosed within geometric patterns. Printer's imprint in lower margin. *Printer:* Waterlow & Sons Ltd., London Wall, London. *Colour:* Blue, green

287 Isle of Man Bank Ltd. Obverse and reverse of one pound note dated 20 May 1940, signed by J. N. Ronan and C. M. Watterson. Reverse design was common to all issues until 1961. [*F. L. Morgan*]

and brown print on white paper, blue and green reverse. *Watermark:* ISLE OF MAN BANK LIMITED and £1. *Dimensions:* 150 x 84mm. *Positional Code Letters:* A/C, B/D, C/A, D/B. *Rarity:* R4 (29 known + 6 in archives).

N/2 0001–10000	1 October 1934
O/2 0001–10000	1 October 1934
P/2 0001–10000	3 April 1935
Q/2 0001–10000	3 April 1935
R/2 0001–10000	2 December 1935
S/2 0001–10000	2 December 1935
T/2 0001–10000	9 June 1936
U/2 0001–10000	9 June 1936
V/2 0001–10000	5 May 1937
W/2 0001–10000	5 May 1937

285 Printer's Proof (1934)
Specification as (284) but no serial numbers or positional code letters. Facsimile signature of John R. Quayle, hand-written date 1 October 1934. *Rarity:* R7 (1 known, in archives).

286   Printer's Promotional Note
Waterlow's promotional note No: 598, as issued note (284). Lilac and green print on white paper obverse and reverse. Positional code letter C on obverse, reverse positional code letter punched out. *Rarity:* R7 (1 known).

287   Issue 12 (1938–1942). Notes signed in facsimile by J.N. Ronan (Manager) and C. M. Watterson (Assistant Manager).
Specification as (284). *Rarity:* R3 (67 known + 6 in archives).

288   Issue 13 (1938–1942). Notes signed in facsimile by J.N. Ronan (Manager) and Edw. Corteen (per pro Assistant Manager).
Specification as (284). *Rarity:* R3 (52 known + 6 in archives).

Notes of Issues 12 and 13 were counter-signed in blocks by either Cecil Mark Watterson in his capacity of assistant manager or by Edward Corteen per pro assistant manager. No details of blocks of serial numbers allocated. Details of prefix letters and dates are given below with indication of which counter-signatory was used. (W = Watterson, C = Corteen).

X/2 0001–10000	4 February 1938		C
Y/2 0001–10000	4 February 1938	W	C
Z/2 0001–10000	21 November 1938	W	C
A/3 0001–10000	21 November 1938	W	C
B/3 0001–10000	27 April 1939	W	
C/3 0001–10000	27 April 1939	W	C
D/3 0001–10000	20 May 1940	W	C
E/3 0001–10000	20 May 1940	W	C
F/3 0001–10000	6 March 1941	W	C
G/3 0001–10000	6 March 1941	W	C
H/3 0001–10000	30 August 1941	W	C
J/3 0001–10000	30 August 1941	W	C
K/3 0001–10000	16 December 1942	W	C
L/3 0001– 2000	16 December 1942	W	

Some of the above serials with a particular signature are very rare. Of 131

288   Isle of Man Bank Ltd. One pound note dated 4 February 1938, signed by J. N. Ronan and Edward Corteen. [*H. F. Guard*]

289   Isle of Man Bank Ltd. One pound note dated 7 January 1948, signed by J. N. Ronan and W. E. Quirk.

specimens only one A/3 Watterson reported, no B/3 Corteen, two B/3 Wattersons and only one E/3 Corteen has been traced.

289   Issue 14 (1942–1948). Notes signed in facsimile by J. N. Ronan (Manager) and W.E. Quirk (Assistant Manager).
Specification as (284). *Rarity:* R3 (46 known + 7 in archives).

L/3 2001–10000	16 December 1942
M/3 0001–10000	28 October 1943
N/3 0001–10000	28 October 1943
O/3 0001–10000	7 January 1948
P/3 0001– 4000	7 January 1948

290   Issue 15 (1948–1955). Notes signed in facsimile by J. N. Ronan (Manager) and R. H. Kelly (Assistant Manager).
Specification as (284). *Rarity:* R2 (186 known + 13 in archives).

P/3 4001–10000	7 January 1948
Q/3 0001–10000	9 February 1949
R/3 0001–10000	9 February 1949
S/3 0001–10000	10 November 1950
T/3 0001–10000	10 November 1950
U/3 0001–10000	24 September 1951
V/3 0001–10000	24 September 1951
W/3 0001–10000	18 October 1952
X/3 0001–10000	18 October 1952
Y/3 0001–10000	1 December 1953
Z/3 0001–10000	1 December 1953
A/4 0001–10000	29 November 1954
B/4 0001– 4000	29 November 1954

Robert H. Kelly was promoted to manager in 1955 with John Edward Cashin as assistant manager but no notes were issued in the name of R.H. Kelly in his capacity of manager due to his death early in 1956. Existing stocks of one pound notes were used countersigned by either W.E. Quirk or J.E. Cashin until notes bearing the facsimile signature of J.E. Cashin were available from the printers later on, blocks of serial numbers being allotted to each counter-signatory, as detailed below.

291 Issue 16 (1955–1956). Notes signed in facsimile by J.N. Ronan (Manager) and W.E. Quirk (Assistant Manager).
Specification as (284) *Rarity:* R7 (6 known + 1 in archives)

B/4 4001–6000	29 November 1954
B/4 7001–7500	29 November 1954
B/4 9001–10000	29 November 1954

292 Issue 17 (1955–1956). Notes signed in facsimile by J.N. Ronan (Manager) and J.E. Cashin (Assistant Manager).
Specification as (284) *Rarity:* R6 (9 known + 3 in archives).

B/4 6001–7000	29 November 1954
B/4 7501–9000	29 November 1954

293 Issue 18 (1956–1961). Notes signed in facsimile by J.E. Cashin (Manager) and W.E. Quirk (Assistant Manager).
Specification as (284) *Rarity:* R (244 known + 13 in archives).

C/4 0001–10000	5 January 1956
D/4 0001–10000	5 January 1956
E/4 0001–10000	24 August 1956
F/4 0001–10000	24 August 1956
G/4 0001–10000	4 April 1957
H/4 0001–10000	4 April 1957
I/4 0001–10000	17 March 1958
J/4 0001–10000	17 March 1958
K/4 0001–10000	2 February 1959
L/4 0001–10000	2 February 1959
M/4 0001–10000	30 December 1959
N/4 0001–10000	30 December 1959
O/4 0001–10000	24 October 1960
P/4 0001–10000	24 October 1960*

* These notes were destroyed, unissued.

293   Isle of Man Bank Ltd. One pound note dated 17 March 1958, signed by J. E. Cashin and W. E. Quirk.

Five Pound Notes

This denomination was first issued in 1894 when notes dated 1 November 1894 were issued. The same basic design continued until 1927 when a new design was issued and remained the same, except for a change of colour, until 1961.

294   Issue 1 (1894–1914). Notes signed by Alexander Hill (Manager) and T. Cubbon (Secretary).
Issued: 20 November 1894. *Obverse:* ISLE OF MAN BANKING COMPANY at top, "LIMITED" below. NO. (serial number) upper left £5 upper right. I PROMISE TO PAY THE BEARER ON DEMAND/THE SUM OF FIVE POUNDS AT THE OFFICE HERE/IN TERMS OF ACT OF TYNWALD, VALUE RECEIVED/ DOUGLAS (date) (serial number) NO.———— FOR THE ISLE OF MAN BANK-ING COMPANY LIMITED. (signature) MANAGER. (signature) SECRETARY at lower right. £FIVE at lower left. Triune and motto centre left. Printer's imprint below. *Reverse:* 5 in circle. FIVE POUNDS in curved frame each side. *Printer:* W. & A.K. Johnston, Edinburgh. *Colour:* Black and blue print on white paper, black reverse. *Watermark:* ISLE OF MAN BANKING COMPANY LIMITED. *Dimensions:* 203 x 112mm. *Rarity:* R7 (none known).

00001–02600	1 November 1894	(5)
02601–05600	1 January 1900	(10)
05601–06600	4 November 1911	(2)

Number in brackets indicate number of notes outstanding in 1961.

295   Printer's Specimen (1894)
Specification as (294), but lacks printer's imprint below Triune and motto. Serial number 02000. SPECIMEN overprint vertically to left and right. Probably prepared as a printer's reference. Dated 1 Novr. 1894. *Rarity:* R7 (1 known).

295   Isle of Man Banking Co. Ltd. Printer's specimen of five pounds note dated 1 November 1894. This omits the printer's imprint. [*Royal Bank of Scotland*]

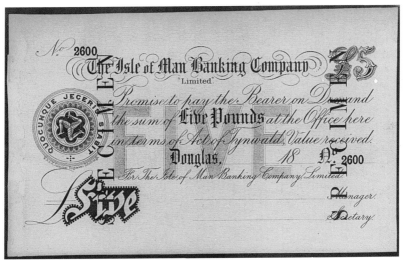

296   Isle of Man Banking Co. Ltd. Obverse and reverse (see following page) of undated printer's specimen of five pounds note. Printer's imprint now included. Design used from 1894–1927. [*Royal Bank of Scotland*]

296   Printer's Specimen (1900)
Specification as (294), bears printer's imprint below Triune and motto. Serial numbers 02600 and 05600. SPECIMEN overprint vertically to left and right.

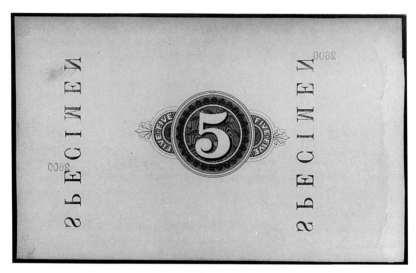

296 (reverse)

Probably prepared as printer's reference. A second specimen numbered 05600 is known but bears the date 1 January 1900. *Rarity:* R7 (1 known + 2 in archives)

297   Printer's Colour Trial (1894)
Specification as (294). *Colour:* Brown print on yellow paper with brown overlay, FIVE in blue. Blue on yellow reverse. *Rarity:* R7 (2 known).

298   Printer's Colour Trial (1894)
Specification as printer's colour trial (297). *Colour:* Blue print on yellow paper with brown overlay, FIVE in brown. Blue on yellow reverse. *Rarity:* R7 (2 known)

299   Printer's Colour Trial (1894)
Specification as printer's colour trial (297). *Colour:* Black print on yellow paper with brown overlay, FIVE in brown. Blue on yellow reverse. *Rarity:* R7 (2 known)

300   Issue 2 (1914–1927). Notes signed by T. Cubbon (Manager) and J. R. Quayle (Secretary).
Specification as (294). *Issued:* 30 November 1914. *Rarity:* R7 (1 known + 2 in archives).

06601–08600	7 August 1914	(7)
08601–09000	1 March 1920	(0)
09001–10600	1 March 1920*	

* Destroyed unissued, 7 March 1928. Terminal note, 10600, preserved for archives. Numbers in brackets indicate notes outstanding in 1961.

301 Isle of Man Bank Ltd. Five pounds note dated 1 November 1927, signed by Thomas Cubbon and John R. Quayle. Same design used until 1961.

301 Issue 3 (1927–1936). Notes signed by T. Cubbon (Manager) and J. R. Quayle (Assistant Manager).
Issued: 1 November 1927. *Obverse:* Vignette of Douglas Harbour and Bay, ISLE OF MAN BANK LIMITED in curved line above, INCORPORATED IN THE ISLE OF MAN 1865 AS THE ISLE OF MAN BANKING COMPANY LIMITED/ UNDER ACT OF TYNWALD in two curved lines below. 5 in upper corners within geometric design. NO. (serial number) to left and right of vignette. FIVE POUNDS below; PROMISE TO PAY/THE BEARER/ON DEMAND in three lines to left, AT THE OFFICE HERE/IN TERMS OF/ACT OF TYNWALD in three lines to right. DOUGLAS (date) below. (signature) ASST. MANAGER lower left, (signature) MANAGER lower right. Lower corners display old and new Arms of the Lords of Man. All within frame of Celtic design. Printer's imprint in lower margin. *Reverse:* Triune and motto within geometric design, centre, 5 within geometric designs to left and right. ISLE OF MAN BANK LIMITED in upper frame; FIVE POUNDS in lower frame. Printer's imprint in lower margin. *Printer:* Waterlow & Sons Ltd., London Wall, London. *Colour:* Blue, green and pink print on white paper, reverse same. *Watermark:* ISLE OF MAN BANK LIMITED and £5. *Dimensions:* 176 x 92mm. *Positional Code Letters:* A/A. Letters will be located on the obverse at junction of interlacing of lower frame and design surrounding lower left hand emblem, and on the reverse at inner corner of frame in lower left corner. Only one impression on the printing plate. *Rarity:* R3 (78 known + 3 in archives).

9001–11200   1 November 1927

302 Printer's Proof (1927)
Specification as (301). No serial numbers, dated 1 November 1927. *Rarity:* R7 (1 known, in archives).

303   Isle of Man Bank Ltd. Five pounds note dated 1 November 1927, signed by John R. Quayle and W. K. Corlett. [*H. F. Guard*]

303   Issue 4 (1936–1937). Notes signed by J. R. Quayle (Manager) and W.K. Corlett (Assistant Manager).
Specification as (301). *Issued:* 1 October 1936. *Rarity:* R7 (4 known).

11201–11400   1 November 1927

304   Unissued Note
Notes of the 1927 design were numbered 9001–14000. Owing to a similarity of colour between the one and five pound notes it was decided to change the colour of the latter, therefore notes numbered 11401–14000 were never issued and all destroyed except for the terminal five, 13996–14000, which are now all in archives. *Rarity:* R7.

305   Issue 5 (1937–1958). Notes signed by J. R. Quayle (Manager) and J. N. Ronan (Assistant Manager).
Issued: 28 April 1937. Specification as issued note (301) but change of colours to brown, pink and green on obverse and brown and pink reverse. *Rarity:* R4 (27 known + 3 in archives)

11401–14400   1 December 1936

306   Issue 6 (1958–1961). Notes signed by J.E. Cashin (Manager) and W.E. Quirk (Assistant Manager).
Specification as (305). *Issued:* 5 December 1958. *Rarity:* (1945) R7 (6 known + 1 in archives), (1960) R7 (5 known + 4 in archives).

14401–15000   3 January 1945
15001–16200   7 April 1960

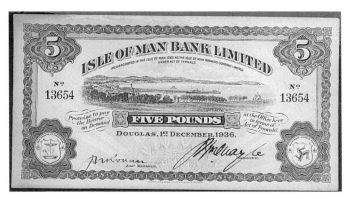

305 Isle of Man Bank Ltd. Five pounds note dated 1 December 1936, signed by John R. Quayle and J. N. Ronan.

307 Printer's Proof (1945)
Specification as (306), but no serial numbers. *Rarity:* R7 (1 known).

The five pound note register was examined in August 1978. Since 1961 no notes have been cancelled on return and therefore only a total number outstanding has been recorded. In 1961 512 notes were outstanding. In the immediate years after 1961 the notes were paid in rapidly and those dated 1945 and 1960 must have seen very little circulation before withdrawal, especially the latter date which were only released on 26 April 1960 and therefore only circulated for 15 months. For many years the number outstanding had remained constant at 295 for all issues, and of these 134 are known to exist.

CHAPTER 6

Douglas & Isle of Man Bank (Dumbell, Son & Howard) Dumbell's Banking Company Ltd.

DOUGLAS & ISLE OF MAN BANK (Dumbell, Son & Howard)

With the closure of Holmes' Douglas & Isle of Man Bank in 1853 a new private bank of the same title was founded by two partners, George William Dumbell and Lewis Geneste Howard. Dumbell was a prominent man of the time, practising as an advocate in Douglas and serving as a member of the House of Keys. Immediately Holmes' bank closed Dumbell applied to the Governor, Charles Hope, for a licence to issue notes. This was granted and the business commenced in November 1853 in St. George's Street, Douglas with Dumbell as the active partner and manager whilst Howard, who took no active part in the bank, remained in the background. The chief clerk was Robert Shimmon, father of John Shimmon the manager at the closure in 1900.

The licence for the note issue permitted up to £5,000 in one pound notes to be issued commencing on 7 January 1854 when the circulation reached £3,800 within a month. An excess in the note issue which occurred before the bank had been in business for its first year, required an increase in the licence limit to £15,000 being granted in November 1854. The following month the note circulation was £8,000.[74]

January 1855 saw the opening of branches at Castletown and Ramsey, resulting in an increase of business and extension of the note circulation. Competition by the newly founded Bank of Mona was quite fierce and all means were used to obtain customers. This rivalry was furthered when the Bank of Mona gave a dinner at the Castle Mona Hotel in Douglas for the benefit of their principal customers.

Less than four years after its foundation, Dumbell's experienced its first failure when the following notice appeared on the bank's door

> The Bank is compelled to suspend business for the present. No doubt need be felt that everyone will be paid in full, and that very speedily.
> Geo. W. Dumbell
> Douglas, 22 August 1857

Several meetings were called and at one of them Dumbell made a statement which so convinced the audience that the meeting closed with a vote of confidence in Dumbell. Early in November 1857 Dumbell had a further meeting with his depositors, resulting in the bank resuming business on 18 November in its former premises with Dumbell still as manager. The note licence was increased to £10,000 in July 1858.

In October 1861 the bank moved from its premises in St. George's Street to new offices at 1 Prospect Hill, which are in use today by the National Westminster Bank Limited. The following year witnessed the securing of a valuable account, that of the Great Laxey Mining Company which had been founded with G.W. Dumbell as its chairman. This proved to be particularly useful since it allowed an outlet for circulation of the bank's notes among the miners, where a pound note was included in the wage packet of every miner earning more than twenty shillings.[75] Another account held by the bank at this time was that of the Isle of Man Bank for Savings, which purchased and presented a large area of land on Douglas Head to the town of Douglas and later laid it out as a pleasure ground.

William Dumbell, the eldest son of George William Dumbell, was admitted as a partner in September 1864 and the note design modified to include the additional name on the obverse. Another rival to the Douglas & Isle of Man Bank appeared in 1865 on the founding of the Isle of Man Banking Company Limited, given in greater detail in an earlier chapter. The period from 1869 to 1874 witnessed the struggle between the banks not only for banking business but even to opposition parties in public bodies and companies.

DUMBELL'S BANKING COMPANY LIMITED

Until 1874 the bank had maintained its position as a private bank, but the provisions of the Companies Act, 1865 compelled it to become a limited company under the title of Dumbell's Banking Company Limited, The prospectus was published in the *Manx Sun* in August 1874 in which the subscribed capital was £180,000 in 30,000 shares of £6 each, of which £2 per share was paid as £1 on application and £1 on allotment thus making a paid up capital of £60,000. Although the prospectus did not include a statement of business by the bank or even an estimate of prospects the confidence of the public in the personality of G.W. Dumbell was such that even though the capital was oversubscribed he was included among the 420 shareholders.[76]

On 2 January 1875 the first list of shareholders was issued of which George William Dumbell was allotted 4,000 shares and his two sons, Alured and William, 200 and 100 respectively.[77] At the first meeting of the shareholders on 19 November 1874 G.W. Dumbell made some remarks which in view of events over twenty-five years later are of interest. He said

"It will be my business particularly to watch over the branches. We have a great variety of checks to ensure safety, especially during our time, so as to prevent any business being done at the branches which is not known at the Head Office. There is no business done at the branches which is not known at the Head Office on the following day. Every transaction at the branches goes through our own books and under our own eyes at the Head Office. It is greater trouble, but it is greater security. We keep a perfect tally by weekly and monthly accounts, showing every shilling that has been advanced and the names of the individuals, and a check is kept showing every man's balance as debtor or creditor, and what security there is for every advance."[78]

In view of subsequent events this system of checking was mentioned to give confidence or it fell into disuse.

The new bank held many important accounts particularly those of the Great Laxey Mines, Foxdale Mines, the Government Account, the Harbour and Highway Boards and several of the Douglas hotels. The first balance sheet dated 31 December 1875 indicated 21,125 pound notes were in circulation and deposits of £128,184.18.2.[79] In 1877 the note issue reached £25,600 thus becoming the largest in the Island.

On closure of the Bank of Mona in 1878 the former manager of the Ramsey branch, Alexander Bruce, was appointed as general manager to Dumbell's Bank. In the same year the manager, William Dumbell, died and John Shimmon was appointed, a position held until 1900. John Shimmon had been the bank's accountant since 1874 when the bank became a limited company; his father, Robert, held a similar post in the private bank until his retirement in 1874. With the promotion of Shimmon to manager the new accountant was John Curphey who held this position until he resigned from the bank in November 1899.

Facts disclosed at a later date indicated that false balance sheets were prepared in which unissued notes were included as cash in hand, and from 1878 the bank started on an adventurous career by the founding and financing of speculative companies, the development of which had been greatly assisted by the increasing popularity of the Island as a holiday resort.[80]

The founder of the bank, George William Dumbell, died on 13 December 1887 aged 83. Popularity of the Island as a holiday resort commenced in the same year and the lack of sufficient hotel accomodation led to hasty land purchasing for erection of hotels, boarding-houses and restaurants. Increasing prices of land in Douglas and Ramsey led to speculators borrowing money from the banks. Alexander Bruce, John Shimmon and Charles B. Nelson, a director of the bank, also joined in by speculating with their own money and later that of the bank until 1892. Whilst in London the following year Bruce and Nelson started further unsuccessful joint speculations with the bank's money. To conceal these losses, which amounted to £34,000 by 1899, an account termed the Nelson Trust Account was opened at Ramsey. Nelson resided at Ramsey and under the bank's rules branch accounts were not audited at the branch but instead were certified by the branch managers for audit. After the bank's closure Nelson had an overdraft of £35,000.

All these speculations and transactions were carried out without the knowledge of the bank's directors, except Nelson. The bank's securities book which had not been written up since 1893 was missing, consequently no record of securities was kept.

1898 was the time for amalgamations and Bruce, realising this, lost no opportunity in his speculations. A successful amalgamation of the Douglas amusement resorts was carried out where premiums of twenty to one hundred per cent were paid to existing shareholders of various separate companies. The shares of the combined company were sold and a profit of £40,000 made. An earlier amalgamation success had been the Isle of Man Tramways and Electric Power Company which yielded substantial dividends. Bruce and his associates built the Snaefell Mountain Railway as a private venture and later sold it to the Tramways Company with a profit to the original owners.[81]

Success of these amalgamations led to a further one in the form of the Isle of

Man Breweries Amalgamation. In 1898 quiet purchases by private individuals and sub-syndicates of grocery stores, public houses, breweries and hotels were undertaken and in June 1899 a prospectus was published inviting a capital of £550,000 in shares and debentures to acquire forty-six licensed houses, three breweries and a number of other properties. The directors of the Amalgamation included Bruce and Nelson but this fact was not publicised at the time.[82]

The appeal for capital was not successful and almost half the stock remained in the hands of the promoters. No doubt the Breweries Amalgamation would have been a dividend-yielding concern but the public were not buying, consequently the properties purchased by the syndicate had to be paid for and by the end of 1899 a high percentage of Dumbell's bank funds were locked up in advances both to the promoters of the scheme and to the directors. Also at this time the London, City & Midland Bank were pressing Bruce for securities for advances made during the past two years which now amounted to £178,000.

The first intimation that the bank was on the brink of disaster came on 2 December 1899 when the directors received a letter of resignation from the bank's accountant, John Curphey, who had been with the bank for twenty-five years. An extract of this letter to the chairman W.B. Stevenson was very prophetic. Dated 1 December 1899 a portion reads as follows:-

"I have thrown up my position as third official to enable me to bring before the directors what, at the present time, I consider to be the most dangerous and critical state of the bank's affairs, brought about by years of gross neglect on the part of the managers; and unless your Board take immediate steps to avert it, a most serious crisis must shortly ensue which will shake the Island to its foundations and ruin thousands of innocent people." [83]

The directors realised this letter was not to be ignored and quickly investigated matters for themselves.

For many years previously there had been attempts by English banks to secure a direct business footing in the Island. Dumbell's had been approached but the idea was discouraged by the managers who knew the bank's true financial position. Now that the position was known to the directors an approach was made to Parr's Bank through the Parr's Superintendent of Branches, T.H.P. Mylechreest, who had once been in the service of Dumbell, Son & Howard.

A provisional agreement was set up in London in which Parr's would take over all the assets and liabilities of Dumbell's and pay £50,000 for the goodwill of the business. The agreement was formally submitted to the Dumbell's directors on 1 February 1900; it was realised a new clause, not discussed at the London meeting, had been added by Parr's. In effect this clause stated that if Dumbell's actual liabilities exceeded £20,000, the amount shown in the balance sheet for 31 December 1899, Parr's would have the right to withdraw from the agreement.[84]

On Saturday morning 3 February 1900 a notice was fixed to the doors of Dumbell's Bank on Prospect Hill indicating that payments had been suspended but Parr's would accept responsibilities and to reduce inconvenience would advance ten shillings (50p) in the pound on all deposits, and the bank would open for business on the following Monday at 10 am.

Soon a great crowd gathered to read the notice, which also appeared at branches at Castletown, Ramsey, Peel and Port St. Mary where similar scenes took place. Pressing demands for the payment of wages for employees prompted Parr's to open the bank at 1.30 pm. on the Saturday. Depositors were informed that they could not draw any of their money, except on loan to the extent of ten shillings (50p) in the pound which had to be repaid with interest.

The collapse of Dumbell's was disastrous. Regarded as a national institution in the Island, the effect of the collapse was equivalent to one of the largest English banks failing.

Within a few days the true position of Dumbell's was known and Mylechreest recommended that Parr's should withdraw from the provisional agreement, but the acquisition of Dumbell's premises should continue. A meeting of the Dumbell's shareholders on 12 February revealed a melancholy state of affairs.[85] The balance sheet for June 1899 was not a true account of the bank's position but assurances from the general manager, Alexander Bruce, and the manager, John Shimmon, as to its correctness allowed the balance sheet to be published. An undisclosed liability was revealed. These discoveries caused Parr's to make formal notification of the rescinding of the contract. Dumbell's tried to make Parr's hold to the contract but this opposition was later withdrawn. Finally Parr's purchased Dumbell's for £40,000 for the premises and goodwill plus £293 representing interest.

Holders of the Dumbell's notes assumed that since the bank had collapsed the banknotes were worthless and foolishly parted with the notes at less than face value. Other banks accepted them at full value, even in gold, but post offices refused them. One of the conditions attached to the issue of note licences was the deposition of securities to the value of notes in circulation, thus the notes could still be retired at full value. This fact was not always known to the public, consequently the notes were disposed of quickly, which accounts for the rarity of issued notes in existence today.

The effect of the suspension was immediately felt by sharp reductions in share values of many Manx concerns including the other two banks which took some time to recover. Public feeling ran high at the apparent lack of action by the authorities in taking proceedings against the Dumbell's officials responsible for the collapse. Eventually they were brought to trial and with the exception of Bruce, who died during the trial, they all served sentences. A full account of the trial was recorded by the Island's two newspapers, *Manx Sun*[86] and *Mona's Herald.*[87]

Winding up of the bank took twenty-two years. The first dividend of 3/4d. (16p) in the pound was paid on 21 June 1900 and the final dividend 6½d. (3p) paid on 24 June 1922 where the total paid was 12/7d. (63p), in the pound.

A fuller and more detailed account of the Dumbell's Bank and its personalities has appeared more recently.[88]

Note Issues

308   Issue 1 (1854–1865). Notes signed by G. W. Dumbell (Manager) and Robt. Shimmon (Accountant).
Issued: 7 January 1854. *Obverse:* Vignette of Triune and motto supported by Lion and Unicorn, motto DIEU ET MON DROIT below. Sailing vessel to left, Tower of

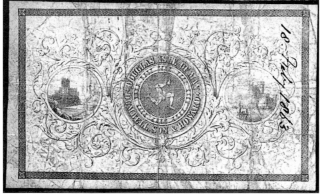

308 Douglas & Isle of Man Bank (Dumbell's). Obverse and reverse of unissued one pound note. [*H. F. Guard*]

Refuge to right. NO. (serial number) upper left and right corners. DOUGLAS & ISLE OF MAN BANK below vignette. WE PROMISE TO PAY THE BEARER/ON DEMAND ONE POUND IN BANK NOTES/OR BILL ON LONDON, AT OUR OFFICE HERE./ENT. (signature) DOUGLAS (date) 18———/FOR GEO. W. DUMBELL & LEWIS G. HOWARD in five lines. ONE POUND to left, signature to right. Vignette at left displays figures, sheep and agricultural implements. All within engine-worked border. Printer's imprint above lower border. *Reverse:* Triune within circle, DOUGLAS, ISLE OF MAN + DUMBELL, SON & HOW-ARD + round. Vignettes display Peel Castle at left, Tower of Refuge at right. The remaining areas filled with a foliate pattern. All enclosed within engine-worked border. Printer's imprint within lower border. *Printer:* W.H. Lizars, Edinburgh. *Colour:* Black print on white paper, reverse same. *Watermark:* none. *Dimensions:* 172 x 103mm. *Rarity:* R7 (1 known). Only one entire unissued note known.

310   Douglas & Isle of Man Bank (Dumbell's). Obverse and reverse of printer's proof for one pound note.

13 half-notes are known with printed serial numbers in the range 2281–3130. Since these are cancelled top halves no further details about dates or signatures are known.

309 Artist's Sketch
Original artist's sketch in pencil and watercolour. As (308) but FOR G.W. DUMBELL AND ALURED DUMBELL in gothic script at lower right corner. *Rarity:* R8 (1 known).[89]

310 Printer's Proof
As (308) but reverse lacks border. *Rarity:* R7 (1 known).

311 Printer's Proof
Proof note prepared by Lizars. As (308) but obverse design and border differ. *Rarity:* R7 (1 known, in archives).

312 Printer's Proof
Similar to (308) but obverse border as (313). Reverse frame as for (308). Bears imprint for W. & A.K. Johnston on both sides. Final line of promissory legend now reads PAYABLE IN TERMS OF ACT OF TYNWALD 7 Wm. 4th. Serial number 50,000 obliterated and new number, 1223, printed below. *Rarity:* R7 (1 known).

312 Douglas & Isle of Man Bank (Dumbell's). Obverse of printer's proof for one pound note. [*H. F. Guard*]

313   Douglas & Isle of Man Bank (Dumbell's). Unissued one pound note signed by Robt. Shimmon. [*H. F. Guard*]

313   Issue 2 (1865–1874). Notes signed by G. W. Dumbell (Manager) and Robt. Shimmon (Accountant).
Issued: 1865. *Obverse:* As (308) but now has additional name of William Dumbell at lower right. Border is now as (312). *Reverse:* As (308). *Printer:* W. & A.K. Johnston, Edinburgh. *Colour:* Black print on white paper, reverse same. *Watermark:* none. *Dimensions:* 191 x 116mm. *Rarity:* R6 (8 known + 3 in archives). Known notes are serial numbered in the block 22815–22955 and bear signature of Robert Shimmon only. A cancelled top-half note, number 11308, is known in archives.

314   Printer's Proof (1864)
Specification as (313), bears pencilled remark 'To this 17 August 1864'. *Rarity:* R7 (1 known).

315   Issue 3 (1874–1875). Provisional Issue. Notes signed by G. W. Dumbell (Manager) and John Shimmon (Accountant).
Notes of Issue 2 (313) overprinted DUMBELL'S BANKING COMPANY/ LIMITED in two lines in red vertically to left of obverse. No signed notes have been traced. All numbered in the series 49886–51080. *Rarity:* R5 (14 known + 16 in archives).

317   Issue 4 (1874–1878). Notes signed by Wm. Dumbell (Manager) and John Shimmon (Accountant).
Issued: 1874. *Obverse:* Vignette of Triune and motto supported by Lion and Unicorn with motto DIEU ET MON DROIT below. £1 with No. (serial number) in upper left and right corners. DUMBELL'S BANKING COMPANY LIMITED below vignette. PROMISE TO PAY THE BEARER/ON DEMAND ONE POUND AT THE OFFICE HERE/IN TERMS OF ACT OF TYNWALD 7th Wm. 4th/ENTD.

315 Dumbell's Banking Co. Ltd. Unissued provisional issue one pound note. [*Manx Museum*]

317 Dumbells' Banking Co. Ltd. Unissued one pound note signed by William Dumbell. A few of these notes bear his signature only, but Dumbell died before the notes could be countersigned and issued. [*H. F. Guard*]

(signature) ACCT. DOUGLAS (date) 18——— in four lines. (signature) MANAGER at lower right, ONE to left. All enclosed in engine-worked border with geometric medallions in four corners. Printer's imprint within border at lower left corner. *Reverse:* Triune and motto within geometric pattern. DUMBELL'S BANKING COMPANY above, LIMITED below. Foliate pattern within. All enclosed within engine-worked border with emblems at each corner. Printer's imprint at lower left. *Printer:* Perkins, Bacon & Co. London. *Colour:* Black print on thin white paper, reverse same. *Watermark:* none. *Dimensions:* 160 x 118mm. *Rarity:* R6 (7 known + 4 in archives). No issued notes known. All known specimens are serial numbered in the block 34701–35000 and bear the signature of Wm. Dumbell only. He died in May 1878.

318   Printer's Proof (1874)
Specification as (317). No serial number, date, etc. Stamped SPECIMEN in space for manager's signature. Pencilled date 'October 1874' in lower right. *Rarity:* R7 (1 known).

319   Issue 5 (1878–18..). Notes signed by John Shimmon (Manager) and John Curphey (Accountant).
Specification as (317). *Rarity:* R7 (1 known, in archives). The only known specimen is number 55095 and dated 17 July 1882.

320   Issue 6 (18..-1900). Notes signed by John Shimmon (Manager) and John Curphey (Accountant).
Issued: ?. *Obverse:* Vignette of Triune and motto supported by Lion and Unicorn with motto DIEU ET MON DROIT below. DUMBELL'S BANKING COMPANY above, LIMITED below. NO. (serial number) either side of vignette. PROMISE TO PAY THE BEARER/ON DEMAND ONE POUND AT THE OFFICE/HERE IN TERMS OF ACT OF TYNWALD 7th. Wm. 4th in three lines on central panel with repeated microprint ONE POUND as background. ENTD. (signature) ACCT.. DOUGLAS (date) 18——— in line below. (signature) MANAGER at lower right, ONE at lower left. £1 at upper corners, ONE at lower corners. All within ornamental border. Printer's imprint in lower margin. *Reverse:* Triune and motto in centre within geometric patterns. DUMBELL'S BANKING above, COMPANY LIMITED below. ONE in each corner of ornamental border. Printer's imprint in lower margin. *Printer:* Waterlow & Sons Limited, Great Winchester Street, London E.C. *Colour:* Slate-grey print on white paper, reverse same. *Watermark:* none. *Dimensions:* 158 x 122mm. *Positional Code Letters:* A/A, B/B, C/C, D/D, E/E, F/F. Letters will be located on the obverse in the area between left hand curve of frame surrounding promissory legend and left hand frame of note, and on the reverse adjacent to the trefoil at a point 48mm. from the left hand frame and 30mm. above the lower frame. *Rarity:* R7 (5 known + 3 in archives) Highest serial number known 120550. *Dates:* (Other dates may exist)
21 December 1891
7 August 1895
21 May 1897
4 November 1899

321   Printer's Proof
Specification as (320). No serial number, date or signatures. *Rarity:* R7 (1 known).

322   Unissued Note. Signed by John Shimmon (Manager).
Specification as (320) but manager's signature only. *Rarity:* R7 (4 known). Specimens bear serial numbers in the range 121469–121495.

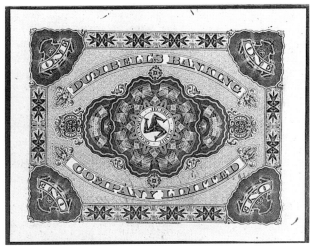

320 Dumbell's Banking Co. Ltd. One pound note dated 4 November 1899, signed by John Shimmon and John Curphey. This was the final date of the note issue.

323 Unissued Note
Specification as (320) but no signatures. *Rarity:* R5 (13 known + 12 in archives). Specimens bear serial numbers in the range 145502–145862.

CHAPTER 7

Establishment of the English Banks – I

Parr's Bank Limited,
London County Westminster
& Parr's Bank Limited,
Westminster Bank Limited

PARR'S BANK LIMITED

Parr's Bank originated in Warrington as Parr, Lyon & Company in 1782 under the partnership of two sugar refiners, Joseph Parr and Thomas Lyon, and a solicitor, Walter Kerfoot. The title was changed to Parr & Company in 1797 shortly before the death of Kerfoot. In 1804 William Hurst was admitted as a partner. On 30 June 1819 a new deed of partnership was entered into by Joseph Parr, junior, Thomas Lyon and Edward Greenall. Exactly six years later the business became known as Parr, Lyon and Greenall with the addition of John Greenall into the partnership until his death some years later when the title was changed to Parr, Lyon & Company on 26 April 1851.

In 1865 the company became a joint-stock bank known as Parr's Banking Company Limited, and later on absorption of the Alliance Bank in 1892, had the new lengthy title Parr's Banking Company and the Alliance Bank Limited. Amalgamation of the Consolidated Bank in 1896 reduced the name to the more convenient form of Parr's Bank Limited which was retained until 1918 on amalgamation with the London County & Westminster Bank under the style of London County Westminster & Parr's Bank Limited, the name being abbreviated to Westminster Bank Limited from 1 March 1923.[90]

With the purchase of Dumbell's Bank the general manager of Parr's investigated the possibility of a note issue in the Isle of Man. On 19 April 1900 a report to the Parr's Board indicated the bank would be able to issue one pound notes subject to the granting of a licence by the Manx Government. A design was submitted to the Board early in May and an order placed with Waterlow & Sons shortly afterwards, the notes being ready for issue by August 1900.[91] T.H.P. Mylechreest acted as manager of Parr's Douglas branch until about 1914 when he was succeeded by H.E.D. Abbott. The accountant, G.W. Fleming, had previously been with Dumbell's Bank.

Note Issues

324   Issue 1 (1900–1906). Notes signed by T.H.P. Mylechreest (Manager) and W.F. Quayle (Accountant).
Issued: August 1900. *Obverse:* Vignette displays Triune and motto supported by Lion and Unicorn, DIEU ET MON DROIT below. PARR'S BANK above LIMITED below. NO. (serial number) to left and right. PROMISE TO PAY THE BEARER/ON DEMAND ONE POUND AT THIS OFFICE/ONLY IN TERMS OF ACT OF TYNWALD 7th. WM. 4th. in three lines, below. ENTD. (signature) ACCT. DOUGLAS (date) 19——— below. (signature) MANAGER at lower right. ONE at lower left. Upper left corner displays Arms of the bank comprising Arms of Warrington, London, Manchester and Liverpool. Other corners are occupied by motifs relating to various bank amalgamations. Ornamental frame surround. Printer's imprint in lower margin. *Reverse:* Triune and motto centre. PARR'S BANK/LIMITED in two curved lines above, HEAD OFFICE/4, BARTHOLO-MEW LANE, LONDON in two curved lines below. ONE POUND on figure 1 to left and right. All on background of geometric design. Printer's imprint in lower margin. *Printer:* Waterlow & Sons Limited, Great Winchester Street, London E.C. *Colour:* Slate-grey print on white paper, blue reverse. *Watermark:* none *Dimensions:* 157 x 118mm. *Positional Code Letters:* C/C (others may exist). These are located in the obverse margin at junction between lower frame and frame surrounding emblem in lower left corner, and on the reverse in the margin at a point 18mm. from lower left corner. *Rarity:* R7 (none known) *Dates:* (outstanding notes in brackets).

000001–025000	20 August 1900	(72)
025001–030000	23 January 1901	(16)

325   Printer's Proof (1900)
Specification as (324). No serial numbers or date. *Rarity:* R7 (2 known, in archives).

326   Issue 2 (1906–1914). Notes signed by T.H.P. Mylechreest (Manager) and Percy Ashbery (Accountant).
Specification as (324). *Rarity:* R7 (3 known + 1 in archives). *Dates:* (outstanding notes in brackets).

030001–035000	1 June 1906	(13)
035001–042500	2 April 1909	(16)

327   Issue 3 (1914). Notes signed by T.H.P. Mylechreest (Manager) and G.W. Fleming (Accountant).
Specification as (324). *Rarity:* R7 (none known). *Date:* (outstanding notes in brackets).

042501–049000	24 March 1914	(11)

326　Parr's Bank Ltd. Obverse and reverse of one pound note dated 2 April 1909, signed by T. H. P. Mylechreest and Percy Ashbery. This was the design for all Parr's note issues and also for the London County Westminster & Parr's provisional issue. [*H. F. Guard*]

328　Issue 4 (1914–1918). Notes signed by H.E.D. Abbott (Manager) and G.W. Fleming (Accountant).
Specification as (324). *Rarity:* R7 (none known). *Dates:* (outstanding notes in brackets).

049001–050000	9 October 1914	(1)
050001–051000	9 August 1915	(2)
051001–052000	9 August 1916	(2)
052001–054000	10 November 1916	(0)

LONDON COUNTY WESTMINSTER & PARR'S BANK LIMITED

Prior to 1923 the Westminster Bank was known as the London County Westminster & Parr's Bank a name derived from amalgamation with Parr's Bank in 1918
before which it was titled the London County & Westminster Bank. The three
main constituent banks of the Westminster Bank were the London & Westminster
Bank which commenced business on 10 March 1834, the London & County Bank
established in Southwark in 1836 as the Surrey, Kent & Sussex Banking Company, and Parr's Bank discussed earlier. These rather long titles for banks were
the result of a policy to retain as many parts as possible of the names of the
constituent banks. To the public these names had a prestige value and in cases
where customers had banked with the earlier constituent banks the change of
title was not easily adopted by the customer. In was in 1923 that a resolution was
passed to change the name to the more convenient form of Westminster Bank
Limited.

The London & Westminster Bank[92] was the first joint stock bank to be founded
in London. Up to 1833 it had been assumed that the Bank of England had the
monopoly of joint stock banking, not only in London but within a radius of sixty-
five miles around the capital. A successful challenge by a London merchant,
W.R.K. Douglas, maintained that this monopoly was confined to the right of note
issue. Under the Bank Charter Renewal Act, 1833 it was declared that a joint
stock bank could function in London on condition that it did not issue notes.
Immediately this was known the London & Westminster Bank was established
with an initial capital of five million pounds composed of fifty thousand shares of
one hundred pounds each. Much of the bank's business consisted of acting as the
London agents for many private and joint stock banks in the rest of the country.

Unlike its competitors a policy of rapid expansion was not adopted and
activities were confined to the London area. Only seven branches had been
established by 1880 when the bank became a limited liability company. In 1909 the
bank was absorbed into the London & County Bank.

The London & County Bank[93] was established in 1836 as the Surrey, Kent &
Sussex Banking Company with a capital of two million pounds composed of forty
thousand shares of fifty pounds each, although only twenty-five thousand pounds
had been paid in 1837. Opening of branches in other counties required a change in
title to London & County Banking Company. A policy of expansion absorbed
many small banking businesses and by the 1870s had become the largest bank in
England and Wales with the majority of branches in the London area. In 1880 the
bank became a limited liability company and amalgamated with the London &
Westminster Bank in 1909 to become the London County & Westminster Bank,
followed later by amalgamation with Parr's Bank under the title of London
County Westminster & Parr's Bank Limited.[94]

Note Issues

The notes were confined to denominations of one pound. Until a definitive issue
had been prepared for the new bank a provisional issue was made by overprinting
stocks of Parr's notes. Definitive issues appeared in 1919 and were of identical
design to the Parr's notes with the substitution of the new bank title.

329   Issue 1 (1918). Notes signed by H.E.D. Abbott (Manager) and G.W. Fleming (Accountant).
Specification as (324) but overprinted in black LONDON COUNTY WESTMINS-TER in the upper margin on obverse and reverse, with ampersand & just above Parr's title. *Positional Code Letters:* f/f (others may exist). Letters will be located in same position as Parr's notes. *Rarity:* R7 (2 known + 3 in archives). *Dates:* (outstanding notes in brackets).

054001–059000	28 March 1918	(16)
059001–062000	25 April 1918	(12)
062001–067000	24 May 1918	(11)
067001–070000	22 November 1918	(6)

330   Issue 2 (1919–1923). Notes signed by F. Proud (Manager) and G.W. Fleming (Accountant).
Design as Parr's notes (324) but new title LONDON COUNTY WESTMINSTER & PARR'S BANK now replaces the Parr's Bank title on obverse and reverse. *Printer:* Waterlow & Sons Limited, Great Winchester Street, London E.C. *Colour:* Slate-grey print on white paper, blue reverse. *Watermark:* none *Dimensions:* 157 x 118mm. *Rarity:* R7 (none known) *Dates:* (outstanding notes in brackets).

070001–072000	11 October 1919	(4)
072001–073000	11 January 1921	(1)
073001–075000	25 November 1921	(3)

WESTMINSTER BANK LIMITED

Note Issues

On the change of title to Westminster Bank Limited in 1923 another provisional issue was prepared by suitably overprinting the notes. There was also a change in title from Accountant to Assistant Manager. This provisional issue continued from 1923 to 1929 when a new design of note of smaller format was issued which continued, with a few minor changes, until 1961.

331   Issue 1 (1923–1924). Notes signed by F. Proud (Manager) and G.W. Fleming (Assistant Manager).
Specification as (330), overprinted in red WESTMINSTER BANK LIMITED in upper margin, FORMERLY below, on obverse and reverse. *Positional Code Letters:* G/D, H/E, I/F, J/A, K/B, L/C, these will be located in the same position as on the Parr's notes. *Rarity:* R7 (1 known + 1 in archives). *Dates:* (outstanding notes in brackets).

075001–081000	4 July 1923	(7)
081001–084000	17 December 1923	(3)
084001–089000	5 February 1924	(7)

332 Westminster Bank. Obverse and reverse of provisional issue dated 16 December 1926, signed by F. Proud and A. O. Christian. [*H. F. Guard*]

332 Issue 2 (1924–1929). Notes signed by F. Proud (Manager) and A.O. Christian (Assistant Manager).
Specification as (331). *Rarity:* R7 (1 known + 1 in archives). *Dates:* (outstanding notes in brackets)

089001–094000	20 October 1924	(6)
094001–097000	23 November 1925	(8)
097001–102000	16 December 1926	(9)
102001–107000	4 April 1927	(4)

Positional Code Letters on notes

These will be located on the obverse and reverse in the bottom margin near lower left corner.

1929–1945
Notes printed in six subjects per sheet with the following layout:-

$$
\begin{array}{ccc}
A/D & & D/A \\
B/E & + & E/B \\
C/F & + & F/C
\end{array}
$$

ie for A/D A = obverse impression, D = reverse impression. In the Table below only the first three digits of the serial number are shown.

A/D	B/E	C/F	D/A	E/B	F/C
107	108	109	110	111	112
113	114	115	116	117	118
119	120	121	122	123	124
125	126	127	128	129	130
131	132	133	134	135	136
137	138	139	140		
157	158	159	160	161	162
163	164	165	166	167	168
169	170	171	172	173	174

This plate produced 58,000 notes before the reverse impression D was renewed. The gap in the above table is due to no notes being examined to confirm if the system was retained. A note in the 155xxx series bears the plate letters D/A which appears to be out of sequence. Observation of more notes will confirm this.

1946–1954
Sometime in the early 1940s the reverse impression D, being last used for notes dated 4 February 1943, was either worn or damaged and a new combination, A/P, used commencing with notes dated 16 January 1946.

A/P	B/E	C/F	D/A	E/B	F/C
175	176	177	178	179	180
181	182	183	184	185	186
187	188	189	190	191	192
193	194	195	196	197	198
199	200	201	202	203	204
205	206				

This plate produced a further 32,000 notes before it was replaced in 1954.

1955–1961
On modification of the note design the printing plate was altered from six to nine impressions per sheet with the following layout. The positional code letters have a small dot above.

$$
\begin{array}{ccc}
\dot{A}/\dot{K} & \dot{D}/\dot{H} & \dot{G}/\dot{E} \\
\dot{B}/\dot{L} \;+\; & \dot{E}/\dot{I} \;+\; & \dot{H}/\dot{F} \\
\dot{C}/\dot{M} \;+\; & \dot{F}/\dot{J} \;+\; & \dot{I}/\dot{G}
\end{array}
$$

Ȧ/K̇	Ḃ/L̇	Ċ/Ṁ	Ḋ/Ḣ	Ė/İ	Ḟ/J̇	Ġ/Ė	Ḣ/Ḟ	İ/Ġ
207	208	209	210	211	212	213	214	215
216	217	218	219	220	221	222	223	224
225	226	227	228	229	230	231	232	233
234	235	236	237	238	239	240	241	242
243	244	245						

This plate produced 39,000 notes.

333   Issue 3 (1929–1935). Notes signed in facsimile by F. Proud (Manager) and A.O. Christian (Assistant Manager).
Issued: 1929 *Obverse:* Vignette of Triune and motto supported by Lion and Unicorn DIEU ET MON DROIT below. WESTMINSTER BANK LIMITED in curved line above. NO. (serial number) to left and right. PROMISE TO PAY THE BEARER/ON DEMAND ONE POUND AT THIS OFFICE/ONLY IN TERMS OF ACT OF TYNWALD 7th. Wm. 4th. in three lines, centre. (signature) ASSISTANT MANAGER to left ONE below, (signature) MANAGER at lower right with DOUGLAS, (date), 19——— above. Arms of the bank in upper corners £1 signs in lower corners. All enclosed by geometric design frame. Printer's imprint in lower margin. *Reverse:* Triune and motto in centre. WESTMINSTER BANK/LIMITED/ HEAD OFFICE-41, LOTHBURY, LONDON. in three curved lines above. ONE POUND below, £1 in panel to left and right of vignette. All within frame of

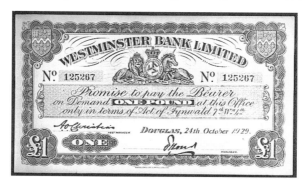

333   Westminster Bank. One pound note dated 24 October 1929, signed by F. Proud and A. O. Christian.

geometric design. Printer's imprint in lower margin. *Printer:* Waterlow & Sons, London. *Colour:* Black and yellow print on white paper, blue and green reverse. *Watermark:* none *Dimensions:* 150 x 84mm. *Rarity:* R7 (1 known + 1 in archives) *Dates:* (outstanding notes in brackets).

107001–112000	9 January 1929	(41)
112001–132000	24 October 1929	(222)
132001–137000	14 November 1933	(38)

Although 222 notes are shown as outstanding for notes dated 24 October 1929 the only two specimens known of this issue are of this date. Whether a large hoard of this date is waiting to be discovered or a large quantity was accidentally destroyed remains to be seen.

334   Printer's Proof (1929)
Specification as (333). No serial numbers, date or signatures. *Rarity:* R7 (1 known)

335   Printer's Proof (1929)
Specification as (333). This proof note bears a five digit serial number, 00000, in red but was altered to black printing to comply with the Tynwald Act, 1817. *Rarity:* R7 (1 known, in archives).

336   Printer's Promotional Note
Specification as (333) but printed in dark brown and yellow, positional code letters E/B. No serial number, date or signatures. *Rarity:* R7 (1 known).

337   Issue 4 (1935–1944). Notes signed in facsimile by A.O. Christian (Manager) and R.E. Callin (Chief Clerk).
Specification as (333). Title of Assistant Manager now obliterated and new title of Chief Clerk printed immediately below. Notes with new title correctly printed

337   Westminster Bank. One pound note dated 17 January 1938, signed by A. O. Christian and R. E. Callin. [*H. F. Guard*]

appeared about 1941. *Rarity:* R6 (13 known + 4 in archives). *Dates:* (outstanding notes in brackets).

137001–141000	22 January 1935	(14)
141001–146000	14 January 1936	(22)
146001–151000	2 October 1936	(23)
151001–153000	9 April 1937	(19)
153001–157000	17 January 1938	(40)
157001–163000	18 January 1939	(75)
163001–166000	21 February 1940	(36)
166001–168000	20 October 1941	(39)
168001–170000	4 February 1943	(29)

338   Issue 5 (1944–1950). Notes signed in facsimile by R.E. Callin (Manager) and W.G. Flinn (Chief Clerk).
Specification as (337). *Rarity:* R6 (9 known + 8 in archives) *Dates:* (outstanding notes in brackets).

170001–172000	11 February 1944	(34)
172001–174000	30 May 1944	(37)
174001–175000	30 January 1945	(10)
175001–177000	16 January 1946	(30)
177001–179000	27 August 1946	(15)
179001–180500	18 February 1947	(18)
180501–182000	15 January 1948	(17)
182001–183500	9 November 1948	(14)
183501–184500	18 March 1949	(9)

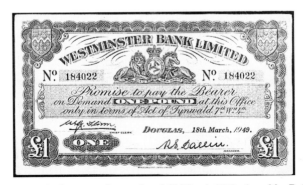

338 Westminster Bank. One pound note dated 18 March 1949, signed by R. E. Callin and W. G. Flinn. [*H. F. Guard*]

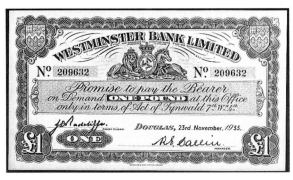

340 Westminster Bank. One pound note dated 23 November 1955, signed by R. E. Callin and G. D. Radcliffe showing sans-serif typeface at dateline.

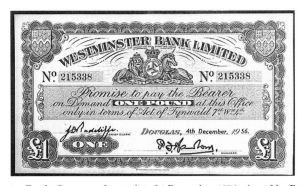

341 Westminster Bank. One pound note dated 4 December 1956, signed by P. F. Barlow and G. D. Radcliffe.

342 Westminster Bank. One pound note dated 10 March 1961, signed by P. F. Barlow and T. D. Russell.

339   Issue 6 (1950–1955). Notes signed in facsimile by R.E. Callin (Manager) and G.D. Radcliffe (Chief Clerk).
Specification as (337). *Rarity:* R4 (20 known + 11 in archives) *Dates:* (outstanding notes in brackets).

184501–186500	7 November 1950	(18)
186501–188500	25 January 1951	(24)
188501–190500	6 March 1951	(21)
190501–193500	14 November 1951	(36)
193501–195500	28 January 1952	(58)
195501–197500	25 September 1952	(29)
197501–199500	14 January 1953	(38)
199501–201500	11 November 1953	(30)
201501–203500	24 March 1954	(41)
203501–205500	5 November 1954	(43)
205501–207500	30 March 1955	(62)

340   Issue 7 (1955–1956). Notes signed in facsimile by R.E. Callin (Manager) and G.D. Radcliffe (Chief Clerk).
Principal design as (333). Two minor modifications occurred in the note design by addition of the words INCORPORATED IN ENGLAND in small print immediately below the bank's title on the obverse and a change in lettering style in the date from serif to sans-serif. Notes now printed from new printing plate. *Rarity:* R7 (2 known + 3 in archives) *Date:* (outstanding notes in brackets).

207501–210500	23 November 1955	(70)

341   Issue 8 (1956–1959). Notes signed in facsimile by P.F. Barlow (Manager) and G.D. Radcliffe (Chief Clerk).
As (341). *Rarity:* R3 (34 known + 17 in archives). *Dates:* (outstanding notes in brackets).

210501–213000	4 April 1956	(79)
213001–216000	4 December 1956	(82)
216001–218000	2 April 1957	(23)
218001–221000	26 November 1957	(49)
221001–224000	13 May 1958	(58)
224001–227000	24 October 1958	(79)
227001–230000	3 March 1959	(75)

342   Issue 9 (1959–1961). Notes signed in facsimile by P.F. Barlow (Manager) and T.D. Russell (Chief Clerk).
As (340). *Rarity:* R3 (51 known + 11 in archives). *Dates:* (outstanding notes in brackets).

230001–234000	8 December 1959	(70)
234001–237000	15 March 1960	(72)
237001–241000	21 October 1960	(134)
241001–246000	10 March 1961	(101)

CHAPTER 8

Establishment of the
English Banks – II

Manx Bank Limited, Mercantile Bank of Lancashire
Limited, Lancashire & Yorkshire Bank Limited,
Martins Bank Limited

THE MANX BANK LIMITED

With exception of the Bank of Mona all the Isle of Man banks of the nineteenth century had been Manx in character. It was not until 1896 that English banks entered the Island on a business footing, by which time only the Isle of Man Banking Company, Dumbell's Bank and the Manx Bank remained.

The Manx Bank[95] commenced business in 1882 at its head office, 57 Victoria Street, Douglas with branches at Castletown, Ramsey and Peel and a sub-branch at Port Erin. The authorised capital of £150,000 was composed of 25,000 shares of £6 each, £25,000 of the issued capital of £75,000 was paid up. At the first ordinary meeting of the bank the directors were Robert Curphey, John Hoyle, Giles Metcalf, William Wade and William Kelly. The chairman was William Kelly and manager James M. Sutherland.

Although the bank started too late in comparison to the two established banks of Dumbell's and the Isle of Man Banking Company, the possession of a well distributed body of shareholders made the bank popular especially with country people and tradesmen.

In August 1896 a deputation from the Mercantile Bank of Lancashire met a similar group of representatives of the Manx Bank with a view to purchasing the latter but in the following month F.H. Smith, the general manager of the Mercantile Bank, saw a report that the Union Bank of Liverpool were interested in purchasing the Manx Bank, consequently negotiations were delayed. Failure of negotiations between the Union Bank and the Manx Bank resulted in the latter again approaching the Mercantile Bank in August 1900.

The original terms were lowered due to the severe financial crisis in the Island resulting from the Dumbell's affair a few months previously. In spite of this stress the bank's deposits were £224,000 with £11,806 of notes in circulation. A profit of £1,611 yielded a dividend of 5%. Conditions of local banking had altered and in the years prior to this small banks, although successful in business, were gradually being amalgamated into larger banks.

Realising this the directors of the Manx Bank suggested the bank should be offered for sale. The Mercantile Bank of Lancashire indicated their interest and

120

in November 1900 a letter was sent to the manager, James M. Sutherland, accepting the offer of par value for the shares of £25,000.

The shareholders were invited to an extraordinary meeting on 5 December 1900, when the provisional agreement for the sale of the bank was read out. It was indicated that the Mercantile Bank would pay £25,000 and the directors of the Manx Bank had to present an undertaking not to carry out banking business in the Island. The chairman, William Kelly, reminded the shareholders of the recent financial crisis and the changes in the structure of local banking systems. After a brisk discussion in which many topics were covered the offer was accepted and transfer of the Manx Bank effected.[96]

Note Issues

The licence limit allowed up to £12,000 of one pound notes to be circulated. Two designs are believed to have been used, the second being a slightly simpler modification of the first. Since the date of change is unknown the list of serial numbers and dates with numbers of notes outstanding is given for the whole period 1882–1900. No circulated notes of the second design have been discovered, the only evidence being presented by a few unissued notes.

343   Issue 1 (1882–18..). Notes signed by James M. Sutherland (Manager) and Robert Callister (Cashier).
Issued: November 1882 *Obverse:* The whole note design is very ornate. Vignette of Tower of Refuge, THE/MANX BANK/LIMITED in three lines above. PROMISE

343   Manx Bank. Obverse and reverse (see following page) of one pound note of the first design dated 21 May 1889, signed by James M. Sutherland and Robt. Callister. Note has been slightly trimmed. [*H. F. Guard*]

343 (reverse)

TO PAY THE – BEARER ON DEMAND/AT THE OFFICE HERE IN – DOUG-
LAS/ONE – POUND/IN TERMS OF ACT OF TYNWALD – VALUE RECEIVED.
in four lines divided by vignette. DOUGLAS (date) 18—— to left, NO. (serial
number) to right. (signature) CASHIER lower left; (signature) MANAGER lower
right. ISLE OF MAN upper border, ONE POUND lower border. Heavy ornamen-
tal border, 1 in each corner. *Reverse:* Triune in centre, *THE MANX BANK
LIMITED*ISLE OF MAN round, all within geometric design. Small vignettes of
Albert Tower, Ramsey above; Laxey Wheel below. Larger vignettes of Castle
Rushen at left and St. Germain's Cathedral, Peel at right. ONE POUND vertically
in geometric pattern at each corner. Printer's imprint in lower margin. *Printer:*
Waterlow & Sons Limited, 27 Great Winchester Street, London Wall, London E.C.
Colour: Black print on white paper, brown on white reverse. *Watermark:* none
Dimensions: 199 x 124mm. *Rarity:* R7 (1 known + 1 in archives).

344   Printer's Proof (1882)
As (343). No serial numbers. *Rarity:* R7 (1 known + 1 in archives).

**345   Issue 2 (18..-1900). Notes signed by James M. Sutherland (Manager)
and Robert Callister (Cashier).**
Basic design similar to (343) but much of the ornate design has been reduced. The
reverse has also been simplified by removal of the four corner elements. *Dimensions:* 168 x 123mm. *Rarity:* R7. No issued notes known. Twelve unissued notes
numbered 28500–28511 were presented to banks and officials during the period
1900–1909, of these one is in a private collection and four, signed by Robert

345 Manx Bank. Unissued one pound note of the second design. [*H. F. Guard*]

Callister only, are now in the Manx Museum. *Dates:* (outstanding notes in brackets).

00001–09000	11 November 1882	(55)
09001–13000	1 November 1883	(19)
13001–15000	1 May 1884	(16)
15001–17000	21 May 1889	(23)
17001–17500	2 December 1889	(4)
17501–18000	1 May 1890	(3)
18001–18500	1 November 1890	(6)
18501–19000	2 February 1891	(6)

19001–20000	1 May 1891	(10)
20001–21000	1 October 1891	(10)
21001–21500	2 April 1892	(5)
21501–22000	1 May 1892	(5)
22001–23000	1 May 1893	(7)
23001–24000	20 November 1894	(8)
24001–24500	20 November 1895	(4)
24501–25000	1 June 1896	(4)
25001–26000	28 April 1897	(5)
26001–26500	1 May 1899	(1)
26501–27000	1 March 1900	(2)
27001–27500	30 May 1900	(1)
27501–29000	not issued	

MERCANTILE BANK OF LANCASHIRE LIMITED

The Mercantile Bank of Lancashire[97] was established in 1890 with its head office in temporary premises in Guardian Buildings, Cross Street, Manchester, with a capital of one million pounds composed of 50,000 shares of £20 each including 100 deferred shares. The prospectus showed the need for a new bank due to an increase in business in recent years in the Manchester area and would provide assistance for new businesses expected to commence when the Manchester Ship Canal, then under construction, was opened. Within a few weeks of opening over 200 accounts were opened and by January 1891 this figure had increased to 300. On 30 June 1891 the bank reported a net profit of £2,806.

After the Baring Crisis in 1890–1891 a number of failures occurred with some of the bank's customers and in turn some losses were incurred by the bank due to overdrafts of failed businesses. Profits increased to £20,564 in 1900 and dividends increased with deposits. The bank was successful and opened several branches in the Manchester area with further branches in Cheshire, Derbyshire, Staffordshire and Yorkshire and in 1900 branches were established in the Isle of Man on amalgamation of the Manx Bank referred to earlier.

Through the establishment of branches in the Island the note issue was continued with a licence limit of £15,000 compared with £12,000 of the Manx Bank. The manager of the Douglas office was Reginald Hirst Milner with Henry Travers Hall as assistant manager.

After absorption of the Manx Bank, deposits with the Mercantile Bank decreased due mainly to withdrawal of deposits from the Isle of Man branches and the effect of the South African War on investments. The Board of the Mercantile realised the situation and decided that because of the relative small size of the bank they could only survive by absorption of other banks or be absorbed themselves. Two possible amalgamations were considered in 1901 by the Whitehaven Joint Stock Bank and another in 1902 by the York City & County Banking Company, but both were declined.

During the early part of 1904 several meetings were held between R.P. Hewitt, chairman of the Mercantile Bank and T.B. Moxon, general manager of the Lancashire & Yorkshire Bank with the result that on 1 July 1904 the business of the Mercantile Bank was transferred to the Lancashire & Yorkshire Bank. The

Mercantile's chairman joined the Board of the Lancashire & Yorkshire Bank with the other directors retained in a consultative capacity for a few years.

Note Issues

346   Issue 1 (1901–1904). Notes signed by R. H. Milner (Manager) and H. T. Hall (Assistant Manager).
Issued: June 1901. Basic design as (345) but slightly smaller format. Bank's title now reads THE MERCANTILE/BANK OF LANCASHIRE LIMITED in two lines above vignette. Title of counter-signatory changed to ASST. MANAGER *Printer:*

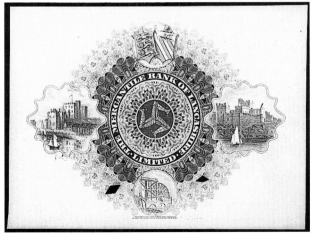

346   Mercantile Bank of Lancashire. Unissued one pound note. [*H. F. Guard*]

Waterlow & Sons Limited. *Colour:* Black print on white paper, reverse same. *Dimensions:* 168 x 117mm. *Rarity:* R7 (2 known + 2 in archives). *Dates:* (outstanding notes in brackets).

00001–02000	13 June 1901	(6)
02001–03000	8 July 1901	(4)
03001–04000	24 August 1901	(2)
04001–05000	5 October 1901	(3)
05001–06000	6 September 1902	(3)
06001–08500	unissued, destroyed*	

* Three of these notes, 06003, 08499 and 08500, have survived, the terminal two now in archives. Numbers of notes outstanding have remained at the above figures since 1935.

347   Printer's Proof (1901)

As (346). No serial number, date or signature. *Rarity:* R7 (1 known).

LANCASHIRE & YORKSHIRE BANK LIMITED

Foundations for the Lancashire & Yorkshire Bank[98][99] were laid in London in 1862 by the establishment of the Alliance Bank, the directors of which pursued a policy of extensions in the provinces by opening branches in Manchester and Liverpool. The Manchester office opened on 1 January 1864 at 73 King Street under the managership of John Mills. Difficulties for banks in general arose due to the Cotton Famine and the failure of Overend & Gurney in 1866, but the stability of the Alliance Bank was not affected.

A decision was taken in 1871 to close the two provincial branches and Mills, having been successful in Manchester, decided to draw up a scheme to form a new bank termed the Lancashire & Yorkshire Bank Limited. The prospectus issued on 30 April 1872 invited a capital of one million pounds divided into 50,000 shares of £20 each. Most of the directors were prominent Manchester businessmen and Mills was appointed as manager. Nearly £4,000 profit was made in the first six months of business giving a dividend of 6%.

Branches were opened commencing in August 1872 and over the next few years a gradual extension of business occurred throughout Lancashire and Yorkshire with profits exceeding £53,000 in 1882 and dividends of 9% in 1883 and 10% in 1886. Some of the bank's deposits were used to finance the construction of the Manchester Ship Canal opened in 1894. Many private banks ceased to exist in the second half of the nineteenth century, especially as a result of the Overend Crisis of 1866, but the Lancashire & Yorkshire Bank emerged without effect.

Other amalgamations of the Lancashire & Yorkshire Bank included the Bury

Banking Company, Preston Union Bank, Adelphi Bank, West Riding Union Banking Company and the Mercantile Bank of Lancashire which was its last absorption and enabled the Lancashire & Yorkshire Bank to continue the Mercantile Bank's note issue in the Isle of Man with branches at Douglas, Ramsey, Onchan, Peel, Castletown and Port Erin. Initially the note licence limit was fixed at £17,000 but was later increased to £20,000. The former manager and assistant manager of the Douglas office retained their positions after the amalgamation and continued to sign the notes.

Reference to the Bank's balance sheets gives some indication of the note circulation in the Island, £9,804 (1915), £17,890 (1921) and £14,000 (1927) but after the note issue was taken over by Martins in 1928 the number of Lancashire & Yorkshire Bank notes decreased. Less than 240 remained outstanding in 1993.

Note Issues

348 Issue 1 (1904–1920), Notes signed by R. H. Milner (Manager) and H. T. Hall (Assistant Manager)
Issued: November 1 ... ign as (346) but bank's title now reads THE/ MANX BANK/BR... HE/LANCASHIRE & YORKSHIRE BANK LIMITED in four c... ve vignette. *Reverse:* Arms of the Lancashire & Yorkshire bank n... hose of the Mercantile Bank of Lancashire. *Printer:* Waterlow... ted, 27 Great Winchester Street, London Wall, London E.C. *Colo...* t on white paper, reverse same. *Watermark:* none

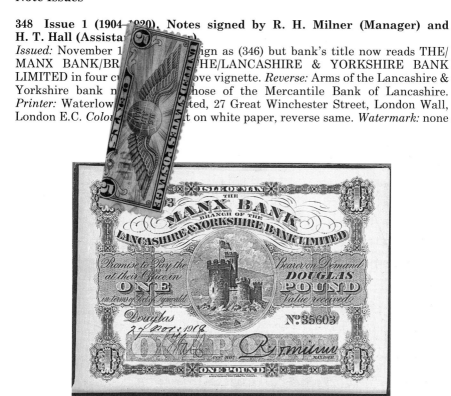

348 Lancashire & Yorkshire Bank. One pound note dated 27 November 1918, signed by R. H. Milner and H. T. Hall. [*H. F. Guard*]

Dimensions: 167 x 120mm. *Rarity:* R6 (17 known + 1 in archives). *Dates:* (outstanding notes in brackets).

00001–01000	10 November 1904	(5)
01001–02000	1 December 1904	(6)
02001–03000	18 March 1905	(3)
03001–04000	15 August 1905	(2)
04001–05000	11 November 1905	(1)
05001–06000	31 March 1906	(5)
06001–07000	6 October 1906	(2)
07001–08000	12 November 1906	(2)
08001–09000	23 March 1907	(3)
09001–10000	31 August 1907	(8)
10001–11000	9 November 1907	(6)
11001–12000	21 March 1908	(1)
12001–13000	17 October 1908	(1)
13001–14000	16 November 1908	(2)
14001–15000	9 April 1910	(4)
15001–16000	9 October 1910	(2)
16001–17000	29 October 1910	(1)
17001–18000	13 May 1911	(0)
18001–19000	10 November 1911	(5)
19001–20000	30 October 1912	(0)
20001–21000	30 April 1913	(1)
21001–22000	14 November 1913	(2)
22001–23000	4 August 1914	(6)
23001–24000	5 August 1914	(2)
24001–25000	7 August 1914	(1)
25001–26000	10 October 1914	(3)
26001–27000	13 November 1914	(2)
27001–28000	22 June 1915	(3)
28001–29000	12 May 1916	(3)
29001–30000	21 November 1916	(2)
30001–31000	27 September 1917	(1)
31001–32000	26 April 1918	(3)
32001–33000	1 November 1918	(2)
33001–34000	5 November 1918	(4)
34001–35000	12 November 1918	(4)
35001–36000	27 November 1918	(4)
36001–37000	18 December 1918	(5)
37001–38000	24 February 1919	(2)
38001–39000	14 April 1919	(3)
39001–40000	17 November 1919	(1)
40001–41000	3 May 1920	(6)
41001–42000	30 October 1920	(2)

349 Printer's Proof (1904)
As (348). No serial numbers. *Rarity:* R7 (1 known, in archives).

350 Issue 2 (1920–1924). Notes signed by R. H. Milner (Manager) and H. T. Hall (Assistant Manager).
Issued: December 1920 *Obverse:* Two vignettes are displayed. The Arms of the bank are depicted at the left and Tower of Refuge at the right. THE/LANCAS-HIRE & YORKSHIRE BANK/LIMITED in three lines upper centre. NO. (serial number) at upper left and right. PROMISE TO PAY THE BEARER/ON DE-MAND AT THEIR OFFICE IN/DOUGLAS/ONE POUND/IN TERMS OF ACT OF TYNWALD. VALUE RECEIVED. DOUGLAS. (date) 19—— in six lines centre below bank's title. (signature) ASST. MANAGER at lower left and (signature) MANAGER lower right. ISLE OF MAN in upper border at left and right, ONE POUND in lower border. All within decorative border. 1 in each corner and lower centre. Printer's imprint in lower margin. *Reverse:* Triune within circle, centre .THE LANCASHIRE & YORKSHIRE BANK LIMITED. round. £1 below. Left vignette depicts Castle Rushen, and Laxey Wheel in right vignette. Geometric pattern. Printer's imprint in lower margin. *Printer:* Waterlow & Sons Limited, London Wall, London E.C. *Colour:* Slate-grey print on white paper, reverse same. *Watermark:* none *Dimensions:* 165 x 85mm. *Positional Code Letters:* A/A, B/B. These will be located on the obverse to the right of the trefoil in the lower left corner, and on the reverse to right of ornament at lower left centre of frame of left hand vignette. *Rarity:* R7 (none known). *Dates:* (outstanding notes in brackets).

00001–01000	13 December 1920	(6)
01001–02000	18 December 1920	(2)
02001–03000	12 February 1921	(4)
03001–04000	30 April 1921	(4)
04001–05000	5 November 1921	(4)
05001–06000	21 November 1921	(6)
06001–07000	13 February 1922	(1)
07001–08000	20 March 1922	(2)
08001–09000	13 November 1922	(2)
09001–10000	9 December 1922	(0)
10001–11000	10 February 1923	(2)
11001–12000	10 March 1923	(1)
12001–13000	12 May 1923	(4)
13001–14000	12 November 1923	(0)
14001–15000	24 December 1923	(3)
15001–16000	1 March 1924	(1)

351 Printer's Proof (1920)
As (350). Serial number 000000, four punch-hole cancellations, no signatures or date. Waterlow's specimen stamp at lower right. *Rarity:* R7 (1 known).

351   Lancashire & Yorkshire Bank. Obverse of printer's proof for one pound note.

352 Issue 3 (1924–1928). Notes signed by R. H. Milner (Manager) and E. S. Oldham (Assistant Manager).
Specification as (350). *Issued:* October 1924. *Rarity:* R7 (6 known). *Dates:* (outstanding notes in brackets).

16001–17000	11 October 1924	(1)
17001–18000	1 November 1924	(1)
18001–19000	15 November 1924	(1)
19001–20000	23 December 1924	(2)
20001–21000	28 March 1925	(1)
21001–22000	23 May 1925	(5)
22001–23000	29 October 1925	(3)
23001–24000	12 November 1925	(7)
24001–25000	5 December 1925	(2)
25001–26000	1 March 1926	(5)
26001–27000	1 May 1926	(3)
27001–28000	5 June 1926	(4)
28001–30000	16 October 1926	(4)
30001–31000	22 December 1926	(0)
31001–32000	2 April 1927	(6)
32001–33000	21 May 1927	(8)
33001–34000	3 August 1927	(3)
34001–35000	22 October 1927	(3)
35001–36000	16 November 1927	(5)
36001–37000	10 December 1927	(4)
37001–38000	24 December 1927	(2)
38001–39000	28 December 1927	(1)

352   Lancashire & Yorkshire Bank. One pound note dated 16 November 1927, signed by
R. H. Milner and E. S. Oldham. [*H. F. Guard*]

MARTINS BANK LIMITED

Through links with many antecedent banks the history of Martins Bank can be
traced back to 1563 when Sir Thomas Gresham, a man of great influence, founded
a Goldsmith's business on the site formerly occupied by Martins Bank at 68
Lombard Street, London.[100] In the sixteenth century the practice of street
numbering was not adopted and signs were used instead. The Grasshopper, used
by Gresham to identify his business house, was used as the family crest of the
Gresham family and Sir Thomas gave the first Royal Exchange to the City of
London, where the Grasshopper adorned the building in its function of a weather
vane. Records from 1563 to 1666 were lost in the Great Fire of London in 1666 but
there is evidence that the Grasshopper continued to be used as a mark on gold
plate.[101]

After 1666 clear documentary evidence traces the subsequent history of banking "at the sign of the Grasshopper in Lombard Street". Between 1662 and 1672
Edward Backwell carried out his banking business until business abroad necessitated Backwell leaving the bank in the hands of Charles Duncombe. In 1681
Richard Smythe was admitted as a partner and two of his assistants, Andrew
Stone and Thomas Martin, became partners in 1699 and 1703 respectively, thus
the continuous connection with the Martin family was founded, an association to
last for eight generations. The Stone and Martin families continued the business
until 1852 due to the extinction of the male line in the Stone family but an interest
was maintained by the Norman family, descendants of the Stones.[102]

Banking continued in London during the eighteenth and nineteenth centuries
and on 25 February 1891 the business was registered as Martins Bank Limited. An
interesting point concerning the bank is the 50,000 shares of £20 with £500,000
paid up were only held by 56 shareholders, principally members of the Martin
family thus ensuring the bank's continuance with as little change as possible.

From 1891 to 1919 Martins expanded but was too small to remain as an independent concern and it was felt by the Board that expansion to the provinces was desirable, but naturally Martins wished to effect this with the minimum of change. Meanwhile, the Bank of Liverpool, which possessed a large number of branches in the North of England, realised the necessity of securing a place in the London Clearing House and like Martins did not wish to lose their identity by absorption. After discussions between Martins and the Bank of Liverpool a compromise was attained by adopting the title Bank of Liverpool & Martins Limited. Objections to this new title were raised by some of the shareholders, but arguments in favour of its retention showed that it was desirable, due to the value of goodwill connected with each of the two banks. In 1928 the title was reduced to Martins Bank Limited and maintained until 1969 on absorption by Barclays Bank.[103]

After World War I further amalgamations took place, notably in Manchester which had been rather independent in banking affairs. Other banks had unsuccessfully attempted to acquire the Manchester banks but in 1919 the Bank of Liverpool & Martins absorbed the Palatine Bank, after failing to acquire the Union Bank of Manchester and Williams Deacon's Bank earlier in the same year. Another important amalgamation was the Lancashire & Yorkshire Bank in 1928 detailed earlier in this chapter. This amalgamation gave Martins a business foothold in the Isle of Man, and were thus able to continue the bank note issue to a limit of £25,000 until the note licence was revoked in 1961, in common with the other commercial banks.

The former manager and assistant manager of the Douglas office of the Lancashire & Yorkshire Bank retained these positions after the amalgamation and their names appeared on the bank notes as before. In 1931 the notes bear the name of Arthur Frederick Shawyer as General Manager with Edwyn Schofield Oldham as District Manager and from 1934 the notes bear the name of the General Manager or Chief General Manager of Martins as indicated in the detail of the note issues. Thus the Martins notes bore signatures of an official not at the Douglas office and in this respect differ from notes issued by other Manx banks.

Note Issues

Only notes of one pound were issued. Until a definitive note was available the initial issue, consisting of a batch of 2,000 notes of the Lancashire & Yorkshire Bank suitably overprinted, was used. This was replaced by the definitive issue in 1929 and continued with few small changes until 1961. Some of these changes occur due to change in title of signatory and are detailed at the appropriate place. Martins issued 180,500 notes of which 1,378 are outstanding and 280 are known.

353   Issue 1 (1928–1929). Notes signed by R. H. Milner (Manager) and E. S. Oldham (Assistant Manager).
Provisional issue of notes of the Lancashire & Yorkshire Bank (352) overprinted MARTINS BANK LIMITED in black in the upper margin and WITH WHICH IS – INCORPORATED in red just above the serial numbers. *Rarity:* R7 (2 known) (one of each date). *Dates:* (outstanding notes in brackets).

353 Martins Bank. Provisional issue one pound note dated 9 October 1928, signed by R. H. Milner and E. S. Oldham. [*H. F. Guard*]

39001–40000	9 October 1928	(3)
40001–41000	3 November 1928	(3)
41001–42000	not issued, destroyed by bank	

354 Issue 2 (1929–1931). Notes signed in facsimile by R.H. Milner (Manager) and E.S. Oldham (Assistant Manager).
Issued: April 1929 *Obverse:* Vignette at left depicts arms of the bank comprising grasshopper and Liver bird. Vignette of Tower of Refuge at right. MARTINS BANK/LIMITED in two curved lines above, centre; PROMISE TO PAY THE BEARER/ON DEMAND AT THEIR OFFICE IN/DOUGLAS/ONE POUND/IN TERMS OF ACT OF TYNWALD. VALUE RECEIVED/DOUGLAS, (printed date)19—— in six lines. (signature) ASST. MGR. at lower left, (signature) MANAGER at lower right. Serial numbers at upper left and right. ISLE OF MAN above numbers, in upper border; ONE POUND in lower border, centre. All enclosed in ornamental border with figure 1 in each corner. Printer's imprint in lower margin *Reverse:* Triune within circle .MARTINS BANK LIMITED. round, left vignette of Castle Rushen, right vignette of Albert Tower. All enclosed within ornamental border. Printer's imprint in lower margin. *Printer:* Waterlow & Sons Limited, London Wall, London E.C. *Colour:* Slate-grey print on white paper, reverse same, red serial numbers. *Watermark:* none. *Positional Code Letters:* A/C, B/D, C/A, D/B. These will be located in the lower left corner of the obverse below the trefoil, and on the reverse at lower centre of frame on left hand vignette. *Dimensions:* 150 x 84mm. *Rarity:* R7 (none known). *Date:* (outstanding notes in brackets).

42001–45000	serial numbers not used	
45001–65000	2 April 1929	(53)

355 Printer's Proof (1929)
Specification as (354). No date, signatures or positional code letters. Serial number 000000 printed in red. *Rarity:* R7 (1 known, in archives).

356   Printer's Proof of Obverse (1929)
Specification as (354). Impression on large piece of paper marked with details of
edges for final format. No serial number, date, signatures or positional code letter.
Rarity: R7 (1 known)

357   Printer's Proof of Reverse (1929)
Specification as (354). Impression on large piece of paper. *Rarity:* R7 (1 known).

358   Printer's Promotional Note
Specification as (354) but printed in green on obverse and reverse. Positional code
letter D on obverse, reverse positional code letter punched out. Number 517 in
upper margin of obverse. *Rarity:* R7 (1 known).

**359   Issue 3 (1931–1934). Notes signed in facsimile by A.F. Shawyer
(General Manager) and E.S. Oldham (District Manager).**
Specification as (354) but with change of titles for signatories. *Rarity:* (1931) R7 (1
known + 1 in archives), (1932) R7 (3 known + 1 in archives). *Dates:* (outstanding
notes in brackets).

65001–75000	1 December 1931	(25)
75001–95000	31 December 1932	(40)

359   Martins Bank. Obverse and reverse of one pound note dated 31 December 1932, signed
by A. F. Shawyer and E. S. Oldham. Reverse design is common to all note issues.

360   Martins Bank. One pound note dated 1 October 1938, signed by J. M. Furniss. Only single signature now used.

360   Issue 4 (1934–1946). Notes signed in facsimile by J.M. Furniss (General Manager).
Specification as (354). Only one signature appears on notes, serial numbers now in black. *Positional Code Letters:* E/C, F/D, G/A, H/B. *Rarity:* (1934) R4 (26 known + 2 in archives), (1938) R4 (35 known + 1 in archives). *Dates:* (outstanding notes in brackets).

95001–125000	1 August 1934	(134)
125001–155000	1 October 1938	(289)

361   Issue 5 (1946–1950). Notes signed in facsimile by Jas. McKendrick (Chief General Manager).
Specification as (354) but with change of heraldic colours in Arms of bank. Also change of title of signatory. *Positional Code Letters:* A/C, B/D, C/A, D/B. *Rarity:* R4 (35 known + 4 in archives) *Date:* (outstanding notes in brackets).

155001–175000	1 March 1946	(131)

361   Martins Bank. One pound note dated 1 March 1946, signed by Jas. McKendrick. From this date the new heraldic Arms of the Bank were used.

362   Printer's Proof (1946)
Specification as (361). No date, serial numbers or signature. *Rarity:* R7 (1 known).

363   Issue 6 (1950–1957). Notes signed in facsimile by C.J. Verity (Chief General Manager).
Specification as (361). *Rarity:* (1950) R4 (32 known + 1 in archives), (1953) R3 (38 known + 1 in archives). *Dates:* (outstanding notes in brackets).

175001–195000	1 June 1950	(187)
195001–210000	1 May 1953	(203)

364   Issue 7 (1957–1961). Notes signed in facsimile by Mungo Conacher (Chief General Manager).
Specification as (361). *Rarity:* R2 (84 known + 15 in archives). *Dates:* (outstanding notes in brackets).

210001–225500	1 February 1957	(310)

CHAPTER 9

Establishment of the English Banks – III

Lloyds Bank Limited, Barclays Bank Limited

LLOYDS BANK LIMITED

Founded in 1765 under the partnership of Sampson Lloyd, John Taylor and their sons also of the same name, the bank opened for business at Dale End, Birmingham on 3 June 1765 with a capital of £6,000.[104] The growing wealth and prosperity of Birmingham greatly assisted in the development of the bank which opened an office in Lombard Street, London in 1771 under the title of Hanbury, Taylor, Lloyd & Bowman but the partner Sampson Lloyd (father) died in 1807 with the result that the connection between the Taylor and Lloyds in Birmingham and the Lombard Street office was temporarily severed. The year 1864 saw the amalgamation of the banking business of Bland & Barnett, who had occupied adjacent premises in Lombard Street, and the new title of Barnetts, Hoares, Hanbury & Lloyd was used. Through this amalgamation the famous sign of the Black Horse was acquired.

The Birmingham business flourished and gained strength which enabled the bank to overcome the financial crisis of bank failures so common in the early part of the nineteenth century. In 1865 the Birmingham bank became a joint stock bank under the new title of Lloyds Banking Company Limited with a paid up capital of £143,415. Rapid expansion resulted in several branches in the Birmingham area. In 1884 amalgamation of Lloyds Banking Company Limited with Barnetts, Hoares, Hanbury & Lloyd gave the status of a London bank to Lloyds. Shortly afterwards new premises were purchased in Lombard Street and the London office opened at numbers 71 and 72, the former being the address of the head office of Lloyds Bank today.

On amalgamation of the Birmingham Joint Stock Bank in 1889 the present title of Lloyds Bank Limited came into use. Later absorption of other banks occurred of which that of Fox, Fowler & Company of Wellington, Somerset in 1921 is well known since this was the last private bank in England with the right to issue its own notes.

On 1 January 1900 Lloyds entered Lancashire by amalgamation of the Liverpool Union Bank which had had close relations with Lloyds for many years previously. The Liverpool Union Bank had been founded in 1835 but had no branches until 1877. The bank's policy to new branches was modified in later years and on amalgamation with Lloyds had eleven branches, mainly in Liverpool and Birkenhead. One in Douglas was opened in December 1896 in Victoria Street and was thus the first English bank to operate in the Island, its contemporary banks being purely Manx concerns. Two branches were later formed at Ramsey in 1900 and Peel in 1901.

Application for a note licence was made about 1918 and issue of one pound notes to a limit of £15,000 commenced on 23 April 1919 and continued until 31 July 1961 when issue ceased due to the issue of the Manx Government notes.

Note Issues

The same basic design was used for all notes. A large format being issued from 1919 to 1927 and a smaller format until 1961. Positional Code Letters were not used.

365   Issue 1 (1919–1920). Notes signed by G.R. Bargery (Manager) and T.C. Good (Accountant).
Issued: April 1919. *Obverse:* Vignette of the Black Horse within circular frame of beehives, FD1677AD below, within foliate pattern. LLOYDS BANK LIMITED in curved line above. NO. (serial number) at upper left and right. PROMISE TO PAY THE BEARER ON DEMAND/ONE POUND/AT THIS OFFICE ONLY IN TERMS OF ACT OF TYNWALD./DOUGLAS (date) 19—— in four lines. (signature) ACCOUNTANT at lower left, (signature) MANAGER at lower right. All within ornamental border. ONE in each corner, figure 1 in upper corners. ONE POUND in centre of upper and lower border. Printer's imprint in lower margin. *Reverse:* Triune and motto, centre. ONE to left and right. LLOYDS BANK LIMITED in curved line above; HEAD OFFICE. 71 LOMBARD STREET. LONDON.E.C.3. in curved line below. *Printer:* W.W. Sprague & Co. London E.C. *Colour:* Black and green print on white paper, blue-green reverse. *Watermark:*

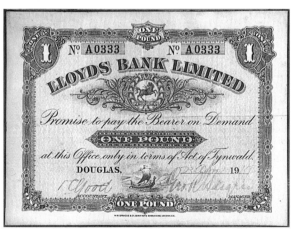

365   Lloyds Bank. One pound note dated 23 April 1919, signed by G. R. Bargery and T. C. Good. [*Manx Museum*]

none. *Dimensions:* 156 x 114mm. *Rarity:* R7 (1 known, in archives). *Dates:* (outstanding notes in brackets).

A0001–A0800	23 April 1919	(3)
A0801–A1000	25 April 1919	(1)
A1001–A1200	28 April 1919	(0)
A1201–A1700	3 May 1919	(1)
A1701–A2300	6 May 1919	(2)
A2301–A2500	10 May 1919	(0)
A2501–A2700	12 May 1919	(1)
A2701–A3100	16 May 1919	(0)
A3101–A3300	24 May 1919	(0)
A3301–A3500	27 May 1919	(2)
A3501–A3700	4 June 1919	(0)
A3701–A3800	6 June 1919	(0)
A3801–A3900	7 June 1919	(0)
A3901–A4000	13 June 1919	(0)
A4001–A4200	25 June 1919	(0)
A4201–A4300	28 June 1919	(1)
A4301–A4600	10 October 1919	(1)
A4601–A5000	6 November 1919	(1)
A5000–A5200	16 December 1919	(0)
A5201–A5400	17 December 1919	(0)
A5401–A5500	19 December 1919	(0)
A5501–A5700	1 January 1920	(0)
A5701–A6000	28 January 1920	(2)

366   Issue 2 (1920–1921). Notes signed by G.R. Bargery (Manager) and E.G. Teare (Accountant).
Specification as (365). *Issued:* 1920. *Rarity:* R8 (none known). *Dates:* (outstanding notes in brackets).

A6001–A6100	17 February 1920	(0)
A6101–A6200	18 February 1920	(1)
A6201–A6600	5 October 1920	(0)
A6601–A6700	15 November 1920	(0)
A6701–A6900	16 November 1920	(0)
A6901–A7000	17 November 1920	(0)
A7001–A7100	9 December 1920	(0)
A7101–A7200	10 December 1920	(0)

367   Issue 3 (1921–1923). Notes signed by T. Priestley (Manager) and E.G. Teare (Accountant).
Specification as (365). *Issued:* 1921. A third colour introduced on the obverse in which the denomination ONE POUND appears in a pink tint. It has not been possible to assign this modification any nearer than 1921 since only one note

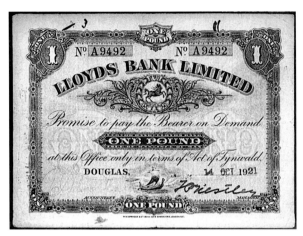

367   Lloyds Bank. One pound note dated 14 October 1921, signed by T. Priestley and E. G. Teare. [*H. F. Guard*]

remains outstanding for Issue 2 and this has not been traced. *Rarity:* R7 (1 known). *Dates:* (outstanding notes in brackets).

A7201–A7700	23 March 1921	(1)
A7701–A8500	27 April 1921	(4)
A8501–A8700	13 June 1921	(0)
A8701–A8800	17 June 1921	(0)
A8801–A10000	14 October 1921	(5)
A10001–A10500	18 January 1922	(0)
A10501–A11000	28 January 1922	(2)
A11001–A11200	15 March 1922	(0)
A11201–A15000	8 April 1922	(15)

368   Unissued Note (1921)
Specification as (367). No serial numbers, unissued. Punch-holed CANCELLED. *Rarity:* R7 (5 known). One of these notes is of interest as it is marked in pencil to show the reduced format and must have been prepared by the printer's for this express purpose.

369   Issue 4 (1923–1929). Notes signed by W.R. Wilson (Manager) and H. Towler (Accountant).
Specification as (367). *Issued:* 1923. *Rarity:* R7 (2 known). *Dates:* (outstanding notes in brackets).

A15001–A20000	29 January 1923	(5)
B0001–B5000	16 April 1924	(10)
B5001–B10000	21 January 1927	(15)

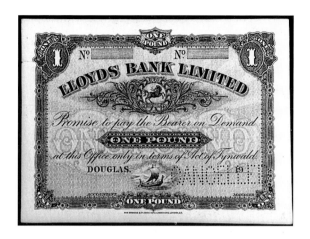

368 Lloyds Bank. Obverse and reverse of cancelled one pound note of the 1921 issue. Reverse design was common to all notes of this format. [*H. F. Guard*]

370 Issue 5 (1929–1935). Notes signed by H. Towler (Manager) and R.A. Hodder (Accountant).
Issued: 1929. Basically same design on obverse and reverse as (367) but smaller format. The words INCORPORATED IN ENGLAND now appear below the bank's title and ISLE OF MAN below DOUGLAS on obverse. The bank's title on the reverse appears in half-shaded lettering. *Printer:* W.W. Sprague & Co. Ltd, London E.C. *Colour:* Black, green and pink print on white paper, blue-green and

pink reverse. *Watermark:* none. *Dimensions:* 150 x 84mm. *Rarity:* R7 (2 known + 1 in archives). *Dates:* (outstanding notes in brackets).

C0001–C1000	1 August 1929	(2)
C1001–C3500	19 August 1929	(2)
C3501–C6000	2 September 1929	(3)
C6001–C7000	12 November 1929	(0)
C7001–C10000	17 December 1929	(0)
C10001–C13000	28 April 1930	(0)
C13001–C18000	14 January 1931	(4)
C18001–C20000	4 December 1931	(2)
C20001–C23000	2 March 1932	(7)
C23001–C26000	17 January 1933	(4)
C26001–C29000	14 February 1934	(5)

371   Printer's Proof (1929)
Specification as (370). No serial numbers, SPECIMEN in typescript in space for manager's signature. *Rarity:* R7 (1 known, in archives).

372   Unissued note (1929)
Specification as (370). No serial numbers. Possibly a printer's trial from a print run. Discovered in the effects of a printer purchased by a London dealer. *Rarity:* R7 (1 known).

373   Issue 6 (1935). Notes signed by H. Towler (Manager) and J. Greenwood (Accountant).
Specification as (370). *Issued:* 1935. Notes serial numbered C29001–C30000 have words INCORPORATED IN ENGLAND as a continuous line below the bank's title. Notes numbered C30001 onwards bear the same wording which is now split by the vignette, ie INCORPORATED [vignette] IN ENGLAND. *Rarity:* R7 (none known). *Date:* (outstanding notes in brackets).

C29001–C30000	28 January 1935	(2)

371 Lloyds Bank. Printer's proof for one pound note of the reduced format. [*Manx Museum*]

374 Issue 7 (1935–1942). Notes signed by H. Towler (Manager) and J. Greenwood (Accountant).
Specification as (370) but with slight modification to legend below Bank's title which is now split by vignette and now reads INCORPORATED [vignette] IN ENGLAND. *Rarity:* R4 (26 known + 2 in archives). *Dates:* (outstanding notes in brackets).

C31001–C32000	28 January 1935	(6)
C32001–C35000	22 February 1935	(8)
C35001–C37000	15 November 1935	(5)
C37001–C40000	23 February 1937	(18)
D0001–D3000	31 March 1938	(20)
D3001–D6000	6 March 1940	(16)
D6001–D8000	12 March 1941	(21)

375 Printer's Proof (1935)
Specification as (374). No serial numbers. *Rarity:* R7 (1 known, in archives).

376 Unissued Note (1935) – Uncancelled
Specification as (374). No serial numbers, unissued. See (372) for further detail. *Rarity:* R6 (10 known + 1 in archives).

377 Unissued Note (1935) – Cancelled
Specification as (374). No serial numbers, unissued. Word CANCELLED in punch-holes appears in centre of note or in area for manager's signature. See (372) for further detail. *Rarity:* R6 (10 known + 1 in archives).

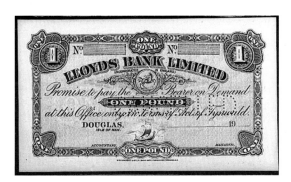

377 Lloyds Bank. Obverse and reverse (see following page) of cancelled unissued one pound note (1935). Probably remainders from print runs, some of which were cancelled. Shows the new modification to obverse design.

377 (reverse)

377A   Printer's Test Piece (1935)
Specification as (373). Printer's testing of machine prior to numbering of batch of notes after printing. This was for the new design of notes with the modified obverse. Note bears serial number C30001 in upper right corner, C30003 in upper left corner, and C30002 vertically at lower left. Probably from same source as (372), (376) and (377). *Rarity:* R8 (1 known).

378   Issue 7 (1942–1948). Notes signed by J. Greenwood (Manager) and C.R. Collister (Accountant).
Specification as (374). *Rarity:* R6 (8 known + 4 in archives). *Dates:* (outstanding notes in brackets).

D8001–D10000	20 November 1942	(20)
D10001–D12000	14 November 1944	(15)
D12001–D14000	6 March 1946	(14)

379   Issue 8 (1948–1951). Notes signed by J. Greenwood (Manager) and R.C. Sale (Accountant).
Specification as (374). *Rarity:* R6 (6 known + 6 in archives). *Dates:* (outstanding notes in brackets).

D14001–D17500	25 February 1948	(35)
D17501–D20000	27 April 1949	(25)

380   Issue 9 (1951–1954). Notes signed by J. Greenwood (Manager) and C.R. Collister (Accountant).
Specification as (374). *Rarity:* R4 (7 known + 31 in archives). *Dates:* (outstanding notes in brackets)

D20001–D24000	27 February 1951	(66)
D24001–D26500	24 March 1952	(69)
D26501–D27500	20 February 1953	(23)
D27501–D30000	26 February 1954	(40)

382 Lloyds Bank. One pound note dated 29 April 1960, signed by D. Berry and C. R. Collister.

381 Issue 10 (1955–1958). Notes signed by J. Greenwood (Manager) and C.R. Collister (Accountant).
Specification as (380) but Bank's title on reverse now printed in full shaded lettering. Also the blue-green print on reverse is now in a lighter shade. *Rarity:* R5 (11 known + 12 in archives). *Dates:* (outstanding notes in brackets).

D30001–D34500	2 February 1955	(46)
D34501–D37000	31 January 1956	(28)
D37001–D39000	25 February 1957	(26)
D39001–D40000	Not issued, destroyed by bank	

382 Issue 11 (1958–1961). Notes signed by D. Berry (Manager) and C.R. Collister (Accountant).
Specification as (381). *Rarity:* R3 (26 known + 42 in archives). *Dates:* (outstanding notes in brackets).

D40001–D42000	28 February 1958	(36)
D42001–D45000	9 December 1958	(53)
D45001–D47000	24 March 1959	(39)
D47001–D49000	29 April 1960	(47)
D49001–D50000	14 March 1961	(34)

BARCLAYS BANK LIMITED

The history of Barclays Bank as a limited company is relatively short dating from 1896 on the amalgamation of twenty banks in various locations in England.[105] Many of these banks were able to trace their foundations back to the seventeenth century. In 1690, John Freame of Lombard Street was in business as a goldsmith and banker and in 1728 his son Joseph purchased adjoining premises in Lombard Street at the sign of "The Black Spread Eagle". Since that date the site has been extended and continuously used by antecedents of Barclays Bank and is now number 54 Lombard Street, the Head Office. In 1733 John Freame's daughter, Sally, married James Barclay who himself entered the business in 1736 in partnership with Joseph Freame. In 1766 Joseph Barclay and John Freame, son of Joseph, died and the bank became titled Freame, Smith & Bening and in the following year Silvanus Bevan entered the business, but apparently was not admitted to the partnership until 1770 when the title was again changed to Freame, Smith, Bevan & Bening. After the death of Joseph Freame in the same year the name of Freame was omitted from the title. On the admission to partnership of David Barclay in 1776 the title of Barclay, Bevan & Bening was adopted until John Barclay was admitted in 1780 when the firm became Barclay, Bevan, Barclay & Bening. In 1783 John Henry Tritton became a partner and the title was changed to Barclay, Bevan, Barclay & Tritton. By 1791 the bank became Barclays & Tritton with the temporary deletion of the name Bevan due to the retirement of Silvanus Bevan but in 1797 when his son, David, was admitted as a partner, took the new title of Barclay, Tritton & Bevan until 1809 on the death of David Barclay. A series of changes in title occurred as new partners were admitted but members of the Barclay, Bevan and Tritton families continued.

In the eastern counties of England there were eight banks in which members of the Gurney family had interests,[106] the Gurneys having been merchants in Norwich since about 1650 carrying out various banking transactions. In 1775 two brothers, John and Henry Gurney, established the first bank as a business separate to other interests under the title of John and Henry Gurney & Company, but within four years the founders died and the business passed to Bartlett Gurney who took into partnership two cousins one of whom, Richard Gurney, had married the only daughter of David Barclay thus bringing to the business a large fortune. Thus began the close association of the two families of Gurney and Barclay and throughout subsequent years various members of the Gurney family served the Norwich bank as partners. During the course of the nineteenth century other banking businesses in East Anglia were absorbed resulting in the strengthening of banking interests in the area, followed in 1896 by the important amalgamation with Barclay & Company and other banks to form Barclay & Company Limited with modification to its present title in 1917.

Joint stock banking commenced with the Act of 1826 but until the principle of limited liability had been admitted in 1856 and the whole complex legislation consolidated into the Companies Act, 1862 many private bankers had held back from the new form. By the end of the nineteenth century the system of joint stock banking had proved successful and many of the private banks had been eliminated by amalgamations with joint stock banks desirous of securing representation in London and geographical extensions. The remaining private banks in considering their future that they would either be absorbed gradually by larger banks or alternatively they could form their own combine. Barclays took the latter course but not without difficulty. Three of the largest banks involved in these discussions realised the dangers of delay and decided to enter into a preliminary agreement to combine their banks. The three banks were Barclay & Company, London, Gurney & Company, Norwich, and Jonathan Backhouse & Company of Darlington. Other banks were given the opportunity of joining, of which seventeen eventually assented. These twenty banks formed the nucleus from which Barclays Bank has grown.

Barclays now had strong connections in many areas of England, particularly in the Eastern counties and during the period up to 1920 the bank was extended and consolidated by amalgamations of other banks resulting in a network of branches throughout England and Wales. But one gap remained in Lancashire which had a number of branches, but it was felt that these were insufficient in number for a heavily populated area. Affiliation of the Union Bank of Manchester in 1919 resulted in the formation of Barclays' branch network in this area.

In 1920 Barclays had interests in banks operating abroad but no branches of its own outside the United Kingdom. Branches were opened in Jersey in 1921, Guernsey in 1923, and the Isle of Man in 1922 when a branch was established in Victoria Street, Douglas, which was the only branch except for a branch at Ramsey. The Ramsey branch opened on 16 October 1967 and closed on 12 December 1969 due to merger of Barclays Bank with Martins Bank with effect from 15 December. The former Martins branch then became Barclays.

Note Issues

One pound notes were the only denomination issued and were the smallest number of the Manx banks. Initially dates on the notes were handwritten but from at least 1927 the date was applied by hand-stamp. The brown plate printing on the obverse was a darker colour on earlier notes and later a lighter shade of printing was used. The obverse design of the note is believed to be the work of the manager's daughter, Miss Swann.

Positional Code Letters

The notes were printed from a double impression plate, notes numbered 00001–35000 were from impressions A and B. These were arranged vertically and each yielded 17,500 notes before replacement. Letters C and D were used for notes numbered 35001–50000. Positional Code Letters are located only on the obverse in the bottom margin at the lower left corner.

Replacement Notes

Owing to the small numbers of notes available for examination it has been difficult to confirm the existence of replacement notes, since the notes were printed from a plate bearing two impressions in multiples of a thousand notes, the sheets cut then numbered. The few notes examined indicate notes bearing the terminal serial number xx001–xx500 would be from one impression and those notes numbered xx501–xx000 are from the other impression. However, a single replacement note has been identified. The batch of notes numbered 35001–36000 bore positional code letter D on notes 35001–35500 and letter C on notes 35501–36000, but note number 35252 bears the letter C instead of the expected letter D and this may confirm the existence of a replacement note. All other Barclays notes examined fall neatly into the two lettered groups of 500 notes each.

383 Barclays Bank. One pound note dated 7 June 1924, signed by E. E. Swann and J. E. Callister. This was the first note issued. [*Barclays Bank*]

383 Issue 1 (1924–1926). Notes signed by E.E. Swann (Manager) and J.E. Callister (Accountant).
Issued: June 1924. *Obverse:* Triune in centre, BARCLAYS BANK/LIMITED in two curved lines above. PROMISE TO PAY THE BEARER/ON DEMAND AT THEIR OFFICE IN/DOUGLAS/ONE POUND/IN TERMS OF ACT OF TYNWALD. in five lines printed over Triune. DOUGLAS (date) 19——— below. (signature) MANAGER at lower right, (signature) ACCOUNTANT at lower left £1 at upper left and right corners; (serial number) to left and right of Triune. All enclosed within ornamental border. ONE POUND in small panel centre of upper and lower border. Printer's imprint in lower margin. *Reverse:* View of Douglas Harbour. BARCLAYS BANK LIMITED/DOUGLAS, ISLE OF MAN in two lines above. HEAD OFFICE, 54 LOMBARD STREET, LONDON E.C. in two lines below. £1 to left and right of vignette. *Printer:* Waterlow & Sons Limited, London Wall, London E.C. *Colour:* Brown and green print on white paper, brown reverse. *Watermark:* none. *Dimensions:* 150 x 84mm. *Rarity:* R7 (1 known, in archives). *Dates:* (outstanding notes in brackets).

00001–01000	7 June 1924	(4)
01001–01500	19 June 1924	(1)
01501–02000	24 July 1924	(1)
02001–02500	1 May 1925	(0)
02501–03000	20 January 1926	(0)
03001–04000	7 April 1926	(2)

384 Printer's Promotional Note
Specification as (383). No date, serial numbers or signatures. Predominantly green colours on obverse and reverse. *Rarity:* R7 (1 known).

385 Issue 2 (1926–1929). Notes signed by E.E. Swann (Manager) and M. Pulman (Accountant).
Specification as (383). *Rarity:* R7 (1 known). *Dates:* (outstanding notes in brackets).

385   Barclays Bank. One pound note dated 23 April 1927, signed by E. E. Swann and M. Pulman. [*F. Swann*]

04001–05000	28 August 1926	(2)
05001–06000	23 April 1927	(3)
06001–07000	15 May 1928	(2)
07001–07500	19 April 1929	(1)

386 Issue 3 (1929–1937). Notes signed by E.E. Swann (Manager) and A. Tranter (Accountant).
Specification as (383). *Rarity:* R7 (1 known). *Dates:* (outstanding notes in brackets).

07501–08000	10 December 1929	(1)
08001–09000	2 May 1930	(4)
09001–10000	20 March 1931	(2)
10001–11000	12 April 1932	(6)
11001–12000	24 March 1933	(5)
12001–13000	21 March 1934	(5)
13001–14000	26 April 1935	(3)
14001–15000	2 April 1936	(3)
15001–15500	7 April 1937	(2)

387 Issue 4 (1937–1950). Notes signed by T.H. Hall (Manager) and A. Tranter (Accountant).
Specification as (383). *Rarity:* R6 (18 known + 1 in archives). *Dates:* (outstanding notes in brackets).

15501–16000	17 December 1937	(5)
16001–17000	24 March 1938	(10)
17001–18000	24 March 1939	(7)
18001–18500	4 April 1942	(13)

18501–19000	15 December 1944	(9)
19001–19500	2 November 1945	(8)
19501–20000	24 August 1946	(10)
20001–20500	24 May 1947	(8)
20501–21000	17 December 1947	(2)
21001–21500	24 March 1948	(4)
21501–22000	7 April 1948	(6)
22001–22500	15 May 1948	(4)
22501–23000	17 November 1948	(5)
23001–23500	22 December 1948	(7)
23501–24000	16 April 1949	(5)
24001–25000	20 February 1950	(10)
25001–27000	20 March 1950	(27)

388   Issue 5 (1950–1954). Notes signed by T.H. Hall (Manager) and J.A. Butterworth (Accountant).
Specification as (383). *Rarity:* R3 (62 known + 15 in archives). *Dates:* (outstanding notes in brackets).

27001–29000	13 November 1950	(10)
29001–30000	15 January 1952	(21)
30001–30500	19 April 1952	(10)
30501–31000	5 May 1952	(10)
31001–31500	7 June 1952	(4)
31501–32000	21 June 1952	(4)
32001–32500	12 September 1952	(7)
32501–33000	28 February 1953	(14)
33001–33500	17 March 1953	(12)
33501–34000	9 May 1953	(19)
34001–34500	6 June 1953	(17)
34501–35000	4 December 1953	(14)

388   Barclays Bank. One pound note dated 15 January 1952, signed by T. H. Hall and J. A. Butterworth. Signatures hand-written.

389   Barclays Bank. One pound note dated 10 April 1954, signed by T. H. Hall and J. A. Butterworth. Signatures now in fascimile and change of title for countersignature.

389   Issue 6 (1954–1958). Notes signed in facsimile by T.H. Hall (Manager) and J.A. Butterworth (Chief Clerk).
Specification as (383) but signatures now in facsimile, and change of counter-signatory from Accountant to Chief Clerk. Positional code letters are C or D. *Rarity:* R4 (36 known + 14 in archives). *Dates:* (outstanding notes in brackets).

35001–36000	10 April 1954	(33)
36001–36500	28 July 1954	(9)
36501–37500	17 December 1954	(16)
37501–38500	16 December 1955	(12)
38501–39500	16 October 1956	(25)
39501–40500	14 December 1956	(17)
40501–41500	1 March 1957	(26)
41501–42000	14 December 1957	(10)
42001–44000	12 March 1958	(30)
44001–45000	25 March 1958	(26)

390   Issue 7 (1958–1961). Notes signed in facsimile by J.A. Butterworth (Manager) and A. Smith (Chief Clerk).
Specification as (389). *Rarity:* R5 (15 known + 7 in archives). *Dates:* (outstanding notes in brackets).

45001–46000	25 March 1958	(23)
46001–47000	10 March 1959	(35)
47001–48000	30 March 1960	(9)
48001–50000	Destroyed, unissued	

Only nine notes, numbered 47992–48000, of the terminal date were preserved, being presented to senior bank officials or archives, the remainder being destroyed in April 1962. Five of these notes have been located of which four are in archives.

CHAPTER 10

Internment Camps

INTERNMENT CAMPS – WORLD WAR 1

On the outbreak of war in 1914 many enemy aliens were gathered and housed at Olympia Hall, London and by early November some 1,500 were held of a total of 10,000 in Britain. Some internees were transferred to moored ships for additional security. With the continued rise in internees a search was made to find more suitable accommodation and the Isle of Man was suggested. In September 1914 a deputation from the Civilian Internment Camps Committee went to the Island resulting in Cunningham's Holiday Camp, Douglas, being subsequently used and known as Douglas Aliens' Detention Camp for which the owner, William Cunningham, received ten shillings (50p) per week paid by the Government to house and feed each internee. The first intake of 200 aliens arrived on 22 September and within a month the number had risen to the official limit of 2,600 but a temporary increase to 3,300 was authorised for a short while. The aliens initially slept in tents but with the onset of winter wooden huts were erected.

A further visit of Home Office representatives on 24 October took place to determine if additional accommodation could be provided and an army camp at Knockaloe near Peel was eventually chosen as it was close to Peel Harbour and had a good water supply.[107] Owing to the heavy clay nature of the ground it was desirable to erect the huts well above ground and lay cinder paths. Sanction of the Manx Government was approved and construction began with the intention of having part ready by 11 November to take 2,500 internees but these plans were not fulfilled. On the set date for opening only 750 could be housed and many more internees were being sent over than could be accommodated. A chaotic state of affairs resulted from over 3,000 men at Douglas which had a capacity for 2,600 and 1,300 at Knockaloe, almost twice its capacity. This led to a demonstration at the Douglas Camp on 19 November during which five internees were killed.

Further reception of internees was suspended until more huts had been assembled at Knockaloe and by the end of February 1915 2,000 could be housed with construction continuing to increase accommodation to a capacity of 5,000. But the flood continued and by the end of 1915 a capacity of 20,000 was attained.

Very little is known about camp currencies of this period, a note for half-crown issued by the Douglas Aliens' Detention Camp is known but this is a relatively high denomination and there is a strong possibility that lower denominations were used. Extensive enquiries have failed to yield more information on this point. A brass token for sixpence inscribed PEEL on the obverse and 6d. on the

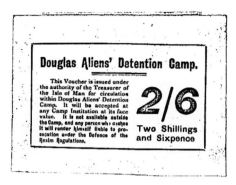

399 Douglas Aliens' Detention Camp. Half-crown voucher. [*Manx Museum*]

reverse is known. Whether this has connections with the Knockaloe Camp has not been verified

DOUGLAS ALIENS' DETENTION CAMP

399 Two shillings and sixpence
Obverse: Title DOUGLAS ALIENS' DETENTION CAMP at top, THIS VOUCHER IS ISSUED UNDER/THE AUTHORITY OF THE TREASURER OF/ THE ISLE OF MAN FOR CIRCULATION/WITHIN DOUGLAS ALIENS' DE-TENTION/CAMP. IT WILL BE ACCEPTED AT/ ANY CAMP INSTITUTION AT ITS FACE/VALUE. IT IS NOT AVAILABLE OUTSIDE/THE CAMP, AND ANY PERSON WHO CASHES/IT WILL RENDER HIMSELF LIABLE TO PRO-/ SECUTION UNDER THE DEFENCE OF THE/REALM REGULATIONS. in eleven lines. To the right is the value 2/6 with TWO SHILLINGS AND SIXPENCE below. All enclosed within border. *Reverse:* plain. *Printer:* unknown. *Colour:* Black print on white paper. *Watermark:* none. *Dimensions:* 103 x 74mm. *Rarity:* R7 (1 known, in archives).

INTERNMENT CAMPS – WORLD WAR 2

On the outbreak of war on 3 September 1939 there were a large number of aliens resident in the United Kingdom and immediately restrictions were applied to them such as restriction of movement within a small radius of their abode, prohibition of visiting certain coastal areas and ownership of cameras, binoculars and radio transmitters. These restrictive conditions continued until 12 May 1940 when the round-up of aliens commenced. In that same month the German armies swept through the Low Countries and it was obvious that Britain could soon be invaded. The British Government quickly reacted by ordering all so called 'enemy aliens' to be interned. Some 1,500 were already under arrest but about 70,000 others were declared to be harmless by the Home Office who had set up special tribunals to examine all aliens. The latter were declared to pose no threat and even contained a large number of political refugees who had sought sanctuary in Britain during the previous seven years.

On 12 May the round-up commenced with internment of Germans and Austrians and on 10 June, when Mussolini declared war, Italians were included. Initially accommodation for these aliens was a problem and consisted of former holiday camps, Scottish castles, hotels and housing estates. Originally the intention was to deport most to Canada and Australia but the first consignment travelled to Canada on the "Arandora Star" which was sunk on 2 July and half were lost.[108] Another attempt at deportation was made when over 2,500 men sailed on the "Dunera" for Australia but the ordeal of these two voyages compelled the British Government to cease deportation.[109 110]

Most aliens commenced internment at various camps in Britain prior to going to the Isle of Man which had been selected by the government. Examples were Warner's Holiday Camp, Seaton, Devon; Wharth Mill, Bury; and Huyton, both in Lancashire, where a newly completed council estate served as a transit camp. In World War 1 the Island had used wooden huts as accommodation but a timber shortage and lack of time meant that hotels and boarding houses were used instead.

The process of requisition of property entailed notification of occupants of selected premises by a Government Commandeering Notice to vacate within a few days and that all furniture, bedding, cutlery, crockery and household utensils be left. An inventory was then made and unwanted items stored at government expense. The government then paid a fee of twenty-one shillings (£1.05) per week per internee to owners.[111] The properties were then enclosed within a wire fence with guard posts, etc. The first camp prepared was the Mooragh Camp, Ramsey in mid-May 1940 followed by the Onchan and Port Erin Camps, the latter being exclusively for women and children who had unrestricted use of the town.

The number of aliens held on the Island fluctuated as they gained their release. In January 1942 the number was c.3,700, in January 1943 2,990 and by January 1944 the number was 2,068. The total number of internees on the Island never exceeded 14,000. By the end of 1944 only 318 men and women occupied Rushen Camp, and just over 1,000 held jointly in the Mooragh and Peveril Camps. All the Douglas camps were by this time closed for internees and were in use as prisoner of war camps or by the military. Finally, on 8 May 1945, only 1,198 internees remained on the Island and gradual releases reduced the final number to 400 at Peveril Camp and 180 at Rushen Camp when they both closed on 5 September 1945.

Not all camps issued their own currency but details of each camp are given for sake of completeness.

CENTRAL INTERNMENT CAMP

Situated on Central Promenade, Douglas, it comprised the "Empress Hotel" and adjacent properties. Opened about July 1940 and closed 27 February 1941 when the remaining 697 internees were transferred to Onchan Camp. The premises were then transferred to the Royal Air Force. No evidence of notes used at this camp.

GRANVILLE INTERNMENT CAMP

Situated in Douglas this occupied all hotels bounded by Loch Promenade, Granville St., Strand St. and Howard St. Opened in July 1940, with a capacity for 750 internees, it closed sometime in 1941 when the premises were used by the Royal Navy as a training establishment, H.M.S. "Valkyrie II". Onchan Camp notes are known stamped GRANVILLE CAMP dated August 1941.

HUTCHINSON INTERNMENT CAMP [112]

Situated in Douglas based on Hutchinson Square, was also known as P Camp, and unofficially as Broadway Camp in its early days. Opened in July 1940 it continued in use until March 1944 when it was closed to internees and the remaining 228 were transferred to the Peveril Camp. The camp may have been used for prisoners of war after November 1944. Notes of the Home Office issue were the only ones used. This camp also published a newspaper titled "The Camp".

METROPOLE INTERNMENT CAMP

Also known as S Camp, it was situated in Douglas just north of the Palace Camp. The Metropole comprised four hotels on Queen's Promenade, "Alexandra", "Metropole", "Milne's Waverley" and "Dodsworth's", the latter being used as the camp infirmary. A detention cell was in a stable formerly used by Douglas Corporation. The camp opened in July 1940 with an intake of 743 internees, mainly Italians, who were later released in 1943 when Italy surrendered. When the Palace Camp closed in 1942 the internees were transferred to the Metropole. The camp housed 482 in October 1944 and by the following month had been cleared. It was then used to house Germans. Other nationalities also lived there from time to time.

The camp issued its own distinctive currency of card halfpence and pence, and notes for ten shillings and one pound.[113]

400 Halfpenny
Obverse: 1/2d in centre, METROPOLE above; CAMP below, all within circular border on rectangular card. *Reverse:* (serial number) within rectangle, centre. Ornament above and below. *Printer:* Norris Modern Press, Douglas. *Colour:* Black print on bright blue cloth lined paste board, grey-green print on white reverse. *Dimensions:* 67 x 68mm (card), 31mm dia.(print). *Rarity:* R6 (8 known + 1 in archives). One block of four known. Another block was discovered in 1972 but was later cut to yield four singles. All known pieces are un-numbered but the specimen in archives is numbered 2164.

401 One Penny
As (400) but reads 1d. *Colour:* Black print on steel-grey cloth lined paste board, brown print on white reverse. *Dimensions:* 73 x 76mm. (card), 31mm dia. (print).

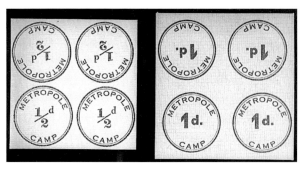

400/401   Metropole Internment Camp. Halfpenny and one penny cards which were printed in four subjects per sheet then cut when required. [*H. F. Guard*]

Rarity: R6 (8 known + 1 in archives). One block of four known, another was discovered in 1972 but was later cut to yield four singles. Known pieces are un-numbered but the specimen in archives is numbered 3837.

402   Ten Shillings
Obverse: METROPOLE INTERNMENT CAMP/DOUGLAS in two lines of gothic script at top, PROMISE TO PAY THE INTERNEE/THE SUM OF/TEN SHIL-LINGS in three lines, centre. FOR METROPOLE CAMP/O.C. PULLEY, MAJOR/COMMANDER in three lines at lower right. M (serial number) at upper right and lower left. 10/- within rectangular block left and right. All on patterned background. within border. *Reverse:* Denomination in figures, centre. All on patterned background within border. Printer's imprint N.M.P. in lower margin. *Printer:* Norris Modern Press, Douglas. *Colour:* Blue print on white paper, blue reverse. *Watermark:* none. *Dimensions:* 140 x 78mm. *Rarity:* R7 (5 known + 1 in archives). *Serial Numbers:* M1001–M3000. The first note printed received mis-matched serial numbers M1000/M1001.

402   Metropole Internment Camp. Ten shillings note. This is the first note printed and received mis-matched serial numbers in error. [*L. G. Burr*]

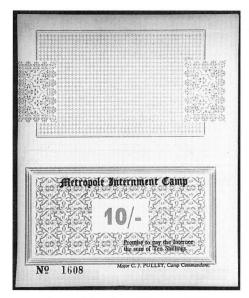

403 Metropole Internment Camp. Printer's trial for ten shillings note. [*H. F. Guard*]

403 Ten Shillings – Printer's Trial
Similar to (402), but printed on double size piece of paper, uniface, bearing trial impressions of obverse and reverse on same side. *Obverse:* METROPOLE INTERNMENT CAMP in gothic script above, PROMISE TO PAY THE INTERNEE/THE SUM OF TEN SHILLINGS/MAJOR C.J. PULLEY, CAMP COMMANDANT in three lines at lower right. NO. (serial number) at lower left. 10/- centre within patterned area, all within border. *Reverse:* As underprint on issued note (402). *Printer:* Norris Modern Press, Douglas. *Rarity:* R8 (1 known). This item carries the serial number 1608.

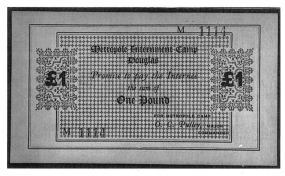

404 Metropole Internment Camp. One pound note. [*L. G. Burr*]

404   One Pound
Obverse: As (402) but reads ONE POUND. *Reverse:* £1 in centre, ONE POUND above. Triune within circle to left and right, all on patterned background within border. N.M.P. in lower margin. *Printer:* Norris Modern Press, Douglas. *Colour:* Red print on white paper, black and red reverse. *Dimensions:* 153 x 85mm. *Rarity:* R7 (6 known + 1 in archives). *Serial Numbers:* M1001–M1500.

405   One Pound – Printer's Trial
Obverse and reverse design and colour identical to reverse of (404). *Obverse:* Camp title METROPOLE INTERNMENT CAMP in gothic script appears in black print at top with serial number 0387 in black at lower left corner. *Reverse:* As obverse but serial number only at lower left, no camp title. *Rarity:* R8 (1 known).
    Notes of the Home Office issue are known to have been used at this camp.

405   Metropole Internment Camp. Obverse and reverse of printer's trial for one pound note. [*H. F. Guard*]

MOORAGH INTERNMENT CAMP

This camp was based on the Mooragh Park, Ramsey and included all properties on the Mooragh Promenade commencing at the "Peveril Hotel" along to the end of the golf links and embraced all properties at the rear as far as "Lake View". Some private bungalows adjacent were also included along with some nearby properties for use as billets for the camp guard. The Mooragh golf links were also requisitioned as a recreation ground for the internees. The small road leading from the Swing Bridge to the Park was kept open to the public but part of the roadway was included within the perimeter fence A barbed-wire fence was constructed close to the sea wall leaving an alley-way for use by the guards. About thirty houses were involved with a total accommodation for 2,000 internees. Previous occupants of the houses had very short notice of requisition and had only five days to quit leaving most of the domestic contents. An inventory was taken by a local valuer and an annual rent paid by the government.

Initially it was intended to limit the number of internees to 1,000 and the first 823 males arrived on 27 May 1940 followed by a further 400 on 4 June. The first commandant of the camp was Capt. Alexander with Lt. E.W. Thornley in charge of the guard. The camp was internally divided into three sections to keep the main nationalities separate. These sections were titled Camp L for Germans, Camp M for Finns and Camp N for Italians, these letters being used at least until 1943.[114 115] The camp finally closed on 2 August 1945 when about 600 men left the Island.

The only currency known to be used at Mooragh Camp was the Home Office issue. A few are known with a circular hand-stamp MOORAGH INTERNMENT CAMP * round, RAMSEY centre, two sizes were used. Another stamp was used consisting of a diagonal bar with letter F in the centre, on the obverse, in blue-green ink. Nothing further is known about this item.

ONCHAN INTERNMENT CAMP

This camp was situated in Royal Avenue West, and adjacent streets on the south side of Port Jack Glen, Onchan. In preparation for the camp a letter was sent on 23 May 1940 to 60 householders informing them that their houses were to be requisitioned and all had to be evacuated by 31 May. The properties were in Royal Avenue West (33 houses), Belgravia Road (12 houses), Belgravia Terrace (8 houses) and Imperial Terrace (7 houses). It was expected that 2,000 aliens would be accommodated and the whole area was wired off.[116]

The first 1,000 internees from Wharth Mill, Bury arrived on 11 June followed by 250 from Huyton on 13 June and the final 250 from Kempton Park Racecourse on 15 June. Lack of work by the internees created boredom but within a few weeks the "Onchan Pioneer" made its appearance as a duplicated newspaper. This is a most useful source of information and has since proved invaluable for detail of camp personalities.[117]

Initially the camp was under the command of Major R.G. Marsh who was succeeded in August 1940 by Capt. (later Major) The Lord Greenway. The population of the camp reduced as internees were released. In February 1941 the number had decreased to 485 but on 27 February the Central Camp closed and the 697 internees transferred to Onchan. About June 1941 the camp's bank manager,

Markus, gained his release. It is understood he was the designer of the camp notes. These were first issued in October 1940 and continued until about October 1941 when replaced by the Home Office issue. The camp was closed temporarily from July to September 1941 when it reopened with Italian internees, all original Germans not released went to Hutchinson Camp. Onchan Camp was cleared again in November 1944 and made ready for prisoners of war.

Note Issues

The camp was one of the earliest to issue its own distinctive currency which was in use for about a year when it was replaced by the Home Office issue. Notes of the latter series are known bearing circular hand-stamps with ONCHAN CAMP round and (date) in centre. Known dates are March and June 1942. A number of Onchan notes are known in which the serial number has been crossed in three red lines and marked 'Not Negotiable' on the reverse. It is believed these are a form of cancellation since some contemporary collectors obtained these and other camp notes at the time of issue and the Onchan specimens supplied bear these lines. Some circulated notes have also been seen and may have been cancelled on redemption and returned to the payee as a souvenir on their release. Some Onchan notes are also known stamped GRANVILLE CAMP and dated variously in August 1941. These are probably notes used by internees transferred to that camp.

406   Half-Crown

Issued: 7 October 1940 *Obverse:* Vignette to left of Tower of Refuge, ONCHAN INTERNMENT/CAMP in two lines above. 2/6 in panel at upper right, HALF-CROWN centre. ISLE OF MAN below vignette. (serial number) at lower right. *Reverse:* plain. *Printer:* Phoenix Printing Co. Ltd., Liverpool. *Colour:* Blue print on white paper, plain reverse. *Watermark:* Printed on Wiggins, Teape paper, bearing watermark of a castle gateway, W T & Co, in script, EXTRA STRONG/ 3009 all in four lines. *Dimensions:* 120 x 70mm. *Rarity:* R4 (28 known + 5 in archives). *Serial Numbers:* 0001–2000.

406   Onchan Internment Camp. Half-crown voucher.

407   Onchan Internment Camp. Five shillings voucher.

407   Five Shillings

Issued: 7 October 1940 *Obverse:* Similar to (406) but reads FIVE SHILLINGS. SHILLINGS on 5, with + at each corner, in panel at upper right. *Colour:* Red print on white paper. *Rarity:* R4 (31 known + 7 in archives). *Serial Numbers:* 0001–5000.

408   Ten Shillings

Issued: 7 October 1940 *Obverse:* Similar to (407) but reads TEN SHILLINGS. SHILLINGS on 10 in panel at upper right. *Colour:* Green print on white paper. *Rarity:* R4 (29 known + 6 in archives). *Serial Numbers:* 0001–5000.

409   Ten Shillings – Essay (1940)

Basically similar to the issued note (408) but with some variations. The title ONCHAN INTERNMENT CAMP/DOUGLAS IoM in two lines appears at the upper left. THE COMMANDANT at lower left. In the area for the serial number there is a reference number 190 731 714 167A1940. All full size of issued note with marginal notes 'INSTRUCTIONS SEE 5 SHILLINGS NOTE' and 'INTENSITY OF SCREEN' with a test blob of printer's colour, in green as used for the issued note. It may have been intended that the commandant would have signed each note prior to issue, but this was not carried through.[118]

This item was only discovered in 1986 amongst the effects of an estate. It appears that there may have been similar essays for the other two denominations

408   Onchan Internment Camp. Ten shillings voucher.

409   Onchan Internment Camp Essay for ten shillings voucher. [*A. E. Kelly*]

and also a set of specimen notes, but were destroyed before their significance was realised. *Rarity:* R8 (1 known).

Although beyond the scope of this work details of the brass tokens are to hand. Messrs. Gaunt of Birmingham supplied the tokens consisting of 2,000 halfpennies, 20,000 pennies and 2,500 sixpences. These were also released at the same time as the notes. No further tokens and notes were supplied. The halfpennies soon became scarce due to use as ornaments in boxes and other items made as souvenirs by the internees.[119]

PALACE INTERNMENT CAMP

Established about July 1940 under the command of Major E.P. Allport, the camp embraced 29 hotels in Palace Terrace, Queen's Promenade, Douglas. Commencing at the "Rookery" and "Daytona", which served as infirmaries, then north to "The Hydro" and terminating at "Edelweiss" in Little Switzerland.[120] The next block northwards was principally the Metropole Camp.

The camp housed mainly Italians and later other nationalities including Japanese. It continued in use until November 1942 when 260 Finns remaining were either released or transferred to the Mooragh Camp. The Palace Camp was then taken over by the Army.

Note Issues

Vouchers for use within this camp were made up in one pound booklets consisting of 4 x 2/6, 6 x 1/-, 4 x 6d., 4 x 3d. and 12 x 1d. Ten shilling booklets were also prepared containing half the numbers of the one pound booklets. All vouchers bore the same serial numbers within the same booklet with the prefix letter 1K for one pound and ½K for ten shilling booklets. Dates of issue unknown. A complete one pound booklet (1K 22806) was discovered in 1972 and part of another pound booklet (1K 8574) with 15/7d. worth of vouchers remaining with a part ten shilling booklet (½K 5616) with 5/8d. worth of vouchers appeared in a London sale in 1974.[121] These three are the only ones known and all have since been disbound to make a few complete sets available. Apart from the special vouchers notes of the Home Office issue were also used bearing the appropriate hand-stamps, some of which were also used at the Mooragh Camp.

410   One Penny
Obverse: PALACE INTERNMENT CAMP centre. (serial number) above, denomination in figures to left and right, and in words, below. *Reverse:* plain. *Printer:* "Examiner" Printing Works, Douglas. *Colour:* Black print on turquoise-blue paper. *Watermark:* none. *Dimensions:* 84 x 48mm (with stub). *Rarity:* R6 (19 known + 1 in archives).

411   Threepence
As (410) but reads THREEPENCE, printed on yellow-orange paper. *Rarity:* R7 (7 known + 1 in archives).

412   Sixpence
As (410) but reads SIXPENCE, printed on sage-green paper. *Rarity:* R7 (6 known + 1 in archives).

413   One Shilling
As (410) but reads ONE SHILLING, printed on yellow paper. *Rarity:* R6 (11 known + 1 in archives).

413/414   Palace Internment Camp. One shilling and half-crown vouchers with examples of covers from ten shillings and one pound booklets.

414   Half-crown
As (410) but reads HALF-CROWN, printed on pink paper. *Rarity:* R7 (8 known + 1 in archives).
   Only five complete sets have been assembled from the one pound booklets, and one complete set from the ten shilling booklet since only one sixpence voucher was known from the ten shilling booklet ½K 5616.

PEVERIL INTERNMENT CAMP

This camp was established in July 1940 at Peel and consisted essentially of two compounds, one for detainees under Defence Regulation 18B and the second for non-enemy aliens of pro-German sympathies interned under Section 12(5A). Neither of these groups were permitted to be transferred to other camps or to be included in working parties outside the camp, but later it was possible for small working parties under escort to assist outside on farms and gardens. The remainder being employed on camp duties. Initially the camp came under military administration but an incident in September 1940 in which three men escaped brought the camp under direct control of the Metropolitan police under the command of Chief Inspector S.M. Ogden with the military retained as guards. The trio had slipped away from a large group returning to the camp one dark evening and managed to acquire a boat from Castletown and planned sailing to Ireland but progress was slow due to the weather conditions in the Irish Sea at that time of year and they were picked up and returned to the Peveril. On return a disturbance commenced which involved much damage to nearby property.[122] This incident led to the Home Office transferring responsibility for the camp to the police. The camp was one of the last to be closed in September 1945. The camp also published a newspaper titled "The Peveril Guardsman" for the benefit of the camp guard.
   On arrival at the camp internees changed their currency for the special camp money. Inside the Peveril the internees had their own canteen organised by themselves using the special vouchers issued by the camp finance department from the individual's accounts. Any internees on outside working parties would have their accounts credited for work done. The canteen vouchers were in a range of denominations and appear to have been issued shortly after the camp opened and continued until 1941 when all camp currencies were withdrawn and replaced by the Home Office issue. On closure of the Peveril Camp all Canteen Vouchers held by the detainees were recalled and retired by the camp authorities for destruction in a furnace. The majority of these were destroyed but a 'handful' were retained as souvenirs. The whole parcel came onto the market in 1971 and the serial numbers recorded.[123] From intensive and exhaustive enquiries it appears these 148 pieces are the only vouchers now extant along with at least three incomplete sets acquired by Maud Lister during the war, which are now in archival collections, amounting to some 172 pieces in all.[124]

Note Issues

The canteen vouchers ranged in denominations from halfpenny to one pound and a variety of colours. It appears some of the halfpenny cards were altered to read

415/416/419/421 Peveril Internment Camp. Canteen vouchers for halfpenny, one penny, one shilling and half-crown. Two examples of hand-stamped signatures shown, N. H. Parker and J. W. D. Kneen.

five shillings but all were detected and destroyed, not more than six were thus prepared. The card stock used for printing the vouchers varied from smooth to a type with a coarse finish.

415 Halfpenny
Issued: ?July 1940. *Obverse:* CANTEEN VOUCHER at upper left, (serial number) upper right. THIS VOUCHER IS VALID FOR/(denomination)/AT THE PEVERIL INTERNMENT/CAMP CANTEEN ONLY. in four lines. *Reverse:* plain. *Printer:* Clarke & Son Ltd., Peel. *Colour:* black print on white card *Watermark:* none. *Dimensions:* 92 x 61mm. or 89 x 63mm. Prefix letter A to serial number. *Rarity:* R6 (11 known + 3 in archives).

416 One Penny
Similar to (415) but reads 1d., printed on yellow card. Prefix letter B to serial number. *Rarity:* R5 (22 known + 1 in archives).

417 One Penny
As (416) but printed on orange card. *Rarity:* R4 (29 known + 3 in archives).

418 Sixpence
Similar to (415) but reads 6d., printed on pink card. Prefix letter C to serial number. *Rarity:* R6 (15 known + 3 in archives).

417/418/426   Peveril Internment Camp. Canteen vouchers for one penny, sixpence and one pound. Showing variety of hand-stamps.

419   One Shilling
Similar to (415) but reads 1/-, printed on purple card. Prefix letter D to serial number. *Rarity:* R5 (30 known + 3 in archives).

420   One Shilling
As (419) but printed on lilac card. *Rarity:* R7 (3 known + 3 in archives).

421   Half-Crown
Similar to (415) but reads 2/6, printed on blue card. Prefix letter E to serial number. *Rarity:* R6 (19 known + 1 in archives).

422   Half-Crown
As (421) but printed on green card. *Rarity:* R7 (5 known + 3 in archives).

423   Five Shillings
Similar to (415) but reads 5/-, printed on pale-green card. Prefix letter F to serial number. *Rarity:* R7 (1 known, in archives).

424 Five Shillings
As (423) but printed on emerald green card. *Rarity:* R7 (1 known, in archives).

425 Ten Shillings
Issued: ?July 1940. *Obverse:* CANTEEN VOUCHER at upper centre, (serial number) at upper left. THIS CANTEEN VOUCHER IS VALID FOR / (denomination) / AT THE PEVERIL INTERNMENT/CAMP CANTEEN ONLY in four lines enclosed within frame. Triune and motto left, denomination within circle right. TEN SHILLINGS at lower left, (signature) FINANCE OFFICER lower right. *Reverse:* plain. *Printer:* Clarke & Son Ltd., Peel. *Colour:* black print on green paper. *Watermark:* none. *Dimensions:* 132 x 80mm. Prefix letter G to serial number. *Rarity:* R7 (3 known + 2 in archives).

426 One Pound
Similar to (425) but black print on white paper. Prefix H to serial number. *Rarity:* R6 (8 known + 3 in archives).
    At least three facsimile signatures on the cards have been identified. N.H. Parker, John G.A. Harris and J.W.D. Kneen. Some vouchers also bore a small hand-stamp 'DETAINEES A/c'. Another rectangular hand-stamp observed reads
PEVERIL DETAINEES A/c C
PEEL I.o.M.
...................MAJOR
COMMANDER, PEVERIL CAMP
in four lines. Some cards are devoid of signatures or hand-stamps.

Group of internees in the Peveril Camp c1943. [*Donald McHardy*]

Front cover of the "Peveril Guardsman", a news-sheet prepared for the camp guard, 30 September 1943. [*H. F. Guard*]

REGENT INTERNMENT CAMP

This camp had an allocation for 700 internees but was never used. Situated on Loch Promenade between the Granville Camp and Douglas Harbour.

RUSHEN INTERNMENT CAMP

The first women and children to be interned on the Island arrived at Douglas from Liverpool on 29 May 1940 and three trains and a fleet of buses transported them across the Island to Port Erin which had been prepared since 3 May. Arrangements had been made for hotel and guest house proprietors to accommodate the internees and since prospects for the 1940 summer holiday season were not good acceptance was agreed on the basis of a payment of three shillings (15p) per person per day with the internees cooking food provided by the proprietors.[125]

Movement within the Rushen area was limited by a fence built across the peninsula to embrace Port Erin and Port St. Mary. This fence commenced near Fleshwick Bay then east of Ballafesson and just avoided Rushen Church, to enable Manx residents to continue attending, then down to Poolvaish Bay. The arrangement enabled all internees complete freedom within the area but residents had to carry special permits to gain access.

The first commandant of the camp was Dame Joanna Cruickshank, appointed by the Home Office, with Miss E.E. Looker as deputy commandant. After one year they were both succeeded by Inspector C.R.M. Cuthbert of Scotland Yard and Miss Joan D. Wilson. For many months there had been agitation to establish a married camp to alleviate the suffering due to separation of families in different camps. Although meetings of family members were permitted each week for a short period, this arrangement was not thought to be desirable. Eventually another camp was established at Port St. Mary on 8 May 1941 for married women and their children.

Soon small workshops were set up for sewing, dressmaking, shoe repairs, hairdressing, etc. As payment for work, tokens were issued with a value of threepence which could then be exchanged for goods and services. This scheme was announced on 19 September 1940 and continued until November 1941.[126] It has been estimated that five thousand tokens per day were circulated. Intensive enquiries have failed to produce details of these tokens except that they were of cardboard, no further description is available. The Home Office issue of notes do not appear to have been used within the camp since the internees were able to use the shops in the normal way.

427 Threepence
Issued: September 1940. No other details known.

SEFTON INTERNMENT CAMP

Under the command of Major Byerley the Sefton Camp was based on the "Sefton" Hotel and "Gaiety Theatre" on Harris Promenade, Douglas. It was requisitioned by the authorities on 11 September 1940 and received its initial intake shortly afterwards. The number of internees was never great, totalling 377 at Christmas 1940 and 261 in February 1941. With the steady decrease of internee population they were eventually transferred to other camps and by 6 March 1941 the camp closed and was derequisitioned on 4 May 1941.

Note Issues

Until March 1982 it was assumed that the Sefton Camp had no special currency due to its short existence, however, the discovery of a few vouchers now confirms a series was issued.[127]

428 Halfpenny
Issued: 1940. *Obverse:* SEFTON I.C. above, denomination in figures, centre; DOUGLAS I.O.M. below. (serial number) vertical at left. *Reverse:* Plain but bear a rubber hand-stamp extending over more than one voucher reading SEFTON INTERNMENT CAMP/ACCOUNTS OFFICE in two lines. *Printer:* unknown. *Colour:* black print on thick pink paper. *Watermark:* none. *Dimensions:* 56 x 30mm. All are perforated on left and right edges indicating they were printed in roll form rather in the style of contemporary cinema tickets. *Rarity:* R7 (1 known + 1 in archives).

429   One Penny
As (428) but printed in black on green. *Rarity:* R7 (7 known + 1 in archives).

430   Sixpence
As (428) but printed in black on blue. *Rarity:* R7 (1 known + 1 in archives).

HOME OFFICE ISSUE

By mid-1941 the Home Office decided to replace all unofficial camp currencies with one common design. Five denominations were produced and a study of these notes shows that five printing orders were placed, probably with His Majesty's Stationery Office (HMSO) since notes of a similar design were printed by HMSO for prisoner-of-war camps.[128] Each printing has been identified by the printer's reference number on the reverse. The initial order was placed about mid-1941 and made up of 10,000 x 3d; 20,000 x 6d; 20,000 x 1/-; 15,000 x 2/6 and 15,000 x 5/- These were ready fairly soon but it was discovered that insufficient notes for threepence had been ordered so another order was placed for this denomination. Early in 1942 a third order was placed and these three printings met all demands until early 1944 when another printing was ordered followed by the final order later that year, probably most of the latter were destroyed unissued, except for a dozen sets which appear to have been acquired by a contemporary collector. Notes of the five printings have not been classed as separate varieties but a list of serial numbers has been given. Halfpenny and penny tokens in white plastic were used for lower denominations.

431   Threepence
Issued: 1941 *Obverse:* CIVILIAN INTERNMENT CAMPS upper centre, CAMP OF ISSUE (name of camp) below. (denomination) in words, within small frame, centre. NO. (serial number) at lower left, (denomination) in figures at lower right. AVAILABLE IN CAMP OF ISSUE ONLY lower centre. All on a coloured patterned background of trefoils arranged to leave the letters HO (=Home Office). *Reverse:* Eight 22mm. circles to admit hand-stamps, FOR CAMP USE

431/432/433   Internment Camps. Examples of the General Issue of vouchers used in the camps until 1945. Showing a selection of the range of hand-stamps used.

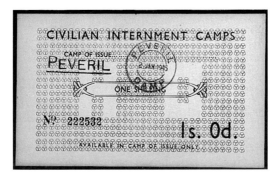

ONLY at upper centre. Printer's reference number at lower left. *Printer:* ?HMSO. *Colour:* Black print on white paper with brown pattern on obverse *Watermark:* none. *Dimensions:* 140 x 83mm. *Rarity:* R5 (19 known + 5 in archives).

432 Sixpence
Similar to (431) but reads SIXPENCE, red patterned background. *Rarity:* R5 (18 known + 6 in archives).

433   One Shilling
Similar to (431) but reads ONE SHILLING, blue patterned background. *Rarity:* R6
(15 known + 5 in archives).

434   Two Shillings and Sixpence
Similar to (431) but reads TWO SHILLINGS AND SIXPENCE, green patterned
background. *Rarity:* R6 (13 known + 6 in archives).

435   Five Shillings
Similar to (431) but reads FIVE SHILLINGS, orange patterned background.
Rarity: R6 (13 known + 5 in archives).
      The majority of these are unissued but known issued notes bear a variety of
hand-stamps and dates. Issued notes are much rarer. This issue is known to have
been used at the following camps and with the dates shown:-

Hutchinson Camp	May, November 1942, April 1944.
Metropole Camp	
Mooragh Camp	
Onchan Camp	March, June, October 1942.
Palace Camp	
Peveril Camp	April 1942, Jan, March, May 1945.

A sixpence note, number 12460, issued in "P" Camp is known bearing the hand-
stamp NOT AVAILABLE IN M CAMP. It would appear that other hand-stamps
may exist and more research is required in this area.

Details of serial numbers and printings are given below:-

Serial Nos:	Denomination	Totals	Imprint
00001–10000	Threepence	10,000	MP-23415
10001–30000	Sixpence	20,000	MP-23415
30001–50000	One Shilling	20,000	MP-23415
50001–65000	Half-Crown	15,000	MP-23415
65001–80000	Five Shillings	15,000	MP-23415
80001–100000	Threepence	20,000	MP-23528
100001–130000	Sixpence	30,000	MP-24061–5
130001–150000	One Shilling	20,000	MP-24061–5
150001–170000	Half-Crown	20,000	MP-24061–5
170001–190000	Threepence	20,000	MP-24061–5
190001–200000	Five Shillings	10,000	MP-25427–31
200001–220000	Half-Crown	20,000	MP-25427–31
220001–230000	One Shilling	10,000	MP-25427–31
230001–255000	Sixpence	25,000	MP-25427–31
255001–270000	Threepence	15,000	MP-25427–31

Serial Nos:	Denomination	Totals	Imprint
270001–275000	Five Shillings	5,000	MP-27980/4
275001–280000	Half-Crown	5,000	MP-27980/4
280001–300000	One Shilling	20,000	MP-27980/4
300001–310000	Threepence	10,000	MP-27980/4

Totals printed

	Threepence	75,000
	Sixpence	75,000
	One Shilling	70,000
	Half-Crown	60,000
	Five Shillings	30,000

CHAPTER 11

Tynwald Act, 1961

Isle of Man Government Notes – Withdrawal of Commercial Bank Notes

ISLE OF MAN GOVERNMENT

With passing of the Isle of Man Government Notes Act, 1961 all licences held by the commercial banks in the Island were revoked and issue of bank notes from these banks ceased after 31 July 1961. Since that date the majority of notes formerly issued by the commercial banks have been withdrawn, cancelled and destroyed and the numbers of notes outstanding have been reduced to 5–7% of the limit imposed by the note licence.

Issues of the Government notes in denominations of five pounds, one pound and ten shillings commenced on 3 July 1961 through the agency of the Isle of Man Bank who still manage the note issue on behalf of the Isle of Man Government.

With nearly a hundred varieties, Government notes can present a complex view of various issues. To make location of a particular note issue easier a summary of main varieties is detailed below.

1961 Design	451–460	Sketches & Essays
	461–463	Printer's Proofs (Garvey)
	464–466	Currency Notes (Garvey)
	467–472	Specimen Notes (Garvey)
	473–476	Colour Trials & Proofs (Stallard)
	477–480	Currency Notes (Stallard)
	481	Specimen Note (Stallard)
1972 Design	482–488	Sketches & Essays
	489–491	Colour Trials (Stallard)
	492–496	Printer's Proofs (Stallard)
	497–500	Currency Notes (Stallard)
	501–510	Specimen Notes (Stallard)
	511–518	Currency Notes (Paul)
	533–534	Specimen Notes (Paul)
	520–530	Currency Notes (Dawson)
	531–536	Specimen Notes (Dawson)

1990 Design   537–541   Currency Notes (Dawson)
                   547–548   Specimen Notes (Dawson)
                   542–546   Currency Notes (Cashen)
                   549–550   Specimen Notes (Cashen)

1961 Design

Note Issues

In 1960 the Manx artist John H. Nicholson was approached by the Manx
Government with a view to preparing suitable designs for the new note issue. A
number of sketches were submitted and slightly modified by the printers, Bradbury, Wilkinson, who retained some of Nicholson's work, ie. reverses of both the
one pound and ten shilling notes.

The original design for the one pound note depicted Tynwald Hill beneath the
special tent used for the Tynwald Ceremony but for greater clarity in the final
design the tent was omitted. Another suggestion was for all captions to be in
Manx but this too was abandoned.[129]

Artist's Sketches & Essays – 1961 Issue

451   Ten Shillings – Printer's Essay – (Obverse)
Colours and design as issued note (464). Lettering, background design, Triune and
motto in watercolours. Annigoni's portrait of H.M. The Queen from stock

451/452 IoM Government. Printer's essay of obverse and reverse for the ten shillings note
(1961). Accepted design.

engraving. Background design in vermilion and sage-green. Serial number
A/1 000000 in black. *Dimensions:* 140 x 67mm. *Rarity:* R8 (unique).

452   Ten Shillings – Printer's Essay – (Reverse)
Design as issued (464) note but in dark-blue. Main design in watercolour, with
border and denomination panels engraved to form montage. Designer's name and
printer's imprint omitted. *Dimensions:* 140 x 67mm. *Rarity:* R8 (unique).
  (451) and (452) mounted on single card.

453   One Pound – Artist's Sketch – (Obverse)
ISLE OF MAN GOVERNMENT across top. PROMISE TO PAY THE/BEARER
ON DEMAND/AT THE HEAD/OR ANY BRANCH OFFICE OF/ISLE OF MAN/
BANK LIMITED in seven lines below centre. (words THE HEAD OR and
BRANCH later crossed through.) ONE POUND below. All on brown background.
1 in triangular shield at upper left and right corners in brown and dark-blue.
Triune and motto to left in circular panel, to the right similar panel with plain

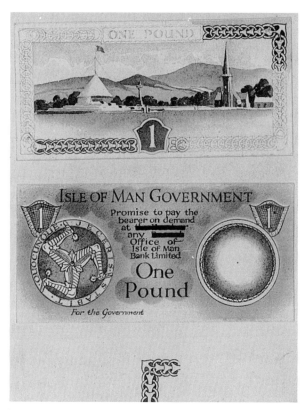

453/454   IoM Government. Artist's sketches for obverse and reverse of proposed one pound
note by John H. Nicholson (1960).

centre. Both in dark-blue. FOR THE GOVERNMENT below at left of centre. Pale-green colour on rest of note. *Dimensions:* 152 x 72mm. *Rarity:* R8 (unique).

454   One Pound – Artist's Sketch – (Reverse)
Similar to issued note (465). ONE POUND in upper border of interlacing Celtic crosses. 1 in panel in centre of lower border. View of St. John's Church and Tynwald Hill, the latter enclosed within tent as used for Tynwald Day Ceremony. All in brown. Denomination in upper border and portions of border design in pencil. Border in upper right corner in dark-blue, lower left corner in green. *Dimensions:* 152 x 72mm. *Rarity:* R8 (unique).
(453) and (454) mounted on single card.

455   One Pound – Printer's Essay – (Obverse)
Watercolour and part engraved montage. Similar to issued note (465) but Triune and motto placed at left to balance Queen's portrait. Position later occupied by Triune and motto in accepted design left blank except for colour tints. All lettering in purple. No £ sign before 1 in upper left and lower right corners. Design behind Queen's head differs from final design also map of Island appears with coloured bars which were later omitted. Serial number A/1 000000 in black. *Dimensions:* 151 x 72mm. *Rarity:* R8 (unique).

455/456   IoM Government. Printer's essay of obverse and reverse for one pound note (1961). Unaccepted design.

457A/458 IoM Government. Printer's essay of obverse and reverse for one pound note (1961). Reverse caption in Manx.

456 One Pound – Printer's Essay – (Reverse)

Similar to first design sketch (453) but 1 in shield in lower border now omitted and placed at lower left and right corners of border. TYNWALD HILL in lower left corner. Colour brown. Vacant area in centre of lower border previously occupied by figure 1 in shield. No printer's imprint or artist's name. *Dimensions:* 151 x 72mm. *Rarity:* R8 (unique).

(455) and (456) are mounted on single card.

457A One Pound – Printer's Essay – (Obverse)

This is the essay for the accepted design. Similar to issued design (465) and in final colours except that Triune & motto now occupy centre position with background colour for Triune in red. Triune appears clockwise. Map of Island in white, ie. no coloured bars. A modification resulting in the final accepted design was effected by preparation of two unmounted pieces, one of the map with modified surrounding pattern and secondly of the Triune and motto arranged counter-clockwise. (457B). Serial number A/1 000000 in black. *Dimensions:* 151 x 72mm. *Rarity:* R8 (unique).

457B/458 IoM Government. Printer's essay of obverse and reverse for one pound note (1961). Design modified by addition of piece showing different Triune.

457B One Pound – Printer's Essay – (Obverse)

As (457A) but with two modified pieces added. *Rarity:* R8 (unique).

458 One Pound – Printer's Essay – (Reverse)

Similar to issued design (465) but CRONK KEEILL EOIN (= Tynwald Hill) at lower right corner. Colour brown. No printer's imprint or artist's name. *Dimensions:* 151 x 72mm. *Rarity:* R8 (unique).

(457A) and (458) mounted on single card.

459 Five Pounds – Printer's Essay – (Obverse)

Watercolour and part engraved montage on card. Similar to issued note (466) in design and colours. Serial number A/1 000000 in black. *Dimensions:* 140 x 84mm. *Rarity:* R8 (unique).

459/460 IoM Government. Printer's essay of obverse and reverse for five pounds note (1961). This design was accepted. Reverse caption in Manx.

460 Five Pounds – Printer's Essay – (Reverse)

Watercolour and part engraved montage on card. Similar to issued note (466) in design and colour but CASHTALL RUSSIN appears in lower left corner. This was later modified to CASTLE RUSHEN, 1775. No printer's imprint. *Dimensions:* 140 x 84mm. *Rarity:* R8 (unique).

(459) and (460) mounted on single card.

461 Ten Shillings – Printer's Proof

Obverse and reverse as issued design (464) and colours. Paper bears security thread and watermark of map of Island. Serial numbers 123456 at lower left and 789012 at upper right in black. Facsimile signature of R.H. Garvey in black. Single punch-hole cancellation above. Letter C penned in upper left corner. Printer's imprint and artist's name on reverse. *Dimensions:* 140 x 67mm. *Rarity:* R7 (1 known).

461/462 IoM Government. Printer's proof for ten shillings and one pound notes (1961). Reverse caption of one pound note now in English.

462 One Pound – Printer's Proof
Obverse and reverse as issued design (465) and colours. Paper bears security thread and watermark of map of Island. Serial numbers 123456 at lower left and 789012 at upper right in black. Facsimile signature of R.H. Garvey in black. Single punch-hole cancellation above. Letter D penned in upper left corner. Reverse in similar design to issued note but coloured brown. TYNWALD HILL replaces CRONK KEEILL EOIN as shown on artists' sketch (458). *Dimensions:* 151 x 72mm. *Rarity:* R7 (1 known).

463 Five Pounds – Printer's Proof
Obverse and reverse as issued design and colours (466). Paper bears security thread and watermark of map of Island. Serial numbers 123456 at lower left and 789012 at upper right. Facsimile signature of R.H. Garvey in black. Single punch-hole cancellation above. Letter G penned in upper left corner. Reverse in design and colour of issued note but caption CASTLE RUSHEN, 1775 now replaces CASHTALL RUSSIN on artists' sketch (460). Printer's imprint in lower margin. *Dimensions:* 141 x 85mm. *Rarity:* R7 (1 known).

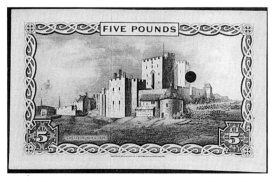

463   IoM Government. Obverse and reverse printer's proofs for five pounds note (1961). Reverse caption now in English.

Issue 1 (1961–1969). Notes signed in facsimile by R.H. Garvey (= Sir Ronald Herbert Garvey, KCMG, KCVO, MBE.) Lieutenant-Governor.

464   Ten Shillings – Notes signed in facsimile by R.H. Garvey (Lieutenant-Governor).
Issued: 3 July 1961. *Obverse:* Vignette of Annigoni portrait of H.M. The Queen appears to the right. ISLE OF MAN GOVERNMENT in single line at upper centre, PROMISE TO PAY THE BEARER ON DEMAND/AT ANY OFFICE OF THE ISLE OF MAN BANK LIMITED in two lines below. TEN SHILLINGS below, centre. Triune and motto occupy area at lower centre. 10 in emblem at upper left and lower right corners, serial numbers at lower left and upper right corners. FOR THE GOVERNMENT (signature) LIEUTENANT GOVERNOR in three lines at lower left. Watermark window to left. *Reverse:* Viking ship in full sail, centre. TEN SHILLINGS in upper border, 10 in shields at lower left and right corners. Border of interlaced Celtic design with a cross at each corner. Printer's and artist's imprint in lower margin. *Printer:* Bradbury, Wilkinson & Co. Ltd., New Malden, Surrey. *Colour:* Predominantly red with multicoloured tints in

centre area, red reverse. On security threaded paper. *Watermark:* Triune. *Dimensions:* 140 x 67mm. *Rarity:* C.

000001–1000000 (3 July 1961)
A000001–A250000 (11 January 1968)

465 One Pound – Notes signed in facsimile by R.H Garvey (Lieutenant-Governor).

Issued: 3 July 1961. *Obverse:* Basically similar to the ten shillings note. ONE POUND above Triune and motto in centre, £1 at upper left and lower right. *Reverse:* View of Tynwald Hill and St. John's Church by John H. Nicholson, ONE POUND in upper frame, 1 in lower left and right corners, TYNWALD HILL at lower right. Border of interlaced Celtic design, printer's imprint in lower margin. *Printer:* Bradbury, Wilkinson & Co. Ltd. *Colour:* Predominantly violet with multicoloured tints in centre. On security threaded paper. *Watermark:* Triune. *Dimensions:* 151 x 72mm. *Rarity:* C.

000001 – 1000000 (3 July 1961)
A000001 – A1000000 (27 February 1964)
B000001 – B200000 (9 March 1967)

466 Five Pounds – Notes signed in facsimile by R.H Garvey (Lieutenant-Governor).
Issued: 3 July 1961. *Obverse:* Basically similar to ten shillings note. FIVE POUNDS above Triune and motto in centre, 5 in upper left and right corners, £5 in lower left and right corners. *Reverse:* View of Castle Rushen from engraving by S. Hooper published on 6 February 1775. FIVE POUNDS in upper frame, 5 within cross at lower left and right, CASTLE RUSHEN, 1775 at lower left. Border of interlaced Celtic design, printer's imprint in lower margin. *Printer:* Bradbury, Wilkinson & Co. Ltd. *Colour:* Predominantly green with multicoloured tints in centre, grey reverse. On security threaded paper. *Watermark:* Triune. *Dimensions:* 140 x 85mm. *Rarity:* S.

000001 – 250000 (3 July 1961)

467 Ten Shillings – Specimen Note
As issued note (464) but diagonally overprinted SPECIMEN in red on obverse. Serial number 000000, two punch-hole cancellations. *Printed:* 150. *Rarity:* R2.

468 One Pound – Specimen Note
As issued note (465) but diagonally overprinted SPECIMEN in red on obverse. Serial number 000000, two punch-hole cancellations. *Printed:* 150. *Rarity:* R2.

467/468/469   IoM Government. Specimen notes of the three final designs as issued. All bear 000000 serial numbers. Signed R. H. Garvey

469   Five Pounds – Specimen Note
As issued note (466) but diagonally overprinted SPECIMEN in red on obverse. Serial number 000000, two punch-hole cancellations. *Printed:* 150. *Rarity:* R2.

470   Five Pounds – Specimen Note
As (469) but bears regular serial number in the block 112001–112170. The original specimen notes (469) had 000000 serial numbers but at a later date it was necessary to re-order another batch of specimen notes and the five pound notes for some unknown reason received regular serial numbers. Only 150 sets were prepared although the serial numbers suggest there were more than this, but 20 of the notes were spoilt during the printing process when the overprint received multiple impressions. These impaired notes were also delivered with the correct notes.

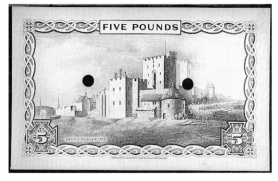

470   IoM Government. Specimen notes of the five pounds. This was from a later batch of specimen notes and bears a regular serial number.

Half the order was made up into display frames (472) and the remainder left as loose sets. Some of the notes have been seen in which the serial number has been crossed out with lines of biro ink (470A). Apparently a few of these specimen notes entered circulation and were promptly returned to the Treasury. To avoid a repetition the five pound notes in the loose sets had the serial number crossed out. Notes without the deletion are scarce by comparison. The specimen notes in sets were arranged loose (467, 468, 469) or framed (472) in a random order, ie. 112051 and 112053 were placed in framed sets and 112052 and 112054 in loose sets. *Prepared:* 75. *Rarity:* R4.

470A   Five Pounds – Specimen Note
As (470) above but serial number obliterated in ink. Further details under (470), about 50 notes were treated in this way and some may have since been destroyed. *Rarity:* R4

470 IoM Government. Five pounds specimen note bearing a regular serial number. This example received multiple impressions of the overprint and cancelled before delivery to the Treasury.

471   Specimen Notes – Framed Set
Framed set of three specimen notes arranged fanwise so that only the ten shilling note is fully displayed, the five pound note bears serial number 000000. *Prepared:* 50. *Rarity:* R4.

472   Specimen Notes – Framed Set
Similar to (471) but the five pound note bears a serial number in the block 112001–112170. *Prepared:* 75. *Rarity:* R4

472   IoM Government. Set of framed specimen notes with five pounds note bearing regular
serial number.

**Issue 2 (1967–1972). Notes signed in facsimile by P.H.G. Stallard (= Sir Peter
Hyla Gawne Stallard, KCMG., CVO., MBE., MA.) Lieutenant-Governor.**

473   Fifty New Pence – Colour Trial (1969)

As issued note (478) but predominant colour is mauve on obverse and reverse.
Serial number 000000 in black. Punch-hole through signature area. *Rarity:* R7
(1 known).

473A   Fifty New Pence – Colour Trial (1968?)

Design as (478), colours unknown. Serial number 000000 in black. Number 12
printed in upper left margin of reverse. No further information. *Rarity:* R7
(1 known)

473B   One Pound – Colour Trial (1961?)

Design and colours as issued note (479) but green print on obverse replaces violet
print of portrait, denominations in corners and Triune. Serial number 000000 in
black. Red SPECIMEN overprint below Triune. Unsigned, single punch-hole
through signature area. Reverse printed in green instead of violet, SPECIMEN
overprint in red. Number 56 printed in upper left margin of reverse. *Rarity:* R7
(1 known).

474   One Pound – Colour Trial (1967)
Design and colours as issued note (479) but violet print on obverse replaced by
green. Serial number A000000 in black. No signature, single punch-hole cancellation through signature area. Overprinted SPECIMEN below Triune. Reverse
printed in green instead of violet. Number 150 printed in upper left margin of
reverse. *Rarity:* R7 (1 known).

475   One Pound – Colour Trial (1967)
Design and colours as issued note (479). Serial number C000000 in black. Single
punch-hole cancellation through facsimile signature of P.H.G. Stallard. Overprinted SPECIMEN in red below Triune. Reverse printed in green instead of
violet. Number 151 printed in upper left margin of reverse. *Rarity:* R7 (1 known).
    Little further information known about the colour trials (473A), (474) and (475).
It appears some consideration may have been given to a change of colour for the
one pound note but was not accepted due to possible confusion with the
contemporary five pound note then printed in similar colours. The decision
was taken to retain the same reverse colour as the predominant colour of the
obverse.

476   Fifty New Pence – Printer's Proof
Specification as for (478) but lacks signature. Serial number A000000, single
punch-hole cancellation in signature space. This is the only specimen of the fifty-
pence note with prefix A to the serial number. *Rarity:* R7 (1 known, in archives).

**477   Ten Shillings – Notes signed in facsimile by P.H.G. Stallard (Lieuten-
ant-Governor).**
Specification as (464) but with new facsimile signature. *Rarity:* C

A250001 – A517000	(17 July 1969)
A517001 – A750000	Destroyed, unissued*

* The terminal note, A750000, is preserved in archives.

478   IoM Government. Fifty new pence, signed by P. H. G. Stallard.

478 Fifty New Pence – Notes signed in facsimile by P.H.G. Stallard (Lieutenant-Governor).
Specification as (464) but new denomination, fifty new pence, replaces ten shillings. Turquoise print. *Rarity:* C.

000001 – 679000	(28 August 1969)
679001 – 1000000	Destroyed, unissued
A000001 – A200000	Destroyed, unissued

From the above it will be seen that no notes were issued bearing the A prefix. The only known specimen is the printer's proof (476).

479 One Pound – Notes signed in facsimile by P.H.G. Stallard (Lieutenant-Governor).
Specification as (465) but with new facsimile signature. *Rarity:* C

B200001 – B1000000	(14 December 1967)
C000001 – C745000	(17 September 1970)
C745001 – C850000	Destroyed, unissued.

480 Five Pounds – Notes signed in facsimile by P.H.G. Stallard (Lieutenant-Governor).
Specification as (466) but with new facsimile signature. *Rarity:* S.

250001 – 500000	(11 December 1968)

481 Fifty New Pence – Specimen Note
As issued note (478) but diagonal overprint SPECIMEN in red on obverse. Serial number 000000, two punch-hole cancellations. *Printed:* 100. *Rarity:* R3.

1972 Design

Issue 3 (1972–1974). Notes signed in facsimile by P.H.G. Stallard.

By 1972 the original Government issue had been in circulation for eleven years and consideration was then given to a new portrait of H.M. The Queen and one by Anthony Buckley was selected. Opportunity was also taken to reduce the format similar to contemporary Bank of England notes and to introduce a ten pound note, the first since circa 1812. All were designed, engraved and printed by Bradbury, Wilkinson and the same basic colours and designs retained with exception of the one pound reverse which was adopted from a photograph.

483   IoM Government. Pencil sketch for obverse of proposed one pound note.

Sketches & Essays – 1972 Issue

482   Fifty New Pence – Pencil Sketch of Obverse & Reverse
Artist's pencil sketches for obverse and reverse of accepted design, mounted on board. *Rarity:* R8 (unique, in archives).

483   One Pound – Pencil Sketch (Obverse)
Artist's pencil sketch of obverse of accepted design, mounted on board. *Rarity:* R8 (unique, in archives).

484   Five Pounds – Pencil Sketch (Reverse)
Artist's pencil sketch of reverse of accepted design, mounted on board. *Rarity:* R8 (unique, in archives).

485   One Pound – Printer's Essay – (Reverse)
Artist's watercolour and part-engraved montage on card of reverse of accepted design. *Rarity:* R8 (unique, in archives).

486   Five Pounds – Printer's Essay – (Obverse)
Artist's watercolour and part-engraved montage on card of obverse. Colours predominantly green and blue similar to Issue 1 (466). *Rarity:* R8 (unique, in archives).

487   Ten Pounds – Printer's Essay – (Obverse)
Artist's watercolour and part-engraved montage on card for obverse design, mounted on card. Colours as issued note (500). *Rarity:* R8 (unique, in archives).

488   Ten Pounds – Printer's Essay – (Reverse)
Artist's watercolour of vignette of Peel Castle within engraved border as montage, mounted on card. Colours as issued note (500). *Rarity:* R8 (unique, in archives).

489   One Pound – Colour Trial
As issued note (498) but mauve print on obverse replaced by green. Serial number C000000. SPECIMEN overprint in red arranged horizontally on obverse and reverse. Punch-hole cancellation through signature. Brown print on reverse. Reference number 42 printed at upper left on reverse. *Rarity:* R7 (1 known).

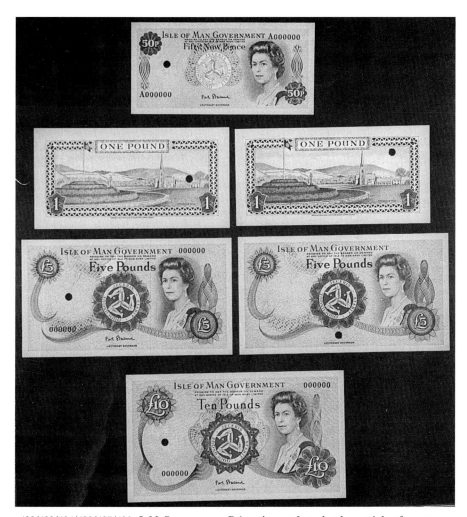

492/493/494/490/495/496. IoM Government. Printer's proofs and colour trials of currency notes. Of the one pound notes shown, reverse of the left-hand note (493) had to have the clouds re-engraved for clarity as shown in the right-hand note (494). The five-pounds note, number 000000, was an unaccepted colour trial (490).

490   Five Pounds – Colour Trial
Obverse and reverse as issued design (499) but colours similar to Issue 1 (466). Paper bears security thread and watermark of Triune. Serial number 000000. *Rarity:* R7 (1 known, in archives).

490A   Five Pounds – Colour Trial
Reported but no further information. Bears number 98 on reverse. *Rarity:* R7 (1 known)

491   Ten Pounds – Colour Trial
Reported but no further information. *Rarity:* R7 (1 known)

492   Fifty New Pence – Printer's Proof
Obverse and reverse as issued design and colours (497). Paper bears security thread and watermark of Triune. Serial number A000000. *Dimensions:* 127 x 61mm. *Rarity:* R7 (1 known, in archives).

493   One Pound – Printer's Proof of unaccepted reverse
Obverse and reverse similar to issued design and colours (498) but reverse required slight modification to enhance clouds as finally used. Paper bears security thread and watermark of Triune. Serial number C000000. *Dimensions:* 136 x 67mm. *Rarity:* R7 (1 known, in archives).

494   One Pound – Printer's Proof of accepted reverse
Uniface proof with re-engraved clouds as used on issued note (498). *Rarity:* R7 (1 known, in archives).

495   Five Pounds – Printer's Proof (Obverse)
The colour trial (490) was rejected and replaced by a new proof submitted in colours as the issued note (499). Uniface printing of obverse, no serial number. *Dimensions:* 141 x 78mm. *Rarity:* R7 (1 known, in archives).

496   Ten Pounds – Printer's Proof
Design and colours as obverse and reverse of issued note (500). Serial number 000000. *Dimensions:* 151 x 84mm. *Rarity:* R7 (1 known, in archives).

497   Fifty New Pence – Notes signed in facsimile by P.H.G. Stallard (Lieutenant-Governor).
Issued: 23 June 1972. Note design and colours basically same as previous issue (478) but with new portrait of H.M. The Queen by Anthony Buckley. Signature now appears lower centre. *Rarity:* C.

A200001 – A800000   (23 June 1972)

498   One Pound – Notes signed in facsimile by P.H.G. Stallard (Lieutenant-Governor).
Issued: 23 June 1972. Note design and colours basically same as previous issue (479) but with new portrait of H.M. The Queen by Anthony Buckley. Signature now appears lower centre. Reverse design now adopted from a photograph otherwise similar to previous issue. Cottages adjacent to church now included. *Rarity:* C.

C850001 – C1000000   (23 June 1972)
D000001 – D970000   (23 October 1972)

499   Five Pounds – Notes signed in facsimile by P.H.G. Stallard (Lieutenant-Governor).

Issued: 23 June 1972. *Obverse:* Portrait of H.M. The Queen by Anthony Buckley at right. ISLE OF MAN GOVERNMENT at upper centre, PROMISE TO PAY THE BEARER ON DEMAND/AT ANY OFFICE OF ISLE OF MAN BANK LIMITED in two lines, below. FIVE POUNDS below, centre. Triune and motto occupy centre within geometric design. £5 within geometric designs appear at upper left and lower right. Other geometric patterns appear on obverse. Signature now appears at lower centre. *Reverse:* Similar to previous issue (466). *Printer:* Bradbury, Wilkinson & Co. Ltd. *Colour:* Dark-blue and maroon with multi-coloured tints in geometric patterns, grey-green reverse. All on white paper with security thread. *Watermark:* Triune. *Dimensions:* 146 x 78mm. *Rarity:* C.

500001 – 950000   (23 June 1972)

500   Ten Pounds – Notes signed in facsimile by P.H.G. Stallard (Lieutenant-Governor).
Issued: 23 June 1972. *Obverse:* Basically similar to five pound note (499). Signature now appears at lower centre. *Reverse:* View of ruins of Peel Castle and Cathedral from a series of topographical prints by A.F. Watts published in 1833–1835. TEN POUNDS in upper frame, 10 in lower left and right corners. PEEL CASTLE, c.1830 at lower centre of vignette. Printer's imprint in lower margin. *Printer:* Bradbury, Wilkinson & Co. Ltd. *Colour:* Brown and green, with multicoloured tints in geometric patterns, dark-brown, blue and orange on reverse. All on white paper with security thread. *Watermark:* Triune. *Dimensions:* 151 x 84mm. *Rarity:* C.

000001 – 050000   (23 June 1972)

501   Fifty New Pence – Specimen Note
Specification as (497) but diagonal overprint SPECIMEN in red on obverse, two punch-hole cancellations. Serial number A000000. *Printed:* 100. *Rarity:* R3.

502   One Pound – Specimen Note
Specification as (498) but diagonal overprint SPECIMEN in red on obverse, single punch-hole cancellation. Serial number C000000. *Printed:* 100. *Rarity:* R3.

503   Five Pounds – Specimen Note
Specification as (499) but diagonal overprint SPECIMEN in red on obverse, single punch-hole cancellation. Serial number 000000. *Printed:* 100. *Rarity:* R3.

504   Ten Pounds – Specimen Note
Specification as (500) but diagonal overprint SPECIMEN in red on obverse, single punch-hole cancellation. Serial number 000000. *Printed:* 100. *Rarity:* R3.

501/502/503/504   IoM Government. Set of specimens of all denominations as issued, showing obverses and reverses. Signature of P. H. G. Stallard.

505   Fifty New Pence – Specimen Note

As (501) but SPECIMEN overprint appears horizontally to centre left of obverse and right on reverse in red. Serial number A000000, diagonal inked bar added after printing at lower left corner of obverse and reverse. No punch-hole cancellation. *Printed: ?. Rarity:* R7 (1 known).

506   One Pound – Specimen Note

As (502). Overprint, etc., similar to (505), SPECIMEN overprint on reverse appears in centre. *Printed: ?. Rarity:* R7 (1 known).

507   Five Pounds – Specimen Note
As (503). Overprint, etc., similar to (505), SPECIMEN overprint on reverse appears at left. *Printed:* ?. *Rarity:* R7 (1 known).

508   Ten Pounds – Specimen Note
As (504). Overprint, etc., similar to (505), SPECIMEN overprint on reverse appears at upper right. *Printed:* ?. *Rarity:* R7 (1 known).
   No further information known about these notes but they may have been specially prepared for advance publicity purposes.

509   Specimen Notes – Framed Set (Obverse)
Framed set of four specimen notes (501–504) arranged to show obverses only. *Prepared:* 70 sets. *Rarity:* R4.

510   Specimen Notes – Framed Set (Reverse)
Framed set of four specimen notes (501–504) arranged to show reverses only. *Prepared:* 10 sets. *Rarity:* R7.

Issue 4 (1974–1980). Notes signed in facsimile by John Paul (= Sir John Warburton Paul, GCMG., OBE., MC.) Lieutenant-Governor.

511   Fifty New Pence – Notes signed in facsimile by John Paul (Lieutenant-Governor).
Specification as previous issue (497) but with new facsimile signature. *Rarity:* C.

A800001 – A1000000	(17 June 1974)
B000001 – B370000	(1 April 1975)

512   Fifty New Pence – Notes signed by John Paul (Lieutenant-Governor).
As (511) but facsimile signature now smaller. *Rarity:* C.

B370001 – B1000000	(28 June 1979)
C000001 – C200000	(23 October 1979)

513   Fifty New Pence – Error: Mismatched Serial Numbers
As (512) but with mismatched serial numbers occurring in multiples consisting of a normal note followed by one or two other notes with the same upper serial number and differing by one digit in the lower serial number. *Rarity:* R7.

514   One Pound – Notes signed in facsimile by John Paul (Lieutenant-Governor).
Specification as previous issue (498) but with new facsimile signature. *Rarity:* C.

D970001 – D1000000	(17 June 1974)
E000001 – E1000000	(8 July 1974)

Notes bearing the D prefix are excessively rare since they were issued in a three

509 IoM Government. Framed set of specimen notes (1972).

511/514/517/518   IoM Government. Notes of the 1972 Issue bearing signature of John Paul. Top three were the first notes issued with the new signature.

week period during the 1974 holiday season and rapidly entered circulation unnoticed. In 1977 several thousand notes were examined to locate this variety which appeared to exist at the rate of one per thousand and these were in well circulated condition. Mint specimens are rarer still as it is believed not more than twenty were preserved by collectors when the new issue appeared. *Rarity:* R6.

515   One Pound Notes signed by John Paul (Lieutenant-Governor).
As (514) but facsimile signature now smaller.

F000001 – F1000000	(1 June 1976)
G000001 – G1000000	(5 December 1977)
H000001 – H440000	(17 May 1979)

The size of the signature was reduced on (512) and (515) purely for the convenience of printing and has no particular significance. *Rarity:* C.

516   One Pound – Error: Missing Signature
As (515) but signature missing. Estimates indicate circa 120 notes were devoid of signature and less than 20 have been traced. *Rarity:* R6.

517   Five   Pounds   –   Notes   signed   in   facsimile   by   John   Paul (Lieutenant-Governor).
Specification as previous issue (499) but new facsimile signature.

950001 – 1000000	(3 December 1974)
A000001 – A1000000	(20 January 1975)
B000001 – B600000	(3 January 1979)

Notes without prefix are difficult to acquire since they were issued just prior to the Christmas period and rapidly went into circulation. Less than ten mint specimens are known of which three are in archives. *Rarity:* C (A and B prefixes only).

518   Ten   Pounds   –   Notes   signed   in   facsimile   by   John   Paul (Lieutenant-Governor).
Specification as previous issue (500) but new facsimile signature. *Rarity:* C.

050001 – 360000	(8 July 1975)

519   Framed Specimen Set
See under (533) and (534).

Issue   5   (1979–1990).   Notes   signed   in   facsimile   by   W.   Dawson (= William Dawson) Treasurer of the Isle of Man.

At this stage of bank note issues there was a change in title of signatory from Lieutenant Governor to Treasurer of the Isle of Man. Under the Governor's General Functions (Transfer) Bill, 1979, the responsibility for signing Government bank notes was transferred from His Excellency to the Government

516/515/522/521 IoM Government. Examples of two error notes with signature missing, with normal notes for comparison.

Treasurer. At the time of issue of the new notes the Bill had been passed by both Branches of the Legislature, and had been signed by Tynwald, but Royal Assent was still awaited. However, under Section 23(1) of the Interpretation Act, 1976, His Excellency issued a Warrant authorising the Government Treasurer to sign Government bank notes.

520 Fifty New Pence – Notes signed in facsimile by W. Dawson (Treasurer of the Isle of Man)
Specification as previous issue (511) but change of facsimile signature. Final issue of this denomination. *Rarity:* C.

C200001 – C750000   (19 February 1981)

520A   Fifty New Pence – Error: Missing Signature
As (520) but signature missing. Only one specimen, number C278522, of this
variety has been recorded. *Rarity:* R7 (1 known).

520B   Fifty New Pence – Error: Mismatched Serial Numbers
Similar to (520). Notes occur in trios in which one will display normal serial
numbers and the other two notes will have numbers differing by one or two digits.
An example will be C224849/C224849 indicating upper and lower numbers,
followed by two notes numbered C224849/C224859 and C224849/C224869. *Rarity:*
R7 (At least four sets are known).

**521   One   Pound   –   Notes   signed   in   facsimile   by   W.   Dawson
(Treasurer of the Isle of Man).**
Specification as previous issue (515) but change of facsimile signature. *Rarity:* C.

H440001 –	H1000000	(13 March 1980)
I000001 –	I1000000	Serials not used
J000001 –	J1000000	(3 December 1980)
K000001 –	K1000000	(4 October 1982)
L000001 –	L1000000	Serials not used

522   One Pound – Error: Missing Signature
As (521) but signature missing. These are numbered

H864998	H874998	H884998
H894998	H904998	H914998
H924998	H934998	H944998

Issued: 9. *Rarity:* R7 (8 known + 1 in archives).

**523   One   Pound   –   Notes   signed   in   facsimile   by   W.   Dawson
(Treasurer of the Isle of Man).**
Specification as (521) but printed predominantly in green on obverse and reverse
on 'Tyvek 919' a polymer material. Notes bear single serial number in lower left
corner, no watermark or security thread. The note was printed on this material
with a view to increasing the life span of the note. Only this denomination was
printed on 'Tyvek'. *Rarity:* C.

M000001 –	M1000000	(23 November 1983)
N000001 –	N1000000	(13 June 1985)
O000001 –	O1000000	Serials not used
P000001 –	P 500000	(17 August 1987)

Tyvek 919 is a synthetic material using fibrous polyolefin specially treated to
produce the smooth high quality surface required for security printing and
therefore resistant to humidity, creasing, soiling, wear and tear compared with
conventional bank note paper. Two main drawbacks are its inability to take a
security thread or watermark and these render it suitable only for low denomination notes where the risk of forgery is minimal. In spite of this the material has a

greater wearing resistance, ie. the standard test is the mean double fold test in which conventional paper will sustain 4,000 to 5,000 folds. Tests on Tyvek 919 exceeded 500,000 folds. The material therefore yields a bank note with a longer life.

524 One Pound – Notes signed in facsimile by W. Dawson (Treasurer of the Isle of Man).
Specification as (521). Notes now revert to original colours and printed on paper. *Rarity:* C.

P500001 –	P1000000	issue date?
Q000001 –	Q1000000	(25 May 1988)
R000001 –	R 500000	(16 June 1989)

525 Five Pounds – Notes signed in facsimile by W. Dawson (Treasurer of the Isle of Man).
Specification as (517) but change of facsimile signature. *Rarity:* C.

B600001 – B1000000	(15 December 1980)
C000001 – C1000000	(17 November 1982)
D000001 – D1000000	(5 August 1987)

526 Ten Pounds – Notes signed in facsimile by W. Dawson (Treasurer of the Isle of Man).
Specification as (518) but change of facsimile signature. *Rarity:* C.

360001 – 1000000	(8 September 1980)
A000001 – A1000000	(17 February 1984)

527 Twenty Pounds – Notes signed in facsimile by W. Dawson (Treasurer of the Isle of Man).
Issued: 19 December 1979. *Obverse:* Basically similar design to the five and ten pound notes (525) (526). TWENTY POUNDS at upper centre, 20 in geometric pattern at upper left and lower right. Bears overprint ISSUED DURING MILLE-NIUM YEAR 1979 just below Queen's portrait. *Reverse:* View of opening of the Great Water Wheel at Laxey in 1854. TWENTY POUNDS at upper centre, all within Celtic ring chain border. Printer's imprint in lower margin. *Printer:* Bradbury, Wilkinson & Co. Ltd., *Colour:* Red and brown with multicoloured tints, reverse red shaded to yellow at each side. Printed on white paper with security thread. *Watermark:* Triune. *Dimensions:* 160 x 90mm. *Rarity:* S.

000001 – 005000	(19 December 1979)

528 Twenty Pounds – Error: missing overprint
Specification as (527) but the Millenium overprint is missing. Five or six of these notes were discovered shortly after issue and apparently most if not all were returned to the sources of issue, so whether any found their way into collections is not known as the significance of this error was not immediately realised. They bore serial numbers in the block 000001–005000. *Rarity:* R7.

527/529/527   IoM Government. Twenty pounds note. Upper note bears special overprint for the Millenium Year 1979. Centre note was the regular currency issue. Reverse design also shown. All signed by W. Dawson.

529 Twenty Pounds – Notes signed in facsimile by W. Dawson (Treasurer of the Isle of Man).
Specification as (527) but no Millenium overprint. *Rarity:* C.

005001 – 150000   (19 December 1979)

530 Fifty Pounds – Notes signed in facsimile by W. Dawson (Treasurer of the Isle of Man).
Issued: 27 April 1983. *Obverse:* Portrait of H.M. The Queen by Peter Grudgeon of Reading at right, Triune and motto centre. ISLE OF MAN GOVERNMENT at upper centre, PROMISE TO PAY THE BEARER ON DEMAND/AT ANY OFFICE OF ISLE OF MAN BANK LIMITED in two lines below. FIFTY POUNDS below. A small representation of the Isle of Man is located to the right of the Queen's portrait. To the left of the obverse is a watermark window. £50 at upper left and lower right in geometric patterns. Other geometric patterns are located in the remainder of the design. Signature at lower centre below Triune. *Reverse:* View of Douglas Bay by W. Kinnebrook published by J. Quiggin in 1841. DOUGLAS BAY 1841 lower centre. FIFTY POUNDS at upper centre, 50 at lower left and right corners. All within Celtic ring chain border. Printer's imprint in lower margin. *Printer:* Bradbury, Wilkinson & Co. Ltd. *Colour:* Light blue and green with multicoloured tints in geometric patterns, reverse blue and green. Printed on white paper with security thread. *Watermark:* Triune. *Dimensions:* 169 x 95mm. *Rarity:* C.

000001 – 250000   (27 April 1983)

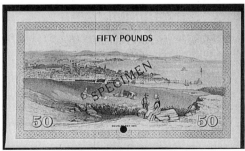

530 IoM Government. Fifty pounds note. This was the first note of this denomination issued on the Island. Signature of W. Dawson. (x⅓)

533 IoM Government. Framed Sets of specimen notes to show obverses. Signature of John Paul on lower denominations and W. Dawson on the twenty pounds.

531   One Pound – Specimen Note
Specification as (523). Overprinted SPECIMEN in red, serial number M000000, single punch-hole cancellation. *Prepared:* ?. *Rarity:* R6.

532   Fifty Pounds – Specimen Note
Specification as (530). Overprinted SPECIMEN in red, serial number 000000, single punch-hole cancellation. *Prepared:* ?. *Rarity:* R7.

533   Specimen Notes – Framed Set (Obverse)
Set of five denominations as specimens mounted in display frame for desk or wall hanging, fifty pence, one pound, five pounds and ten pounds bear facsimile signature of Sir John Paul. Twenty pounds bear facsimile signature of W. Dawson. Overprinted SPECIMEN in red, single punch-hole cancellation through signature. One pound has additional punch-hole through serial numbers. All notes arranged to display obverse only. Serial numbers (50p) C000000; (£1) G869001–G869100; (£5) B000000; (£10) 000000; (£20) 000000. These sets were intended to publicise Manx Government notes and were distributed to Government offices, banks and Post Offices. *Prepared:* 50. *Rarity:* R4.

534   Specimen Notes – Framed Set (Reverse)
As (533) but display reverses only. *Prepared:* 50. *Rarity:* R4.

535   Specimen Notes – Framed Set (Obverse)
Six denominations as specimens mounted in display frame. Fifty pence, one pound, five pounds, ten pounds twenty pounds and fifty pounds all bear facsimile signatures of W. Dawson. Treasurer of the Isle of Man. Overprinted SPECIMEN in red. Serial numbers (50p) C346xxx; (£1) M000000; (£5) B861xxx; (£10) 603xxx; (£20) 027xxx; (£50) 000000. *Prepared:* 200. *Rarity:* R6.

536   Specimen Notes – Framed Set (Reverse)
As (535) but display reverses only. Serial numbers probably similar. *Prepared:* 100. *Rarity:* R6.
   As with previous issues of framed specimen sets these were mainly issued to banks as publicity. Very few have reached collectors.

1990 Design

Issue   6   (1990–1992).   Notes   signed   in   facsimile   by   W.   Dawson (= William Dawson) (Chief Financial Officer).

Notes very similar to 1972 Design but smaller format and now printed by Thomas De La Rue. Also change in title of signatory. It is the intention of the Isle of Man Government to withdraw all notes of the earlier designs as soon as possible after issue of notes of the new design to avoid confusion.

MANX GOVERNMENT NOTES

534 IoM Government. Framed Sets of specimen notes to show reverses. Signature of John Paul on lower denominations and W. Dawson on the twenty pounds.

537 IoM Government. One pound note printed by De La Rue, signed by W. Dawson. [*L. G. Burr*]

537 One Pound – Notes signed in facsimile by W. Dawson (Chief Financial Officer).
Issued: 7 February 1990. *Obverse:* Design similar to previous issue (521) but with some minor variations. Single tactile dot at lower left as an aid to visually handicapped. Print-free watermark window to left. *Reverse:* As (521) but right hand side of vignette has been deleted. Originally this displayed a tree in front of the cottage but the tree was removed a little while ago so the design was amended to show its absence. Printer's imprint in lower margin. *Printer:* Thomas De La Rue & Co. Ltd. *Colour:* Purple with multi-coloured tints of pink, turquoise and mauve, purple reverse. Printed on white paper with security thread. *Watermark:* Triune. *Dimensions:* 128 x 64mm. *Rarity:* C.

R500001 –	R1000000	(7 February 1990)
S000001 –	S1000000	(10 April 1990)
Z000001 –	[Z007739]	Replacement notes*

* These are the first identifiable replacement notes. None were known amongst the Bradbury, Wilkinson printings and this system appears to be normal practice with notes printed by De La Rue. Number in brackets is the highest reported.

538 Five Pounds – Notes signed in facsimile by W. Dawson (Chief Financial Officer).
Issued: 1 February 1991. *Obverse:* Similar to previous issue (525) with minor variations. Two tactile dots in the lower left corner, print-free watermark window above. *Reverse:* Vignette of Castle Rushen reduced in size and moved to left-hand side. Vacated area to right now occupied with watermark window and geometric design with cross emblem. Printer's imprint in lower margin. *Printer:* Thomas De La Rue & Co. Ltd. *Colour:* Mauve and blue with multi-coloured tints of brown,

538   IoM Government. Five pounds note printed by De La Rue, signed by W. Dawson. [*L. G. Burr*].

turquoise mauve and green, reverse green-grey with multi-coloured tints of brown and pink. Printed on white paper with security thread. *Watermark:* Triune. *Dimensions:* 135 x 70mm. *Rarity:* C.

E000001 –	E1000000	(issue date?)
F000001 –	F 100000	(29 November 1991)
Z000001 –	[Z003986]	Replacement notes*

* See note after (537) above.

539   Ten Pounds – Notes signed in facsimile by W. Dawson (Chief Financial Officer).
Issued: 28 June 1991. *Obverse:* Similar to previous issue (526) with minor variations. Three tactile dots in lower left corner, print-free watermark window above. *Reverse:* Vignette moved to left, vacated area to right now occupied with watermark window and geometric designs. Printer's imprint in lower margin. *Printer:* Thomas De La Rue & Co. Ltd. *Colour:* Brown, purple and green with multi-coloured tints of orange, grey, pink and blue, reverse brown and orange with multi-coloured tints of turquoise and ochre. On white paper with security thread. *Watermark:* Triune. *Dimensions:* 141 x 76mm. *Rarity:* R4.

B000001–B 010000   (28 June 1991)

540   Twenty Pounds – Notes signed in facsimile by W. Dawson (Chief Financial Officer).
Issued: 12 June 1991. *Obverse:* Similar to previous issue (529) with minor variations. Four tactile dots at lower left corner, print-free watermark window above. *Reverse:* Vignette moved to left, vacated area to right now occupied with watermark window and geometric designs. Printer's imprint in lower margin. *Printer:* Thomas De La Rue. *Dimensions:* 148 x 80mm. *Rarity:* C.

150001– 450000   (12 June 1991)

540 IoM Government. Twenty pounds note printed by De La Rue, signed by W. Dawson. [*L. G. Burr*].

541 Fifty Pounds
Not printed due to sufficient stocks of previous issue.

Specimen Notes

See (547) and (548)

Issue 7 (1991–). Notes signed in facsimile by J.A. Cashen (= John A. Cashen) (Chief Financial Officer).

542 One Pound – Notes signed in facsimile by J.A. Cashen (Chief Financial Officer).
Specification as previous issue (537) but change of signature. *Rarity:* C.

T000001 –	T1000000	(10 July 1991)
U000001 –	U1000000	(30 November 1992)
V000001 –	V1000000	not yet released
W000001 –	W1000000	not yet released

542 IoM Government. One pound note, signed by J. A. Cashen. [*L. G. Burr*].

543   IoM Government. Five pounds note, signed by J. A. Cashen. [*L. G. Burr*].

543   Five Pounds – Notes signed in facsimile by J.A. Cashen (Chief Financial Officer).
Specification as previous issue (538) but change of signature. *Rarity:* C.

F100001–F1000000	(19 December 1991)
G000001–G1000000	not yet released

544   Ten Pounds – Notes signed in facsimile by J.A. Cashen (Chief Financial Officer).
Specification as previous issue (539) but change of signature. *Rarity:* C.

C000001 –	C1000000	(16 August 1991)
D000001 –	D450000	(13 July 1992)
E000001 –	E1000000	not yet released
Z000589 –	Z004885	Replacement notes*

* Lowest and highest serial numbers reported. No evidence of these numbers commencing at Z000001 with this signature.

544   IoM Government. Ten pounds note, signed by J. A. Cashen. [*L. G. Burr*].

545   IoM Government. Twenty pounds note, signed by J. A. Cashen. [*L. G. Burr*].

545   Twenty Pounds – Notes signed in facsimile by J.A. Cashen (Chief Financial Officer).
Specification as previous issue (538) but change of signature. *Rarity:* C.

450001–750000   (29 October 1991)

537/544   IoM Government. Examples of replacement notes with Z prefix, as printed by De La Rue. [*G. Bridson*].

546   Fifty Pounds – Notes signed in facsimile by J.A. Cashen (Chief Financial Officer).
Believed due for release in 1994, dimensions same as for the forthcoming new Bank of England fifty pound note.

028001–   (1994)

547   Specimen Notes – Framed Set (Obverse)
Set of five denominations as specimens mounted in a glazed aluminium frame. One pound, five pounds, ten pounds, twenty pounds and fifty pounds with mixed signatures of W. Dawson, Chief Financial Officer (£5 and £20), W. Dawson, Treasurer (£50) and J.A. Cashen, Chief Financial Officer (£1 and £10). Overprinted SPECIMEN in red. Serial numbers (£1) U000000; (£5) E000000; (£10) C000000; (£20) 000000; (£50) 026xxx. *Prepared:* 50. *Rarity:* R6.

548   Specimen Notes – Framed Set (Reverse)
As (547) but display reverses only. The fifty pound note bears the serial number 000000 and signature of W. Dawson, Treasurer. *Prepared:* 50. *Rarity:* R6.
The same remarks following (536) also apply to these two sets.

549   Specimen Notes – Framed Set (Obverse)
Set of five denominations as specimens. One pound (542), five pounds (543), ten pounds (544), twenty pounds (545) and fifty pounds (546) all bearing signature of J.A. Cashen, Chief Financial Officer. Due for release in 1994.

550   Specimen Notes – Framed Set (Reverse)
As (549) but display reverses only. Due for release in 1994.

Appendix I

BANKERS' NOTES ACT, 1817

An Act to prevent the Negotiation of Promissory Notes and Inland Bills of Exchange within the said Isle under a limited Sum.

Whereas divers Persons have of late years issued Promissory Notes payable to bearer, for fractional Sums of Money under twenty Shillings, whereby the public Credit of the Island hath been most materially injured, and the Crime of Forgery greatly facilitated and increased, and the legitimate Currency of the Realm nearly banished from the said Isle. And whereas it is expedient to abolish the Issuing and Circulation of Notes or Cards for the Payment of any Sum or Sums of Money under twenty Shillings British. We, therefore, your Majesty's most dutiful and loyal Subjects, the Lieutenant-Governor, Council, Deemsters, and Keys of the said Isle, do humbly beseech your Majesty, that it may be enacted, and be it enacted, by the King's Most Excellent Majesty, by and with the Advice and Consent of the Lieutenant-Governor, Council, Deemsters and Keys of the said Isle, in Tynwald assembled, and by the authority of the same.

1. That from and immediately after the Promulgation of this Act, all the Estate, real and personal, of every Description and Quality whatsoever, whether Quarterland, or Lands of Inheritance, descendible from Ancestor to Heir, or acquired in any other Manner whatever, belonging to, or in Trust for the Issuer of any Promissory or other Note, Bill of Exchange, Draft or Undertaking in Writing, being negotiable or transferable, now in Circulation, or hereafter to be issued, by any Person or Persons as Bankers, under the Provisions of this Act, shall be subject and liable to the Payment of all and every such negotiable Instrument whatsoever.

2. And be it further enacted by the Authority aforesaid, That every such Person or Persons as aforesaid, who, after the Promulgation of this Act, shall make and issue within the said Isle any such Promissory or other Note, Bill of Exchange, Draft, or Undertaking in Writing, being negotiable and transferable, for the Payment of any Sum or Sums of Money, less than twenty Shillings British, shall severally forfeit and pay the Penalty of fifty Pounds for each and every Offence, One-half to and for the Use of his Majesty, and the other Half to the Informer, such Penalty to be recovered by Suit in the Court of Exchequer of this Isle, in the Name of the Attorney-General of the said Isle for the Time being.

3. And be it further enacted, That all Promissory or other Notes, Bills of Exchange, Drafts, or Undertakings in Writing, being negotiable or transferable,

for Payment of any Sum or Sums of Money less than twenty Shillings British, which are now in Circulation within the said Isle, shall, from and after the Expiration of three Calendar Months from the Promulgation of this Act, be, and are hereby declared to be null and void, to intents and Purposes whatever; and that the Holder or Holders of any such unlawful Note, Bill, Draft, or Undertaking aforesaid, shall not have or be entitled to any Relief or Recourse, for the Amount of the same or any Part thereof, upon or against the Maker or Makers, Indorser or Indorsers, of any such unlawful Note, Bill, Draft, or Undertaking aforesaid, or any other Party, Person or Persons whatever; save and except in Cases of Fraud practised upon the innocent.

4.   And be it further enacted by the Authority aforesaid, That from and after the Promulgation of this Act, no Person or Persons shall make and issue any Bills, Notes, or other negotiable Paper or Instrument whatever, for the Payment of twenty Shillings British or upwards, by way of a circulating Medium, without the Licence of the Governor or Lieutenant-Governor of the said Isle, for the Time being, to be granted or refused at their Discretion, under Penalty of fifty Pounds for every such Bill, Note, or other Instrument issued contrary to this Act; which Licence shall remain in force for one Year only, and be rewardable from Year to Year, at the Discretion of the said Governor, or Lieutenant-Governor, and Council, and that the Sum of twenty Pounds British, shall be paid for each and every such Licence into the Hands of the Clerk of the Rolls, to be added to the Highway Fund.

5.   Provided, also, that Nothing herein contained shall extend, or be construed to extend to hinder, prevent, or restrain the making or passing of Notes or Bills of any Amount, without a Licence, so as the same be done in the common and ordinary Course of Trade or Business, and not in the way of Cash Notes or Bills, or Banker's Notes or Bills.

6.   And be it further enacted, That every such Banker or Bankers as aforesaid shall be bound to take up and pay all such Notes or other negotiable Paper or Instruments whatever, made and issued by them or any of them, within the said Isle, by paying the full value in Gold, Silver Coin, of the legal currency of Great Britain, Promissory Notes of the Bank of England, or by direct Bills of Exchange on London, at a date not exceeding two months.
    The Act received the Royal Assent on 1 July 1817 and promulgated at the Tynwald Court on 31 July 1817.

BANKERS' ACT, 1836

Section 6 of the 1817 Act was amended by substitution of the words twenty-one days for two months in the final line. This Act received the Royal Assent on 21 September 1836 and promulgated at the Tynwald Court on 25 October 1836.

NOTE

The final part of section 4 of the 1817 Act regarding the payment of the licence fee was repealed by the Highway Act, 1921.

Appendix II

CURRENCY AND BANK NOTES (Legal Tender) ACT, 1955

An Act to amend the law relating to legal tender of currency.

1.(1)   A tender of payment of money in the Isle of Man if made in the currency of the United Kingdom shall be legal tender-
(a) in the case of bank notes for the payment of any amount;
(b) in the case of silver or cupro-nickel coins for the payment of an amount not exceeding forty shillings;
(c) in the case nickel-brass coins for a payment of an amount not exceeding two shillings;
(d) in the case of bronze coins for a payment of an amount not exceeding one shilling.
(2)   The Governor may by proclamation make as respects the currency of the United Kingdom not being such currency as it mentioned in paragraph (a), (b), (c) or (d) of the preceding subsection the like provision as is made thereby.

2.   Notes payable to bearer on demand issued by bankers in the Isle of Man by virtue of a licence granted under section four of an Act passed in the year 1817, intitled "An Act to prevent the negotiation of Promissory Notes and Inland Bills of Exchange within the said Isle under a limited sum" (which Act may hereafter be cited as the Bankers' Notes Act, 1817) shall be legal tender in the Isle of Man for the payment of any amount.

3.   Every contract, sale, payment, bill, note, instrument and security for money or involving the payment of or the liability to pay any money which is made, executed or entered into, done or had shall be made, executed, entered into, done and had according to the currency which is legal tender in the Isle of Man under the provisions of this Act, and not otherwise unless the same be made, executed, entered into, done or had according the currency of some country or territory other than the Isle of Man or the United Kingdom.

4.   In this Act the following expressions have the meanings hereby respectively assigned to them, that is to say:-

"bank notes" means notes of the Bank of England payable to bearer on demand.
"currency of the United Kingdom" means coins and bank notes which for the time being are legal tender in the United Kingdom or in England and Wales.

215

5.   An Act passed in the year 1840, intituled "An Act for the assimilation of the currency of the Isle of Man to that of Great Britain" is hereby repealed.

6.   This Act may be cited as the Currency and Bank Notes (Legal Tender) Act, 1955.

7.   This Act shall come into operation when the Royal Assent thereto has been by the Governor announced to Tynwald and a certificate thereof has been assigned by the Governor and the Speaker of the House of Keys.
    The Act received the Royal Assent on 17 March 1955 and announced to Tynwald on 19 April 1955.

Appendix III

ISLE OF MAN GOVERNMENT NOTES ACT, 1961

An Act to authorise the issue and recall of currency notes of the Isle of Man Government and for other purposes connected therewith.

1.(1)   The Treasurer, may with the sanction of the Governor and the approval of Tynwald, may, from time to time, issue Government notes to such an amount and of such denominations and in such series as he shall be so authorised.
(2)   Any authority so given may be renewed or varied at any time.

2.(1)   Government notes shall be in such forms and of such designs and printed from such plates and on such materials as the Governor may direct.
(2)   Government notes shall be authenticated by the signature of the Governor, by mechanical means, shall be as valid as if it had been subscribed by the Governor in his proper handwriting.

3.   Government notes shall, subject to the provisions of subsection (2) of section six of this Act, be legal tender in the Isle of Man for the payment of any amount and shall, for the purposes of section three of the Currency and Bank Notes (Legal Tender) Act, 1955, be deemed to be legal tender under the provisions of that Act.

4.   A holder of any Government notes shall be entitled, on demand made by him at any place of payment at any time during the ordinary hours of public business of that place, to receive in payment for such Government notes their equivalent face value in Bank of England notes in such denominations as he may specify, provided that payment of any Government notes shall not be compellable other than in Bank of England notes.

5.   A holder of any Government notes shall be entitled, on a demand made by him at the place of payment at any time during the ordinary hours for public business of that place, to receive in exchange for such Government notes in such denominations as he may specify and which, at that time, are legal tender in this Isle.

6.(1)   The Treasurer shall have power, on giving not less than one month's public notice, to call in the Government notes of any series on exchanging them for the same value in Government notes of a new series or, at the option of the Treasurer, in Bank of England notes.
(2)   Any Government notes with respect to which public notice has been given under this section shall, on the expiration of the notice, cease to be legal tender.

7.(1)   The Treasurer may, with the sanction of the Governor, and upon such terms and conditions as the Governor may approve, appoint an agent or agents to act on his behalf in the performance of any of his powers and duties under this Act in relation to the issuing, exchange and payment of Government notes. The Treasurer may pay any such agent such remuneration as the Governor may allow.
(2)   The Treasurer shall give public notice of every appointment made under this section.

8.   If any person prints, or stamps, or by any like means impresses on any Government note any words, letters or figures, he shall, in respect of each offence, be liable on summary conviction to a penalty not exceeding five pounds.

9.   Government notes shall be deemed bank notes within the meaning of the Forgery Act, 1952, and to be valuable securities within the meaning of the Larceny Act, 1946.

10.(1)   Notwithstanding the provisions of sections four of the Bankers' Notes Act, 1817, a banker's licence which is in force at the time of the coming into operation of this Act, or which may be granted after this Act shall come into operation, may be revoked by the Order of Governor at any time not being less than one month after the date on which such Order shall have been made, and any such licence shall thereupon cease to be in force.
(2)   On the revocation of a bankers' licence under this section the Treasurer shall remit to the banker who held the licence a proportion of the fee paid in respect thereof, such proportion to be calculated by reference to the number of days by which the term of such licence has been reduced by virtue of such revocation.
(3)   Where a bankers' licence has been revoked under this section and it is shown, to the satisfaction of the Trustees named or approved of under Article III of the General Orders as to Banker's Licences made by the Lieutenant Governor in Council on the 25th day of October, 1867, that the value of bills, notes or other negotiable papers or instruments issued under such licence and still remaining in circulation has been reduced as a result of such revocation, the Trustees may, from time to time, release to the banker who issued the same such amount of the security given to him under the said Article III as the Governor may approve.

11.(1)   Where a banker's licence has been revoked under the last foregoing section the person who was the holder of that licence shall not thereafter put into circulation any bill, note or other negotiable paper or other instrument made and issued by him under such licence or any former banker's licence.
(2)   A person who contravenes the provisions of this section shall be liable on summary conviction to a penalty of fifty pounds for every such instrument so put into circulation.

12.   The Governor may from time to time give such directions to bankers in the Isle of Man as the Governor may think necessary, in relation to the circulation or withdrawal of Government notes, which directions shall be carried into effect by bankers in the Isle of Man.

13.   The Governor may make rules with respect to any matter or thing required for the purposes of carrying this Act into effect.

14.   The expenses of the Treasurer under this Act shall be payable out of the General Revenue of this Isle.

15.(1)   For the purposes of this Act-

"banker's licence" means a licence granted under section four of the Bankers" Notes Act, 1817;

"Bank of England note" means a note of the Bank of England payable to bearer on demand:

"Government note" means a promissory note issued by the Treasurer under this Act, payable to bearer on demand;

"place of payment" means such place as the Governor may by Order appoint;

"Public notice" means a notice inserted once in each of not less than two newspapers printed and circulating within this Isle.

(2)   Any reference in this Act to any enactment is a reference thereto as amended by or under any subsequent enactment.

16.   This Act may be cited as the Isle of Man Government Notes Act, 1961, and shall come into operation when the Royal Assent thereto has been by the Governor announced to Tynwald and a certificate thereto has been signed by the Governor and the Speaker of the House of Keys.

The Act received the Royal Assent on 14 April 1961 and announced to Tynwald on 16 May 1961.

The above Acts were replaced by the present Currency Act, 1992.

Appendix IV

Catalogue Numbers – Cross Reference List

Readers using the first edition may wish to locate the new catalogue number by use of the following list of old/new numbers.

OLD/NEW	OLD/NEW	OLD/NEW	OLD/NEW	OLD/NEW
1 201	24 241	46 300	75 352	104 435
2 202	25 242	47 301	76 353	105 400
2 203	26 243	48 303	77 354	106 401
2 204	27 246	49 305	78 359	107 402
2 205	28 250	50 306	79 360	108 404
3 207	28 251	51 308	80 361	109 406
4 208	28 252	52 313	81 363	110 407
5 209	29 253	53 315	82 364	111 408
6 210	29a 254	54 317	83 365	112 415
7 211	30 261	55 320	84 366	113 416
8 212	30 262	56 324	85 367	114 417
9 213	31 264	57 326	86 369	115 418
10 214	32 269	58 327	87 370	116 419
11 216	32 271	59 328	88 374	117 421
12 217	32 273	60 329	89 378	118 422
13 218	33 276	61 330	90 379	119 423
14 219	34 277	62 331	91 380	119 424
14a 221	35 280	63 332	91 381	120 425
15 222	36 281	64 333	92 382	121 426
16 223	36a 282	65 337	93 383	131 464
17 224	37 283	66 338	94 385	132 465
18 225	38 284	67 339	95 386	133 466
19 231	39 287	68 340	96 387	134 477
20 232	40 288	69 341	97 388	135 478
21 233	41 289	70 342	98 389	136 479
22 234	42 290	71 343	99 390	137 480
22a 235	43 291	71 345	100 431	
22b 236	43a 292	72 346	101 432	
23 238	44 293	73 348	102 433	
23a 240	45 294	74 350	103 434	

Acknowledgements

Grateful thanks is due to Dr. Larch Garrad of the Manx Museum, Douglas for her kind help with various aspects of the card money and allowing me access to her listing of the Museum's holdings.

Various bank officials have been particularly helpful by allowing me access to their records over many years and provided useful data and recollections. In particular I wish to thank Dr. Booker, Lloyds Bank, London, J.E. Cashin and J.R. Cannell of the Isle of Man Bank, Douglas, Jessie Campbell, Barclays Bank, Manchester and Mrs. Christine Mallon, Government Treasury, Douglas.

A number of dealers and collectors provided useful data, especially George Bridson and Godfrey Burr who provided much valued information, also G.W. Charman, John Corrin, Alan Kelly, Claire Lobel and Leslie Morgan for their help over the years.

An especial thanks is due to Hilary F. Guard of Douglas who, through 25 years, helped to trace many elusive Manx notes and also located numerous helpful contacts who gave so freely of their time with interviews relative to Manx banking and Internment Camps. Also for proof reading this edition and for constructive criticism.

Finally a special thanks to my wife, Brenda, who tolerated mounds of books, papers, etc. for over a year whilst this book was in preparation, and also for her patient help in checking the text and tables of serial numbers, dates, etc.

References

1   Clay, Charles: *Currency of the Isle of Man* (Douglas,1869).
2   Isle of Man Bank Limited. *Annual Report, 1993*.
3   Kisch, Cecil H. *The Portuguese Bank Note Case* (London, 1932) 45ff.
4   Waldron, George. *The History and Description of the Isle of Man* (1744).
5   *Jenkinson's Guide to the Isle of Man* (1874), 4–5.
6   Norris, Samuel. *Manx Memories and Movements* (Douglas,1938), 70–71.
7   Isle of Man Tourist Board. *Lady Isabella, the World's Greatest Waterwheel* (Douglas, nd.).
8   Jespersen, Anders. *The Lady Isabella Waterwheel of the Great Laxey Mining Company, Isle of Man, 1854–1954* (Virum, Denmark, 1970).
9   Stenning, E.H. *Portrait of the Isle of Man* (1968), 99–105.
10 Stenning, 96–99.
11 *Proc. I.M. Nat. Hist. & Antiq. Soc.* Volume V, (Douglas, 1948), 161–188.
12 Stenning, 157–158.
13 Craine, David. *Tynwald, Symbol of an Ancient Kingdom* (Douglas nd.).
14 Stenning, 58–62.
15 Kinvig, R.H. *History of the Isle of Man.* (Liverpool, 1950), 82–83.
16 Clay, 114–149.
17 *Manks Advertiser*, 17 June 1809.
18 ibid 13 April 1811.
19 ibid 30 July 1808.
20 ibid 13 August 1808.
21 ibid 6 April 1811.
22 ibid 26 July 1806.
23 ibid 4 May 1811.
24 ibid 13 September 1806.
25 Clay, opp. 146.
26 *Manks Advertiser*, 7 March 1816.
27 *Isle of Man Weekly Gazette*, 4 July 1816.
28 Manks Advertiser, 4 September 1817.
29 ibid 26 January 1811.
30 ibid 30 September 1809.
31 ibid 23 July 1808.
32 ibid 18 February 1809.
33 ibid 4 May 1811.
34 ibid 16 October 1817.
35 Sargeaunt, B.E. *The Royal Manx Fencibles* (Aldershot, 1947).

36   Cowin, W.S. 'An Old Castletown Banking House' *Proc. I.M. Nat. Hist. & Antiq. Soc.* Volume V (1948), 161–188.
37   ibid 75–77.
38   ibid 78.
39   ibid 83.
40   Clay 163.
41   Clay 177.
42   Clay 153–154.
43   Clay 139.
44   Clay 175–176.
45   Clay 176.
46   Pridmore, F. *Coins of the British Commonwealth of Nations* Volume 1, (1960) 24–25.
47   Cubbon, W. *Bibliographical Account of Works relating to the Isle of Man* Volume II (1939) 1141–1144.
48   Clay 178.
49   Clay 179.
50   Clay 181–182.
51   Clay 153–154.
52   Cowin 71.
53   Quarmby, Ernest, *The Isle of Man Joint Stock Banking Company Cross Bill* (in preparation).
54   Information via Claire Lobel, Coincraft, London.
55   *Manx Sun*, 10 June 1836, 8b.
56   Clay 154.
57   *Deed of Co-partnership of the Isle of Mann Commercial Banking Company* (Douglas, 1838) 6.
58   ibid 7.
59   Clay 154.
60   Isle of Mann Commercial Banking Company. *Circular to shareholders from the committee appointed to wind up the Company's affairs* (3 December 1858).
61   Christie's Sale, 25 May 1976, Lot 101.
62   *The Courier* (Isle of Man), 2 August 1968.
63   *The Great Bank Robbery in the Isle of Man*, full report of the proceedings (Douglas, 1878).
64   Gregory, T.E. *Select Statutes, Documents & Reports Relating to British Banking, 1832–1928.* Volume II (London, 1964) 288–297.
65   City of Glasgow Bank. *Report of the Trial of the Directors . . . Edinburgh, 1879* (Edinburgh, 1879).
66   Christie's Sale, 25 May 1976, Lot 96.
67   Ralfe, Pilcher G. *Sixty Years of Banking, 1865–1925: A Short History of the Isle of Man Banking Company Limited* (Douglas, 1926) 21.
68   Ralfe 7–8.
69   Ralfe 24–46.
70   Ralfe 11.
71   Norris 99.
72   Ralfe 60.
73   *Isle of Man Bank Limited, 1865–1965. 100 Years of Banking* (Douglas, 1965).

74   The *"Manx Sun" History of Dumbell's Bank, and Account of the Trials* (Douglas, 1900) 1.
75   ibid 3.
76   ibid 4–5.
77   ibid 5–6.
78   ibid 6.
79   ibid 7.
80   ibid 11.
81   Pearson, F.K. *Isle of Man Tramways* (Newton Abbot, 1970) 160.
82   *"Manx Sun" History* . . . 14.
83   Norris 95.
84   *"Manx Sun" History* . . . 25–26.
85   ibid 23–31.
86   ibid.
87   *The Failure of Dumbell's Bank: The Great Bank Trial. "Mona's Herald" History and Report* (Douglas, 1900).
88   Chappell, Connery. *The Dumbell Affair* (Prescot, 1981).
89   Christie's Sale, 25 May 1976, Lot 99.
90   Gregory, T.E. *The Westminster Bank through a century* Volume II (London, 1936) 24–28.
91   ibid Volume II 72–73.
92   ibid Volume I 63ff.
93   ibid Volume I 322ff.
94   ibid Volume II 16–19.
95   Chandler, George. *Four Centuries of Banking* Volume II, (London, 1968) 475–479.
96   ibid Volume II 477–479.
97   ibid Volume II 462–483.
98   ibid Volume II 516–588.
99   McBurnie, James M. *The Story of the Lancashire & Yorkshire Bank Limited, 1872–1922* (Manchester, 1922).
100 Chandler Volume I 21ff.
101 ibid Volume I 40–41.
102 ibid Volume I 58–139.
103 ibid Volume I 443–474.
104 Sayers, R.S. *Lloyds Bank in the History of English Banking* (Oxford, 1957) 1–22.
105 Matthews, P.W. and Tuke, A.W. *The History of Barclays Bank Limited* (London, 1926) 1–50.
106 ibid 103–151.
107 Sargeaunt, B.E. *The Isle of Man and the Great War* (Douglas, 1921) 58–86.
108 Stent, Ronald. *A Bespattered Page? The Internment of His Majesty's 'most loyal enemy aliens'* (London, 1980) 95–113.
109 Gillman, Peter & Leni. *'Collar the Lot'* (London, 1980) 185–201.
110 British Broadcasting Corporation, Broadcast, May 1980.
111 *The Isle of Man Weekly Times*, 8 June 1940.
112 Stent 156–179.
113 Peter Norris, Douglas. Interview October 1969.
114 Donald McHardy, Newton-le-Willows Interview 1973.

115 Chappell, Connery. *Island of Barbed Wire* (London, 1984) 31–35.
116 Stent 180–185.
117 *Onchan Pioneer* (Onchan, 1940–1941).
118 Information via Mr.Alan E. Kelly, Douglas.
119 Letter from Lord Greenway (c1940).
120 Giovannelli, L.N. *"Paper Hero – At His Majesty's Pleasure"* (Douglas, 1971) 16.
121 Letter from Major Allport, 1 July 1941.
122 Chappell (1984) 120–137.
123 Information via Mr. Richard Garlick, Burnley.
124 Information supplied by Miss Maud Lister, 1952.
125 Chappell (1984) 45–58.
126 ibid 54–58.
127 Information via Gary Charman, Birmingham, 1982.
128 Glynn, John. 'United Kingdom Prisoner of War Money' in *International Bank Note Society Journal*, 1983 22 4.
129 John H. Nicholson, Interview, October 1969.

Index